With Love + Light

Resha

oneness

$12

oneness

received and transcribed by

rasha

Earthstar
P R E S S

Earthstar Press
369 Montezuma Ave. #321
Santa Fe, New Mexico 87501
www.onenesswebsite.com
contact: onenessmailbox@gmail.com

ISBN 978-0-9659003-1-7
Previously ISBN 1-58872-049-7
First edition, May 2003
Second edition, January 2006

Book and cover design by Charles McStravick

contents

introduction

In February 1998, I had my first dialogue with Oneness. "What is Oneness?" I asked, silently. "Are you God?"

"As the drop of water is to the ocean—that is what Oneness is. The essence of the drop is every bit the essence of the totality. As you would understand God to be—yes, we are God. We are Oneness," came the astounding reply.

So began a profound relationship, a love story experienced within the sanctity of my consciousness that continues to this day. In that moment, I embarked on the epic journey that culminated in transcribing and living-out the teachings contained in this volume. It was a labor of love, and a voyage of discovery, that took over four years to complete.

Back then, I never would have dreamed how my life would turn upside down and then, miraculously, right itself while, through these teachings, Oneness provided humanity with a startling new vision of the true nature of who we are and the world around us that reflects it.

Never suspecting what was, eventually, in store for me, I had been carefully prepared for a Divine encounter of this magnitude for over a decade. It all began on a gorgeous Tennessee summer day in 1987, when Rama, the Hindu God, silently whispered "I love you," and blasted my heart chakra—and my seemingly normal world—wide open. I was a Nashville songwriter in those days, momentarily lost in a love song I was scribbling on the back of an envelope. In no time at all, I was lost in a world of mind-stretching spiritual concepts, received telepathically, that helped me begin to look at life in a very different way.

In the years that followed, I went on to document hundreds of pages of Divine teachings from Amitabh, "God of Infinite Light," the beloved aspect of The Father Consciousness who became my spiritual teacher. In 1998, I published *The Calling,* a volume of Amitabh's channeled wisdom that has now touched the hearts of thousands. Yet, even after so many years as a courier of Divine guidance, nothing could have truly prepared me for the impact of Oneness and the incredible journey that had only just begun.

As Oneness guided me step-by-step through the agonies and the exultation of the experiential voyage described in this book, I painstakingly documented the principles— word for word, like a secretary taking dictation—directly onto a computer. I had never encountered concepts like this before. And I started to realize that what was *writing itself,* through me, was a foundation for a totally new level of understanding of the phenomenon we call *life.*

As this material began to unfold, I found I was able to grasp the concepts I was transcribing—in theory. Yet, it was hard to come to grips with the realization that even though I could now explain what was happening to me, and to the rest of the world, my life was still a textbook example of "Murphy's Law": everything that *can* go wrong, will go wrong.

What was I doing wrong? I pleaded to Oneness. "You can't teach this if you haven't lived it, Rasha," became the mantra that

I heard in reply, more times than I'd care to count. Then, slowly, as I continued to stumble into all my predictable dramas, an entire lifetime worth of "stuff"—all the chaos, all the upheavals, all the frustration, and all the flashes of déjà vu—the whole roller-coaster of experience started to make sense.

At the same time, I began watching the world as I knew it, changing before my very eyes. I came to terms with the daunting realization that this was, literally, not the same world I was born in. Through these teachings, I started to recognize the fluid nature of a reality in the throes of metamorphosis. The rules of the game—the way we were taught life was supposed to work—clearly didn't work anymore. Why was that? I wondered.

As I wrestled with the endless stream of questions offered by my logical mind, the teachings of Oneness began to lay the foundations for seeing everything in our present-day world from the timeless perspective of *energy*. Oneness explained that the vibrational momentum driving all Creation toward unity is the same momentum that people everywhere are experiencing in their daily lives. And, everywhere I looked, I began to see the effects of the accelerated frequencies all around us, playing out as human experience.

I came to understand the dynamics of how we manifest our reality, vibrationally, and how our emotional response mechanism sets up the parameters for drawing our life experiences to us. I saw the symptoms of the process of *ascension*, the phenomenon of shifting into accelerating levels of reality, all around me. I began recognizing the signs, applying the teachings, and discovering their potential.

After awhile, to my amazement, most of the down-to-earth, life-theme issues I had struggled with all my life—the endless re-runs of the same old movie—started to ease up. Over time, those kinds of experiences stopped happening, altogether. It was a miracle.

The teachings in this book took me to the outer reaches of my own humanness and to the depths of the Divinity I discovered within. Oneness, the presence that encompasses the full spectrum of that awesome journey, is the universal common thread that we all share with each other. It is a touch that is indescribable. Through tears of joy, I remind myself, daily, that I could not have imagined it.

Now, I understand the significance of the choice each of us has made to be here, in physical form, in these extraordinary times. It's a level of understanding that came, not as a learned, philosophical concept with which to stimulate my mind, but as a timeless sense of *knowingness* that I unearthed from within. Like the touch of Oneness, with which I have been so blessed, it's something that has to be experienced to be believed.

— Rasha

chapter one

Oneness.

We are Oneness. We are the embodiment of the God force, as are you. We are as a drop of water is to the ocean— bonded in Oneness to it, being of it and unto it, yet having identity and self-perception. The perception of self would be as the totality. The all-encompassing. The antithesis of limitation, in all respects. It is toward this pinnacle of focus that you strive in the present moment, regardless of whether you are aware or unaware of such concepts.

In uniting in Oneness with all Creation, you give full expression, in the context of linear form, to the multidimensionality that is your true state of beingness. By consciously recognizing the connection and allowing its unlimited expression through your form and through your consciousness, you open the door to the possibility of expansion and encompass the understandings and perceptions that characterize those states of being. It is toward that state of bonded union with the expanded levels of self that you strive in these times.

By virtue of the fact that you are drawn to reading these words, you are functioning at a heightened level of awareness. Your perceptions and understandings regarding the nature of reality would by now have transcended what most concede to be the nature of what *is*. What *is* or *is not* has come to be the focus, in your culture, of considerable speculation. Some would have you believe that what you perceive as your reality is merely an illusion. And though your perceptions are symbolic representations of the thought forms that precipitated them, they are most decidedly real.

Your experience, the reality as your senses have shown it to be—is real. Your world, the reality that your actions and thought forms have manifested, in tandem with the others who cohabit it—is real. And your instinctive sensing of your own connectedness to the tapestry of life, which is not discernible to the physical senses, is very real indeed. It is toward the exploration of those connections—toward the understanding of a destiny that is interwoven of intent and desire—that we strive mutually.

Reality as you would know it to be will cease to be. You will not experience the shift that is to come as *loss*, though the circumstances that will transpire might indicate that interpretation. For in shifting to a higher octave of perception, you will come to embody, in the moment of that shift, the awareness and the innate understandings that accompany the heightened states of beingness toward which your energy flows at an unprecedented pace. You will begin to experience glimpses of that expanded reality as you move closer to the shift in consciousness to come.

You will be able to *see* aspects of reality that most, whose perceptions are limited to the physical senses, are unable to sense. You will know the nature of your unlimited state of being without having read about it in books or heard the concepts spoken of by those who herald visions and prophecies of a new paradigm. You will, ultimately, defer to no one, as you come to be empowered and to experience yourself as the aspect of the Oneness that you, indeed, are.

The enhanced perceptions to come will serve as a foundation for transcending those perceptions entirely. For they are limited to a view of a reality expressed within the context of time and space. The reality toward which you flow—effortlessly, if you allow it—is unbound by the linear concepts of time and space. It is a reality where physical perception, by definition, is superfluous. It is the result of a melding, a bonding, a joyful unity of the totality of your essence in harmony with what is now perceived to be "others." Ultimately, there will be no distinction between the perception of "self"and that of "others." For all will be Oneness.

We are that Oneness. We are the unity of All That Is. We are the unity of which you are indeed a part, and toward the experience of which you strive, whether knowingly or not. We are your hearts longing to reunite with the Source of your beginnings. We are your deep-seated dream of bonding with the fragmented aspects of your own essence, scattered since time immemorial throughout Creation. And we are the impetus toward that unification.

We are the invitation that calls you to action and awakens you from the stupor you call your life. We are the opportunity to purge yourself of the karmic baggage you carry, as a testimony to the state of *separation* you embody. We are the farthest-reaching cry of your very soul to have the self-imposed blinders removed that you may be permitted to truly *see*.

We are the aspect of your own selfhood that transcends every level throughout Creation, yearning in unison with you to be freed of the shackles of a reality defined by linear limitation. We are the ultimate end result of what has been referred to as ascension. We are as you are—and as you are yet to be.

You are a piece of Divine essence—with consciousness, with identity. You are a fragment of your own expression and experience of the One. You are a programmed time capsule that is coming to fruition on schedule, having harvested a wealth of physical experience on your journey. Ultimately, the understandings reaped from those adventures will have turned you toward an undisputed attunement with the higher vibration that resonates within you now.

You have begun the process of unraveling the threads that have been interwoven throughout your lifetimes in the dream that you regard as your reality. And you have achieved a measure of clarity that enables you to recognize, amongst your life dramas, a commonality of intent and a commonality of result that has shaped the identity that you recognize as *you*.

Far from view are experiences that would transcend, in their depth of perception, the awareness you garner from present experiences. Far from view, yet firmly entrenched beneath the surface of your awareness, are experiences of ancient incarnations whose influence helps to choreograph the dramas of your life. In many respects, that which you *are* is a resonance of the sum-total vibration of all you have ever been. The opportunity afforded you in this lifetime is to transcend some of that programming.

The opportunity before you now is to embody your history and simultaneously to reach for and to integrate the timeless aspects of self that have thus far eluded you. In so doing, you will experience yourself as the Oneness that you Are. And you will come to be that Oneness in conjunction with the full collective of every aspect of *you*—aspects that *are* what you are in *their* core essence, but recognize themselves as separate from you.

This is the process at hand. This is the momentum toward which you strive with all else in your reality, and beyond your reality, in these times. This is the journey you have undertaken by coming into form in this lifetime. And this is the journey that could take you beyond the limitations of form—in this lifetime. This is the journey that will carry you the full distance, beyond the parameters of the entire concept of a *lifetime*— to a state of being that is the embodiment of timelessness. A state of being known as Oneness. We are that Oneness. And we have come to guide you home.

chapter two

A glimpse into the experience of ascension.
Integrating fragmented aspects of consciousness.
Attaining the perspective of one's own expanded,
multidimensional self.

You have come to this place in time for a multiplicity of reasons. You have come for the opportunity to transcend the parameters that define your existence. And, in the same breath, you have come to deepen your connection with the interwoven aspects of your beingness that give your life definition in the truest sense. You have come to this experience you know as your life in order to be able to reject, completely, the consensus view of reality imprinted upon you since birth, and to replace that structure of understanding with a perspective that totally transcends it.

This is the first time in your personal history as an incarnate individual that your conscious awareness has been augmented with levels of energy that enable you to transcend your physical senses. This is the first incarnation in which you have been able to reinforce intuitive knowingness with experiential knowingness. This is the moment you have been waiting for, for eons of existence. For, this is the lifetime that will catapult you beyond all you know to a depth of awareness and understanding you are as yet unable to fathom. Trust that this process, in which you are, by now, deeply invested, is unfolding as it is meant to. And that everything is, indeed, in "Divine order."

You are a spark of Divinity in the throes of activation. The programming for the process is deep-seated within you. And it will unfold at its own pace, regardless of steps you might be encouraged to take to accelerate that momentum. You may experience a sense of reassurance by participating in group activities targeted at expanding your consciousness. And you may, indeed, experience sensations indicative of amplified levels of energy during such activities. But know that the results of such exercises are, for the most part, short-lived. For, the foundation for sustaining that energy is built from within. And the momentum of your growth is rooted in stillness.

There is a place within the depths of one's being where opportunities that defy linear logic are able to unfold. The key to maximizing the pace of your process lies in the degree to which you are able to let go and cease directing the scenarios of your drama. Allow life to unfold for you. And recognize the potential in the synchronicity that presents itself. Note the perfection in the results. And consider the possibility that your best interests are best served by a level of awareness that transcends your conscious mind.

Recognize your tendencies, rooted in fear of a less than optimum outcome of your efforts, to attempt to direct that outcome. Dispense with your prior understanding of how results are manifested. And allow the circumstances that present themselves to nudge you in the direction of your highest possible good. As you become more comfortable with the process, you will begin to notice how easily the opportunities flow and how effortlessly you are able to manifest results that serve you at the highest level.

You stand at the threshold of a grand adventure. And the extent to which you are able to experience the fullness of that journey is determined by the extent to which you are able to let go of the scenarios that no longer serve you. You have noticed, with rare exception, that the circumstances of your life are unraveling at an unprecedented pace. You have begun to question what is happening, as the structure of life as you know it, begins to crumble.

You look around you for explanations. And you probe your own circumstances for clues that would justify the destruction of the familiar. At first, you may resist the impetus to dematerialize what has been the foundation of your reality. In time, you will come to recognize the inevitability of the momentum that guides you. For, the momentum is unyielding, carrying you in a direction that is new, yet feels comfortable and familiar.

As you begin to release the constraints that bind you to circumstances you have outgrown, you will discover that the direction of choice is found on a road you must travel alone. As you gather the fragments of the structure that crumbles around you, and as you cease trying to "make sense of it," you will come to embrace the peace of knowing that the struggle is, at last, coming to an end. And you will experience a sense of sweet detachment from what was and an openness to what is yet to be.

As you extract yourself from your previous life script, you will feel deep compassion for the effects of your actions on the circumstances of others with whom you have shared history in this lifetime. Yet, your focus remains clear, as your recognition of the shift taking place within you provides the impetus to move forward, and to release the ties that would bind you and hold you back.

It is for you who now struggle with the circumstances of that shift in orientation to recognize the inevitability of that process. It is for you who struggle to hold on to know that the key to all you could become lies in your willingness to let go, and to allow the metamorphosis, in which you are deeply enmeshed, to proceed.

Once the initial resistance is overcome, there comes a total shift in focus to heart-centeredness. In this state of being, your perception of self and that of the world around you become intertwined. You begin to dance with the energies of life, allowing the ebb and flow to determine the direction. You begin to recognize the potential in the joyous adventure that beckons to you to venture forth. And choices that might once have appeared to be reckless come to be viewed as Divinely guided. You become aware of the heart space within and the song that emanates from it. You begin to harmonize with the breath of life pulsing within that core essence. And in that moment, you awaken to the recognition of the key to all you are and are yet to be.

The rise and fall of the breath of life determines the pace at which one can travel on one's journey. There is a quickening that occurs quite naturally when you allow the breath to guide you into the depths of your very being. Relaxing the physical senses, relinquishing the sense of conscious direction, being willing simply to be in the moment with *All That Is*: these are the parameters of the process that will guide the way, if you permit the process itself to be in control.

There is little distinction between the in-breath and the out-breath when one shifts into the heart-centered state. Ultimately, there is no conscious awareness of breath at all, merely a connectedness to a sense of Self that transcends one's definition of self. One experiences a sense of peace that is both profound and inconsequential, as it is one's very birthright. One *becomes* the rise and fall of the breath. And in that rhythm, one begins the process of expansion that opens the door.

Riding on the wings of the rise and fall of the breath, one begins to experience a perception of self that transcends the limitations of physical form. One's energy field expands. One begins to encompass, in actuality, the expanded parameters of that field. And one bonds in Oneness, in that moment, with an expanded aspect of self—an aspect of who one truly is.

Initially, the expanded state is experienced in the moment and surrenders to the moment. Ultimately, one becomes that moment and becomes One with that expanded sense of self. The higher understandings and heightened perceptions of the expanded self become integrated into one's conscious awareness. And one

is able to make the shift that enables one to transcend completely the limitations that bind one to an earthbound existence.
Through the vehicle of breath, one is able to embody the higher
state of beingness, while retaining physical form.

This is the experience you would refer to as ascension. One does
not, as is popularly believed, cease to materialize in physical form,
in this process. Rather, one comes to embody each successive
level, as each is embraced and encompassed. One retains form, as
the heightened sensibilities are integrated. And one is able to
resonate at the higher level of the expanded consciousness, and to
perceive the world as it truly is, and increasingly comes to be. The
understandings expand, exponentially, as each level is attained and
integrated.

Ultimately, one comes to embody all aspects of one's inter-dimensional lineage simultaneously. One comes to perceive as superfluous
the physical definitions of identity that would keep one tethered
to a reality that, increasingly, lacks relevance. One walks with an
awareness of all that *was* recognizable reality, and is keenly
attuned to what *is* recognizable reality. And one is able to distinguish amongst simultaneous perceptions of what becomes an
increasingly multifaceted world.

There are many who have glimpsed this state of being and have
explored fleetingly the perceptions it offers. Inherent in the process is
the opportunity to retain those levels of beingness, and ultimately, to
experience embodiment in the realities they represent, simultaneously. One can anticipate being able, for example, to experience multiple levels of reality, not by relinquishing one for another, but by
encompassing, sequentially, each of those levels and "becoming"
each expanded state of being—all of which are, in fact, *you.*

Although your path is your own and the pace at which you
travel is a matter of choice, you will not be expected to make the
journey "alone." Each progressive level of self is an investment in
consciousness that is as committed to the process of integration
as you are. As you reach energetically for—and merge with—each

successive level of *self,* you embrace the loving intent of that expanded identity to integrate all that *you* are into its repertoire of awareness and response. As the levels of your consciousness intertwine, the distinction between those aspects of self ceases to be. And *Oneness* is achieved.

There may be multiple levels of integration, as fragmented aspects of what is, in fact, *you* merge in consciousness and become a collective of beingness that attains Oneness, simultaneously, with a mutually shared "higher self." It is indeed possible, when integrating what could be considered to be *lost* aspects of self, to lose conscious awareness of the differentiation of one's original identity. One bonds, energetically, with the collective and, ultimately, the sense of separation is obscured and gives way to the perception of one's expanded, multidimensional self as that which one *is.*

Once integration has taken place, one is able to transcend the limitation of one's previous focus. In so doing, one is able to remain in harmony with all that previously defined one's existence while, simultaneously, opening to encompass the fullness of the totality at that stage in one's process. There is no need to direct this process through your intent. For it is you who will be directed and not the other way around. One's sense of it is of being in a state of absolute receptivity, of surrendering totally, on every possible level, the need— the compulsion—to control the process.

One becomes as a leaf on the wind, embodying a willingness to be carried with the momentum of the process, knowing unquestioningly that one's best interests and one's well-being are being seen to in every possible way. In a sense, one *becomes* the wind, while retaining the self-perception of the leaf. One embodies self-definition and form while merging in totality with momentum and direction. The energies become one. And the transference of the form from *here* to *there* is achieved.

Once *there,* the qualities of momentum and direction are retained as an integral part of one's self-perception. And one is able, eventually at will, to merge with that momentum. One is able to *ride* the energy of momentum in the direction of that momentum, for one would be in complete harmony with that momentum. One would *be* the harmony that unites momentum and form.

This is the direction in which you are headed in these times. This is a fragmentary glimpse of the world that awaits you. The *world* would be less the sense of a destination than of the journey itself. For the *destination* would be in relinquishing the need for destination. The objective would be in releasing the need to *know*. The opportunity would be in turning over the reins that would govern momentum and direction, and to experience the perfection of the ride.

The question is, are you willing to risk relinquishing all that you know—the entire structure of the belief system that defines and constricts your reality—for the chance that you may experience the perspective of your own expanded self? Are you willing to acknowledge that "truth," as your experience has shown it to be, may not be the entire picture? Are you willing to consider the possibility that all you may value could, in fact, be worthless in the higher sense? Are you willing to accept that you are, in fact, ready for this journey?

By virtue of the fact that you are even considering such questions, know that the process has indeed begun. It is not a question of if so much as a question of how and at what pace you will proceed. From the perspective of a being immersed in a linear, physical reality, your challenge now is in your willingness to risk that the information that resonates to you as truth *is* actually truth. And that your objective in this stage in your development is to relinquish your hold on the limitation imposed by reality as you have known it to be. You are here to consider, and ultimately to embrace, the full multidimensional spectrum of your beingness as that which *you* are. You are here to begin to experience that expanded sense of self. And to walk in the fullness of that state of beingness one step at a time.

In this moment, you *are* all you are yet to become. For "time," as you know it to be, is not a factor in what is transpiring in what you consider to be "the Now." All that is to happen *has* happened, energetically. What is left to achieve is the physical manifestation of that expression of energy. This would explain why, at times, you are seemingly *drawn* to a particular set of circumstances. This would explain why you experience what you would consider to be "synchronicity." And this would explain why you experience a sense of disharmony when you resist suggestions that nudge you to act upon certain opportunities.

There are any number of avenues to the crossroads in which you may be headed at any given moment. When you take up the threads of a scenario that presents itself to you as "synchronicity," you experience the manifestation of that particular avenue—those particular sets of circumstances and the individuals who feature in it. Were those threads not taken up, be assured that other potentially "life-altering" events would present themselves to you, scripted to deliver you to the very same crossroads, albeit via a different route. Forgive yourself the misdirected notion that you have strayed offtrack by letting certain opportunities pass you by. Know that you *will* get to where you are going by any number of alternative means. By definition, it cannot be otherwise.

Likewise, forgive yourself the misdirected notion that you have impeded your own progress by your own judgment of your performance in a given set of circumstances. The very responses those scenarios invoked within you are those calibrated, energetically, to deliver you to the state of beingness in which you recognize, consciously, your tendency to respond in that way, and relinquish your need to do so. Once you see the pattern, it is likely that you can cease repeating it and experience arrival at a crossroads that will carry you in a different direction entirely.

In the present period, it is likely that you will experience a sense of coming to completion, on a multitude of levels, with the recurring themes that have dominated this lifetime. As a way of punctuating the point in question, it is likely that your experience will begin to serve you extreme variations on that theme. This is an indication that you are at completion with a particular leg of your journey and that it is, indeed, time to move on.

"Time," as you know it to be, is moving forward at an unprecedented pace. Events appear to be crammed into an improbably short space, and at times seem to be happening simultaneously which, in fact, they are. It is crucial, as your rendezvous with Oneness draws you ever nearer, that you come to completion with the life themes that tether you to this reality. It is crucial that you attain a state of detachment from the energy charges that have magnetized you, habitually, throughout this lifetime. It is crucial that you recognize the common thread in the web of dramas that you have woven—that continue to ensnare you. And it is crucial that you allow yourself the grace of your own humanness in responding to these recurring situations—and love yourself for it.

When you are able to stand back from the overview of the dramas in which you have played a starring role and see yourself as the award-winning performer that you truly are, you are well on your way to completing the journey. Until you have mastered what you have come here to experience, the level of beingness that seeks to integrate *you* in *its* journey to Oneness cannot do so.

As you reach out energetically, with a heartfelt desire to bond with your own higher expression of beingness, know that that aspect of self reaches for you too and adds its energy to the equation of your totality. Until you are able to liberate yourself, vibrationally, from the chronic patterns of response that keep you "stuck" in endless repetitions of the same old song, your higher aspect of self is unable to integrate you without jeopardizing its own vibrational levels.

Likewise, you may sense a tethering, beneath the surface of your conscious awareness, to deep-seated emotional patterns of response, which are out of proportion to the circumstances that evoked them. Consider the very real possibility that what links energetically to you in these moments are aspects of your own being who have been excluded from *you* and who seek to integrate with you, in *their* journey toward Oneness.

From their perspective, you are the heightened state of being-ness toward which they strive. You are the mastery they seek. You are the enlightened perspective that they have tasted fleetingly and with which they yearn to bond at the deepest heart level. Your own emotional responses to given situations in your life open the door to parallel scenarios with parallel energetic "triggers" at other levels of Creation. The common ground and the paths upon which you will merge, energetically, with all aspects of self are the emotions you share at the deepest level.

When you experience a particularly poignant response to a given situation—one that you may judge to be extreme—consider, before judging yourself too harshly, that what you may be feeling is depth of emotion you share mutually with an aspect of self that has been *denied* and was left behind along the way. By repressing the expression of the depths of your feeling, you only serve to pro-long the separation between you and that aspect of self, and to invite repeat performances of scenarios which are calculated to produce the same emotional response.

It is imperative that you open your heart to the very real sensations of hurt, sorrow, or outrage summoned to you by circumstances in the dramas in which you play a part. In so doing, you pave the way for the reintegration of a missing piece of your own being whose life theme may be the embodiment of those very responses, and who strives from his depths to transcend them.

Without the reintegration of these lost fragments of your own consciousness, you will be unable to complete your journey in the way the sum-totality of your beingness would wish to. Without giving yourself permission, in this time frame, to truly feel the depths of your emotional response mechanism, you are holding yourself back, in the way that really matters, at every level of Creation.

You are a multidimensional being. You are not limited to the particular identity that you have come to regard as *you*. There are viable aspects of self that live, unbeknownst to you, in parallel real-ities, who reach out, instinctively, for the lost aspect of self that you would consider to be *you*. To these beings, you are a missing note in a chord that defines their very existence. You are the harmony toward which they strive and without which they are unable to achieve it. The key to your full participation in this multidimensional effort is to *be present* in all that you are and in all that you do so that you are able to be present in all that you are to become.

Be conscious of what you are feeling and how you are responding in the dramas of your daily life. Be honest with yourself in your acknowledgment of your emotional responses. And be not so hasty in rejecting, within your own repertoire of sensibilities, the poignant feelings that you might have yourself believe are "beneath you." Your emotional response mechanism is very real. The key to all you would accomplish in this lifetime hinges upon your willingness to embrace all that you are, for the chance that you may come to experience—in Oneness—all that you truly Are.

chapter three

Your energy field as the co-creator of your circumstances.
The power of your thoughts and words
as tools of manifestation.
Breaking the patterns that create unwanted outcomes.

A vast inter-dimensional conversion in consciousness is presently transpiring throughout every level of Creation. Awareness of your own involvement in this process marks the onset of shifts in life circumstances calculated to carry you to a level of consciousness that is unprecedented in your dimension. As you experience these shifts, and the energies carry you to ever-higher levels of awareness, your attunement to the higher frequencies becomes stabilized. And the transition to an augmented perspective is achieved. By monitoring your responses and catching your logical mind as it attempts to censor your experience, you allow for the optimum state of heightened sensibilities in any given moment.

Sensitivity to the subtle shifts in your own energies is your barometer to the levels of experience you are able to draw to you. Experiences that evoke what you might consider to be lower emotions are magnetized to you, in part, by your conditioned tendency to sustain the familiar, diminished vibrational state. And it becomes a matter of choice as to whether or not you remain at those ʄ energy levels and thus attract experiences, energies, and consciousness that do not necessarily support your highest potential.

You are fully responsible for your vibrational state of being-ness in any given moment. It becomes abundantly clear when you are vibrationally balanced and heart-focused. Your life experiences reflect it. Likewise, it becomes obvious, both from the standpoint of how you feel and by considering your circumstances, when you are operating from the lower end of your own energy spectrum.

It is not necessary to experience repeat performances of painful dramas, simply because you have neglected to release the energy charge carried by those experiences, by expressing the emotions they are calculated to trigger. By numbing yourself to the crescendo of your emotional responses, you nullify the charge and invite a set of parallel circumstances to be drawn to you. The only way to end this vicious cycle of events is to become very clear about the connection between your vibrational state and the life dramas it creates for you to live out.

Your energy field is both your doorway and your shield. The field you maintain around you can be vulnerable to interference by energies and consciousness that you might deem uninvited and undesirable. In so stating we do not intend to imply judgment as to the merits of particular forms of consciousness, but to point out that drawing such forces into your energy field may not serve your best interests. Random, negative thought patterns on your part help to open the door to thought forms and levels of consciousness that add a diminished charge to your energy equation and help to magnetize more of the same. It is a self-perpetuating cycle that can set spinning a downward spiral of circumstances and create an ongoing series of adverse situations. The key to halting and ultimately reversing such conditions lies in attaining and maintaining a state of conscious, heart-focused intent.

When circumstances deliver you to a state of being that you recognize to be unbalanced, take the opportunity to step back for a moment. Withdraw your energies and cease conscious interaction with all that surrounds you, all that is external to the your own being. And allow your awareness to guide you to a place of stillness deep within. Become centered in the silence of that space. And breathe deeply, with conscious connectedness, through your heart center. Detach your awareness from the circumstances that have engaged you. And allow yourself to feel, in the sanctity of that stillness, the Light energy of unconditional Love as it fills you completely.

Surrender to the sense of peace that washes over your entire being, filling you with a feeling of calm serenity. And as you bask in the sanctity of that blessed state, allow your heart to memorize it. Know it as your natural state of beingness. Recognize it as a reference point, a gentle loving reminder of who you really are, to which you can refer at will. This place within is one you carry with you at all times. It is a haven to which you are able to retreat whenever you choose.

Making that choice in the face of adversity is a learned reaction that you are encouraged to adopt and to practice in response to life's dramas. Shifting your energy in this way serves to dispel the spiraling wave of diminished vibration that, once magnetized to your field, can manifest as circumstances calculated to draw you ever deeper into a state of imbalance. Taking conscious command of the moment as it presents itself is the strongest possible response you can make, regardless of the nature of the circumstances.

Know that you are in command of your situation at all times. You are able to choose to step back, at will, from the heat of the moment, and make the conscious choice to shift the energy to one emanating from the place of heart-centeredness. When you are coming from that place, your circumstances reflect it. In shifting the energy *you* project onto any moment or situation, you consciously shift the outcome to one that will give you a more advantageous result. By embodying this training, your life becomes one directed by intention rather than the unconscious reflection of happenstance. For you do create all of it. Know that.

There are no victims. Surely, you have heard these words spoken. It is important to understand, with absolute clarity, the role you play in the creation of scenarios that would not be of your conscious choosing. For at the accelerated levels of vibration you are now integrating into your being, the results of your choices and responses manifest as your reality far more quickly than what once was considered to be "normal" in your dimension. Beings who have integrated heightened levels of vibration as their "norm" will experience extreme results when shifting into an imbalanced vibrational state. You can expect to experience the manifestation of "worst-case scenario" results, when entering any situation in a depleted, unbalanced state. It cannot be otherwise.

In order to break a pattern of adverse circumstances, recognize that those types of situations are self-perpetuating. The diminished energy of adversity often invokes an emotional response that, in itself, adds a measure of diminished energy to the vibrational equation and magnetizes more of the same. The vibration of every thought pattern that passes through your consciousness carries an energy charge; particularly the thought patterns that are *materialized* in the form of verbal communication. By releasing that energy charge in the form of speech, you set into motion an imprint that magnetizes to it circumstances of a corresponding vibration. That is what is meant by the expression: "your thoughts create your reality" in the most simplistic sense.

In order to break a cycle of manifestation of negative occurrences, it is important for you to be keenly aware of the vibration of all you communicate to others. Monitor your speech. Do not utter a negative sentiment about anything, regardless of whether or not you feel it is justified. Make a conscious effort that every word that passes your lips is uplifting to the listener. Closely monitor the way you respond to adverse circumstances and insure that your response is not one calculated to produce for you more of the same.

Speak only the most positive possible statements regarding any situation. Speak ill of no one, lest the energy be mirrored back upon you. Choose to partake, or to pass. Simply that. Gossip, complaining, or speech in the guise of asking for help you do not really require, is a recipe for reprisal in the form of circumstances that would not be pleasing to you. Your speech is a powerful tool when carefully employed. It is a danger to you when used carelessly.

Likewise, your thought patterns, even when not expressed verbally, carry an energy charge that sets in motion circumstances of a corresponding vibration. When one is mistrustful, for example, one manifests the experience of being deceived. When one is fearful, one manifests the experience of frightening situations. When one is anxious and feeling unworthy, one manifests the experience of the rejection of one's efforts. When one becomes the hunter, the hunted feel the predatory energy and flee. When one is obvious in what one wants from another, it is virtually guaranteed that the desired outcome will not be manifested.

Dwell not upon what is lacking in your life, but regard those circumstances with gratitude. Understand that they pave the way for the shift in consciousness that would put you in a position to manifest precisely what you have come into this lifetime to do. A seemingly negative situation may well be the gateway to the precise shift in focus that will deliver you into the arena where you can do your life's work.

It is crucial for all who consider yourselves to be spiritually focused in these times to cultivate a conscious awareness of your responses to the dramas in which you find yourselves. And become aware of the time lag between an emotionally charged response and the next negatively charged occurrence. It will become painfully obvious that there is an indisputable connection between cause and effect, amplified by the accelerated vibrational frequencies now flooding your dimension.

Those of you who have risen to the new heights of human vibrational experience must become extremely clear on the ever-widening gap between the accelerating energy levels all around you and the energies invoked by unconscious patterns of emotionally charged response. As the vibration of the planet continues to accelerate, and your dimension enters the realm of instantaneous manifestation, those who are vibrationally attuned to the pace of that acceleration will have widened the gap between themselves and the masses, and amplified the magnitude of the energy charge expressed as their reality.

It is for you, who consider yourselves to be the forerunners of the shift in consciousness that marks these times, to be keenly aware of the ramifications of consciously accelerating your vibrational frequency. Monitor your responses such that you maintain a state of balance and heart-centeredness. For it is here, in the heart-centered core of your being, that the timeless connections with the multidimensional aspects of self will be made manifest. And it is here that you will encounter the gateway to reunification with the Oneness that you are.

chapter four

Bringing the "recurring dream" of this lifetime to completion.
Learning to recognize and to decline
the invitation of conflict.
How the collective will has helped transcend
the prophesies for these times.

The lessons upon which you have chosen to focus in this lifetime represent categories of experience that you are now working to bring to culmination. It is likely that you are able to isolate certain recurring themes in your present life history. And it is likely that you have completed the necessary number of episodes on those themes to drive the point of the exercise home. There is no need to continue to subject yourself to the "recurring dream" that has been your reality in this lifetime unless you choose to. Now, it is time to turn the page, and to begin the work that you have prepared yourself to do by mastering these life lessons.

It may seem like your life has become a testimony to uncertainty in the present period. By virtue of the fact that you are reading these words and have been drawn to the energy of this communication, you are completing "the course." Yet, the sense of direction toward the next phase of your life continues to elude you. It should be fairly obvious, in light of the dismantling of much of your life's structure, that extensive preparation has been done. And there is a sense of *waiting* for someone or something to give you the "go-ahead" and tell you what's next.

It is not necessary to try to second guess the process, but merely to be present. Observe your situation: your whereabouts, your companions, your current focus, and the synchronistic events that have brought you to this moment. And it is likely that you can discern a sense of the direction in which those factors are combining to draw you toward a new life's focus.

As you grow to trust the process, you will be able to allow the future you are co-creating with other aspects of self to evolve in a natural way. If you are not yet at a point of absolute clarity about the nature of your participation in your *life's work*, it may be that all the information has not yet been presented. Be patient and loving with yourself in this time period. Allow yourself ample time for meditative practices that permit a focus of your energies in your heart center. For, it is from that place of peace and harmony that the real work in these times will be drawn.

You have been given a rare opportunity. You have been given a reprieve from the tedium of your life's script. And you have been given a glimpse of the overview of the dramas you have created. You have drawn certain conclusions, and you are in the process of integrating those understandings. Once you are at peace with all you have done thus far in this lifetime, you will be ready to let go of it. Only then will you be ready to embrace a state of being-ness that transcends the sense of separation reinforced by those experiences. Only then will you be ready to step onto a parallel track with others who have reached the same sense of completion in the same time frame. And you will begin to move forward in unison with those others toward the experience of Oneness that is your birthright.

By remaining focused in the present moment, and resisting the temptation to jump ahead of yourself and *plan* the future before it is ready to evolve, you will be in a position to make the highest choices. Trust that you have choreographed your journey perfectly so that you will arrive at your destination right on schedule. There, you will reunite in a loving bond of Oneness with the multidimensional facets of your own being that await your return to the sanctity of the whole. It is toward this blessed end that you strive in the present moment, whether you are aware of it or not.

There is much that can be said about what is transpiring in your dimension. And the prognosis for a more positive outcome than had originally been anticipated is very good indeed. The addition of the free will factor of the collective consciousness to the equation has resulted in a shift in what might have been a cataclysmic period in the history of your planet. These events are not carved in stone, but are very much dependent upon the actions of humankind as a whole and the choices made by those in a position of leadership.

It is entirely possible to transcend a prophesied series of events that once seemed so likely as to have been considered inevitable. There is no event that is so inevitable as to be resistant to the focused intent of the beings present. Efforts to orchestrate a common focus on a given concept, in unison with vast numbers of other beings, have a profound effect on an outcome that may have been predicted. Humankind has succeeded in altering that outcome and has manifested in its stead a radically modified version of what had once been foreseen.

The real work has now begun. The collective consciousness of those incarnate in your dimension has exercised the power of its will and has manifested an unprecedented result. The harnessing of this power is the opportunity being presented in this time frame. In so doing, it will begin to become obvious to many of you that you are, indeed, creating your reality. As each adds the power of personal intent to the collective, the sum-totality moves that much closer to the point at which a measurable result can be made manifest. And an obvious correlation will emerge between the implementation of the collective will and the modification of anticipated events.

With this tool in hand, you are empowered in the collective to co-create a reality as you would wish it to be. Once you know that you are not living at the mercy of events beyond your control, but are indeed drawing the blueprint for those events with your thoughts, attitudes, and presumptions, you will begin to take very seriously the responsibility each of you has for your part as the co-author of the "movie" you call *life*.

You will awaken to the realization that you are responsible, through your actions and choices, for setting the stage for parallel efforts on the part of those within your sphere of influence. You will begin to understand that the magnitude of the difference you are able to make is in direct proportion to the degree to which you are able to live your word. And you will teach what you know by practicing what you know.

Your word can become a powerful tool through which you are able to cultivate awareness in others who are magnetized to your energy. Yet, the word alone is but an outline for concepts that take root and blossom as deeds. The choices you make in every moment exert their influence vibrationally, and by example, on all whose lives you touch. And as each touches and is touched in return by the actions of the collective, a harmony of intent begins to resonate. When that intent is heart-centered, it is indeed possible to alter the course of what you would consider to be "destiny."

Recognizing your power to create your reality is your key to turning the page and beginning a new chapter in your own life story. Having released the ties that once bound you to repetitive patterns of experience, you have emerged with a fresh perspective and a new sense of self-definition. And you have come to understand the potential in sculpting that identity, as you would like it to be. For the tools for creating your personal reality as a masterpiece of manifested intent are right there within the parameters of your consciousness.

The opportunity for you now is to breathe new life into the blessed creation of self, through heart-centered focus. Then, to stand back and allow that identity the scope of full expression, without the influence of past beliefs, feelings of limitation, or any of the dogmas you have accumulated in your travels. There is no place in the transcendent consciousness for any of the baggage you may still be carrying. All the *shoulds* and *shouldn'ts* that may have dominated your consciousness, are to be released and left at this crossroads.

The path before you now requires a lightness of spirit that allows for ample freedom of motion. One must be able to respond to the opportunities presented without reservation, from a place of heartfelt recognition of the direction of choice. One needs to be able to move forward, unbound by considerations that would limit what is possible in deference to *priorities* that no longer resonate with one's highest good. And one must bestow upon oneself the latitude to distinguish with honesty between what does and what does not serve that end.

The final phase in lightening the load is the task at hand. Much, if not most, of the work has been done. You have come to this moment in time, having surmounted so many of the hurdles that were thrown in your path. Now, what remains to be cleared are remnants of learned responses, which would have you stumble, out of habit, over brambles that are clearly in view. Recognize when you encounter one, and observe the response those situations trigger within you. Consider, before releasing a conditioned response, whether it is possible for you to sidestep the situation entirely and decline the invitation of yet another drama. Your objective now is moving forward. Anything that does not support that momentum, is a situation you have the opportunity to transcend by exercising the power of choice.

Once you have transcended your inclination to stage repeat performances of the dramas that have dominated your life, you are able to move forward to the next phase of your participation in the work at hand. Ideally, the choices you encounter from this point forth represent opportunities to translate discord into harmony. They are opportunities to transcend the need to be "right" on particular issues, in deference to the possibility of emerging with a sense of completion. They are opportunities to respond in ways that shift the dynamics of the interaction and allow all parties concerned to walk away without carrying the energy charge that would invite a repetition. You will observe that you are now able to just "let it go," where once you felt compelled to engage in battle. And you will begin to see the process of transcending ego, in action.

When you are able to recognize conditioned responses that are rooted in the need to "win" a given encounter, you take the first step toward transcending the sense of separation with which you have been equipped. Separation was considered to be a necessary survival mechanism in times where violent confrontations were the order of the day. These times are about changing that pattern. These times are about shifting that energy. These times are focused on recognizing the opportunities for reinforcing separation in action— and choosing to disengage.

The objective in this phase of your development is not to win or be right, but rather, to recognize that the choices that are implemented are the ones that determine what the next set of choices are to be. Winning, losing, and begrudging compromise, are recipes for repetition of the same script, albeit perhaps, with a different cast of characters. For, all are outcomes that would manifest, vibrationally, a sense of separation for all concerned.

Your objective now is to recognize all encounters as the opportunities for achieving harmony that they truly are. By presenting your own perspective without attachment to outcome, you allow for the manifestation of the optimum outcome for all concerned. The keyword here is "allow." By planting the seed of your intent— vill—by presenting your viewpoint without the need to into fruition, you best serve your own interests as well as he others with whom you are engaged.

at seed is released energetically, it has the opportunity the circumstances that best address the interests of the collective will, which strives toward the manifestation of the experience of Oneness. When potential conflict is nullified and the intent of each is the harmonization of will, rather than the manifestation of one's own will over that of another, the outcome is consistently one that serves the highest good of all concerned.

It may take a bit of practice before you become accustomed to recognizing the point of the exercise inherent in each life drama that now presents itself to you. But once you become attuned to the resonance of harmony, that vibration will permeate all you do. You will find that your life experiences flow with ease, one to the next, as examples to you and to all you encounter, of the manifestation of harmony in your reality. You will find that you are less concerned with triumphing over adversity than with maintaining equilibrium. For, in the attainment of balance, you are in the best position, energetically, to create the circumstances that reflect your highest intent.

There is surely an element of trust necessary in the process. And recognizing and releasing the need to "control" your life situations are an important part of the exercise. This *trust* is not the kind that is bestowed upon another, as a way of relinquishing responsibility and turning over the reins of your life. Rather, this sense of *trust* is instilled in the Source that emanates from the core of your own being. It is a trust in the sacred Self that oversees all you do to orchestrate scenarios that serve your highest possible good.

When you relinquish the need to mastermind the labyrinth of your existence and reach deeper to the level where you can *feel* rather than think, and *know* rather than believe, you will have arrived at the place where you can create a reality in which you truly move forward. Until you are able to release the fear-based conditioning that prompts reflex responses, you will continue to manifest circumstances focused on warding off conflict.

The ability to trust in the reality that the energy of your world has indeed shifted, and that there is a higher perspective to be attained, heralds the turning point toward which you strive in these times. Once you have turned that corner and tuned-in to the higher resonance of the harmonization of your personal will with the Will of Creation, the walls of separation will have dematerialized and you will come to experience life as the expression of Unity that it truly is.

chapter five

Releasing the cellular imprinting of your experiential history.
Peeling back the layers of emotional density
that have been dormant for lifetimes.
Navigating the depths of your own experiential rites of passage.

The higher purpose to which you have directed the focus of your intent in these times has recognized that desire within you and has responded. The nature of that response is oftentimes not discernible until one is well invested in the process. And the evidence that heralds that profound shift in focus often simulates symptoms that are more indicative of a setback than of progress.

It is essential that the peeling back of the layers of experiential history, imprinted within your cellular structure, be accomplished systematically and completely so that you are able to liberate yourself from the constraints of the themes that characterize this lifetime. Were this cellular imprinting to remain unreleased, the energy patterns would continue to trigger repetitions of situations calculated to stimulate dramatic emotional responses in areas where resolution and completion may have been achieved.

It is entirely to be anticipated that dramas and interactions transpire that bring into definition and absolute clarity the key emotional issues with which you have been working toward resolution in recent times. It is in your highest possible interests that you permit yourself the experience of these emotional responses, when circumstances manifest them for you, in order that the corresponding patterning can be eliminated from your energy field. By resisting the inclination to repress such responses, when, on an intellectual level, one would believe oneself to have transcended such feelings, one is able to make the shift to a new level of consciousness, unencumbered by a lifetime of experiences that have reached completion.

As the energies continue to accelerate, you can expect to experience profound levels of emotional response, as each life theme, like a chapter unto itself in an ongoing saga, is permitted to culminate as vivid awareness. And simultaneously, one can anticipate the feeling of being intellectually and emotionally uninvested in the outcome of such dramas. One experiences a sense of total detachment from the very situations that might have led one into battle previously. One feels indifferent to issues that might once have characterized one's entire personal history in this lifetime. And one arrives at a state of being that, at last, appears to be free of the constraints of the past and is ready to begin anew.

This is the process in which you are engaged in the present period. And this is the process of many with whom you interact daily. It is a footnote to these times, provided here as a reminder to you, that the dramas into which you may be drawn as either observer or participant may not need to be taken at face value. It is with an informed and elevated perspective toward the concept of emotional processing that you are best equipped to deal with it. The consideration you are able to extend to another being who is in the throes of transformational completion can impact the duration of that process and the role you play in it.

It may well be that you have been cast in the role of *trigger* for the emotional release work in which another being is engaged. And it may appear to you that the individual in question is overreacting to your prompts. Yet, from that other person's perspective, *your* reactions are extreme aberrations of a movie that is worn thin from endless reruns. Both are correct. For differences in perspective characterize the perfection of this process and enable each participant to glean the appropriate insights inherent in the drama.

Once this often-painful period is completed, the horizon once again comes into view and one ceases to see oneself as lost in a momentum that seems devoid of direction. For the direction is within the depths of one's own cellular structure. And the process of combing those depths for displaced fragments of one's consciousness is the way out of a lifetime that may have come to be imprisoned by them.

Approach with gentleness and with compassion the beings with whom you share experience in this time frame. For each of you is performing to the very best of his abilities, playing out roles that have been preordained and not without a certain measure of discomfort all the way around. Know that it is in the highest interests of all concerned that one is prepared to see the experience through to completion and not succumb to the temptation to exit the stage in a fanfare of self-righteousness.

It is far too easy to see the flaws in the thinking and responses of another being than to see the same in one's self. Rest assured that your own performance is equally marred from the perspective of the beings with whom you co-create your end-dramas. And the tendency toward the necessity to appear *right* in the eyes of onlookers only serves to undermine the objective of the interchange. Ultimately, you are able to perceive the overview of the drama. You are able to release the energy charge inherent in attachment to a conditioned perspective. And you are able to move forward, in tandem with those whose differences were catalysts for the monumental shift that is the end result of the process.

Once you have arrived at a place of balance with the energies in question, you will be able to recognize, in retrospect, the significance of scenarios that have surfaced for resolution. You will perceive instantly the sense of familiarity about the dramas that have unfolded. And your recognition of the common theme being represented, once the heat of the moment has passed, will continue to reinforce for you the identification of the patterns of experience that are presenting themselves to you for completion in these times.

Each time you complete a poignant episode and the emotional release of the underlying energy charge has been achieved, you will be able to see that it is yet another example of an experience that has happened over and over again. You can expect the pattern to continue to repeat itself for some time to come, as you bring to the surface and release the layers of vibration held within your energy field.

Allow the episodes of greatest intensity to play out unimpeded. For, your judgment of the depth of your feelings could serve to inhibit the authenticity of your response, should you permit your mind to get in the way. The objective here is not restraint, but rather, release. Your most profound emotions are being triggered intentionally—not for the purpose of reinforcing your proficiency in repressing them, but with the objective of stimulating a profound reaction.

In this way, you can begin to anticipate categories of interaction you are likely to experience. Yet, recognition of the underlying theme being represented does not eliminate the need for experiential episodes to continue to manifest. For it is in the repeated stimulation of the feeling body that the vibrational release is achieved. Your mentalized tracking of the journey is merely a fascinating footnote for you of the actual work being undertaken here. For your cognitive grasp of the process is far less significant than the manifestation of the emotion your circumstances are stimulating.

You can expect familiar episodes of dramas on key themes in your life to intensify, as you delve deeper into the process of release. The manifestation of situations that are even more intense than before does not indicate that you have failed to release the emotional charge or to grasp its significance. The escalating intensity of your life experiences in this phase of your journey indicates a progression in the release work being undertaken. The more significant levels of this work cannot be approached before certain preparatory experiences are allowed to transpire and to be processed.

This aspect of the journey is a product of peeling back the layers of experiential density to reveal levels of intensity that lay dormant, often for lifetimes. As you begin to piece together your core understandings of the categories of experience you are resolving, you will have the sense of the timelessness of some of these themes. Profound levels of pain, grief, hurt, disappointment, and other reactions to the cataclysmic events in your cellular history now have the opportunity to be revealed to you, through the vehicle of your emotions. When you encounter a depth of emotional intensity that is disproportionate to the incident at hand, know that it is entirely possible that you have arrived at the point where *past-life* energetic patterning is able to surface and be released.

It is not necessary for you to know or to understand the significance or the details of these dramas that are being acted out by other levels of your own consciousness. What is needed on your part is your willingness to be present in the authenticity of your reactions to the extreme levels of feeling prompted by catalysts in *this* life drama. And be less concerned with whether or not your reactions are out of character or out of proportion to the instances in question.

You will come to understand, in the fullness of time, the necessity to go through the depths of your feeling body with the objective of coming face to face with the vibrational evidence of your complete personal history. All elements must be brought into balance, in the fullness of this stage of your journey, in order for you to be ready to approach the deeper levels of this process.

The significance of this part of your transformational work is not to be underestimated. For, it will not be possible for you to move forward, and ascend to the higher levels of perception that are possible for you, with retained levels of emotional density. These times are about tuning-in fully to the vibrational history imprinted within you, and allowing yourself, and the others in your inner circle, the grace of expressing fully what is represented there.

You can anticipate being taken to the heights and to the depths of your feeling body's capacity to attune you to subtle levels of perception and response. Your vibrational structure is being recalibrated to the higher frequencies, so that you can withstand the intensity of the new levels without succumbing to the backlash of unreleased residual density. Your awareness of the reality of these changes and your willingness to allow yourself to flow with the pace of this process will ease for you the trials of this transformational period.

You will be guided from within, at levels beyond your conscious awareness, to navigate the depths of some of these experiential rites of passage. The keywords here are trust and surrender. And your willingness to relinquish the need to control and direct your transformational journey will ease for you some of the roughest terrain. Trust that there are levels of consciousness within you that understand precisely what is happening and why it is necessary that you be subjected to this period of upheaval. Your own inner trust, demonstrated at the times when your feelings defy your logical mind, will help you to complete the experiences with ease and to accomplish the objective in drawing them to you.

Know that you are most decidedly on track, despite the sense that life, as you know it, often seems to be derailed. For, radical change is the order of the day in these times, and this level of change is experienced by everyone and everything in your physical world. Life was never meant to be the straight and narrow road you were taught to envision. This lifetime was preprogrammed with a rich itinerary of convoluted detours to the destination toward which you travel. It is the deviation from what you may have expected that makes this journey fascinating and rewarding in the ways that really matter.

You will look back upon this time of intensity and upheaval with a rarefied perspective that is only possible in retrospect. For, by that time, you will be able to integrate new levels of perception into your understanding of what really happened to you in these times, and why. And although that depth of clarity may elude you for some time to come, you can anticipate a time when the dust will have settled. And, in the peace of that time of resting, you will have embraced a new direction and a new level of focus that would not have been possible, had you not traversed the rocky patches of these times.

Many are traveling by your side whose experiences may or may not parallel your own. And it is best to resist the inclination to judge your own process or that of others. For, each of you is engaged in the perfection of his own personal journey to Oneness. And each is contending with an individualized program of experiences calculated to bring you into the fullness of your capacity for the transcendence of this level of reality.

None of you has the same burden to bear, in terms of the levels of density brought forth into this incarnation. And none has been afforded a shortcut that would eliminate the need to detoxify your energy field of all that it carries on every possible level. Each of you is engaged in the process of cellular purification, on physical and non-physical levels, that will enable you to rise to the fullness of your capacity for humanness in this physical form. And each of you is realizing that potential according to your own timetable and in your own way.

Allow the brothers and sisters who journey by your side the grace to experience their experience as they see fit. And resist the inclination to attempt to direct the process of others according to understandings you may have realized along your own path. You are here for your journey alone. And even though you have been provided the comfort of much camaraderie along the way, each of you is, in actuality, flying solo in your "moments of truth."

You will "touch-down" in this reality repeatedly along the way, as a reference point. And there will be the familiar landscape of fellow beings and circumstances to give the journey definition. Yet, in essence, you are making the pilgrimage on your own. You are often bouncing between realities without even knowing that it's happening. And you are learning how to stabilize the energies of those moments and to take command of their effects on the reality you perceive as *your life*.

These are the skills to be garnered now, as you come to grips with the ever-shifting scenery before you. Do not expect your life to "return to normal." That's not what you had in mind when you embarked on this odyssey. "Normal" is a concept that has no frame of reference in the realities for which you are preparing. What can be expected, from this point forth, is the magical fluidity of every moment, and the sense of peace in knowing that your life will never be the same again.

chapter six

Refining your understanding of the momentum
known as "ascension".
Achieving emotional detachment.
Reintegrating fragmented aspects of consciousness.
The significance of the karmic adversary.
The fallacy of "forgiveness".

There are significant changes taking place in the cellular structure of every life form on your planet in the present time period. And there are far reaching ramifications of these changes that enable each and every expression of consciousness to manifest as an accelerated version of one's vibrational fingerprint, in physical form.

The core essence of one's being is not altered in the process at hand. Rather, that essence is enhanced, expanded, and allowed to express as a higher octave of that original essence. The process is accomplished in incremental stages that allow for the integration of subtleties of perception into one's field of awareness. At the same time they allow for the harmonization of one's energies with a diversity of life forms that share the core resonant essence that is identifiable as *you.*

It is within this reintegration process that most "awakened" individuals find themselves in the present period. And it is within the confines of physical form that most who struggle with the symptoms of this process find the key to liberation from that structure. The very limitations of physical self-definition lay the foundations for self-perception that is free of structure entirely. It is in the embracing of physicality, rather than in denial of that reality, that the path is cleared for the transcendence of all limitation.

The truth you seek is not in your mentalized denial of the state of beingness that your physical senses have shown you to be so. Rather, it is in your perception of the fullness of that state that you are able, simultaneously, to embody the limitlessness of the totality and to perceive that blessed state as that which you Are.

Thus, a mind-set that would have you believe that "you are not your body" is misguided. You are very much your body. You are very much your thoughts. You are very much your doubts and fears. You are very much your dreams. You are very much your unfulfilled longings. You are very much your mentalized anticipation of the end to the limitation you would perceive to be your physical identity. And at the same time, you are very much the embodiment of a momentum that is surging toward the completion of a timeless process. That process is the reunification of all that you are, all that you have ever been, and all that you are yet to be, in a simultaneous expression of Oneness.

The misconception that you will be relinquishing identity and form in your journey toward unification has gained popularity in your culture in recent times. You will be no less *you* at the culmination of this process than you were at the onset. The difference will be in the expanded perception of all that *you* really are, not in the substituting of one expression of limitation for another. For, were you to perceive yourself as having relinquished the identity you know, at present, to be *you*, that very notion would constitute a limitation of the totality of the Oneness that considers *you* to be a very important part.

You are not, as a popular notion would have it, a figment of your own imagination. Your reality is not merely a dream. And your world is not simply a crossroads of happenstance where one gets caught and tossed about in the rapidly shifting currents of change. As your individual vibration accelerates in relation to your dimension at large, your reality manifests, recognizably, as a reflection of your choices. There is no longer the luxury of being able to delude yourself into believing that you are subject to the effects of random occurrences. For, as the time lag between the inception of thought and the manifestation of reality diminishes, it becomes obvious to you that you are creating all of it. The realization then dawns that one is able to choose what one wishes to experience. And the true challenges of a physical incarnation have the opportunity to express, through you, as reality.

What do you wish to experience, in physical form, in this lifetime? What do you wish to leave behind, discarded, as excess baggage on your journey? Who do you really wish to be in your own eyes? Knowing now that all things are possible, you are able to make significant choices. And at the same time you are able to take full responsibility for the ramifications of those choices. One becomes the creator and the creation simultaneously. And one is able to experience the fullness of limitless expression as the embodiment of the harvest of all seeds sown.

As your journey toward Oneness accelerates, your experience as a physical being takes on the breadth of perspective and the heightened awareness characteristic of the higher dimensions of existence. As you merge and become integrated with higher aspects of your own being, your experience *here* takes on the coloration of that heightened level of perspective. And even though your reality, as you perceive it to be, will remain as the "here and now," your sense of your self within this reality expands in scope. In essence, you come to embody your own heightened awareness *here* and at the same time are present energetically, at the next level, adding your own piece to the energetic equation that is the sum-totality of all that you are.

Likewise, as you integrate fragmented pieces of your own consciousness, those aspects of your beingness are able to take on *your* heightened perspective. In the simultaneous momentum that drives all aspects of self, expressed in all dimensions in which *you* have a presence, all are able to embody the expanded perspective of *higher consciousness*. And all, in unison, become part of the momentum that is known as "ascension."

You are well within the process of ascension now. For, ascension is not an "event" but rather, a momentum. It is not something that "happens" to an individual at a given moment, and thereafter one's reality is instantaneously different. Ascension is a gradual shift. It is a shift in awareness, a shift in perspective, a shift in vibration, a shift in attunement, and a shift in conscious alignment with who one truly is, so that there is agreement and full participation in the process.

Ascension is a universal motion, a yearning, a striving, a releasing, a surrendering—a joyous culmination of your journey here in physical form. It is not something that is done *to* you. It is a process that is initiated *by* you, orchestrated by you, and experienced fully as an evolutionary journey by you. In order to make the shift, preparation has been made by you, over the course of much time, to bring you to the place that you are able to be a fully conscious participant in the culmination of the journey.

For many of you, the initial stages of the transformation process are now nearing completion. And those aspects of the work have been quite painful in many cases. For, what has been required is a confrontation, within the depths of your conscious awareness, of the negative patterns and the stagnant energies that you have carried within your energy field. Repressed emotions, negative inclinations, habitual behaviors, addictions, and victim consciousness have been raised to the surface, blatantly, so that you would be able to scrutinize the evidence of the misguided energy harbored within your physical form.

Much work has been done, in conjunction with higher aspects of your own consciousness, to prepare you for your liberation from these self-limiting patterns. Much work remains to be done, as the process itself nears fruition. For, the subtleties of the advanced stages of this work are not to be underestimated. And the far reaching consequences of even the most seemingly inconsequential tendencies can have an extraordinary effect on whether or not one is able to move forward from a given experiential theme, or whether further "repeat performances" are necessary to give blatant definition to the drama you call your life.

You will become keenly aware of the threads that are woven, now almost instantaneously, into the tapestry of experience on given themes in your life. You will have spontaneous recall of related occurrences and a sense of understanding that pulls the experiences together into a cohesive document. You will be able to identify the evolution of the levels of experience within certain categories of your life themes. And you will begin to marvel at the most basic examples of certain kinds of experiences that happened to you, even in childhood.

As your life accumulated a track record within certain major categories of experience, the level of sophistication and the intensity of the experience evolved accordingly. In recent times, you are likely to have witnessed the most poignant examples of the issues on which you have been working all your life and which may continue for some time to come. Ideally, as you near the final stages of the completion of this process, these experiences will not ensnare you in the dramas presented. Rather, it is hoped that you will be able to transcend the "hook" built into the experience and deal with the circumstances at hand, free of the lifetime of emotional conditioning with which it is *charged*.

To accomplish this level of detachment is no small feat. For the levels of testing being presented in the final stages of your process are complex and filled with potential "time bombs" preset to detonate should the emotional charge hit home. The opportunity when encountering such experiences is to recognize the theme being presented without allowing the "trigger" to be activated. One evolves, over time, into the state of beingness that responds with detachment to all such emotionally *charged* occurrences.

Eventually, that very detachment becomes the catalyst for totally different categories of experience to manifest for you. The emotional charge, carried at the cellular level within each of you, will by then have been released on each of those life themes and will not be able to magnetize experiences of a corresponding vibration. Once you transcend the automatic response patterning—the reaction of ego-centered emotion—and replace it with an automatic response of indifference to outcome, you shift to a state of being in which you are able to manifest what you would like to experience in your life.

As your journey progresses, the role you are inclined to play becomes more the one of the observer, than the object of your experience. Your finest teachers are those beings who have played the role of nemesis throughout your life. The beings with whom you have had the most caustic and severe interactions are those who were painstakingly cast—by you—for that role. And you will begin to see, in retrospect, that most have played their parts superbly. You, in turn, have been an energetic catalyst for many beings with whom you have had conflict interactions. Your own self-righteous stance in these instances does not negate the effect of your own participation from the perspective of an adversary in a given drama.

Ideally, as your process culminates with an overview, you are able to take responsibility for the parts played from all standpoints of an issue. For rarely does one experience a life theme from one vantage point alone. Chances are, you will have played a life theme from both sides, often simultaneously. It can even appear amusing when you begin to recognize the pattern of the theme and see yourself as both the perpetrator and the object of the adversity.

Some would have you believe that certain interactions and relationships between individuals are *karmic*. And to the extent that the energy charge built into certain issues does not dissipate when one departs one's physical body at the end of a lifetime, this explanation could be said to be true. What is meant here by the term *karmic* is that certain agreements are in place between individuals that transcend a given physical incarnation. And those agreements are in place to continue to work on that given theme in a subsequent lifetime. Thus, one would continue to be drawn into dramas with beings who have played these roles for one another for eons, and will continue to do so until, eventually, they are able to transcend their need to do so.

The fallacy inherent in the common usage of the term *karmic* is that there is a certain degree of inevitability built into the relationship and, with that, a degree of relinquishing of responsibility for one's own role in the interaction. The blessed opportunity built in to relationships that are said to be *karmic* and that are predominantly adversarial, is that each person who is cast in lifetime after lifetime of the same old story is a seasoned actor, who knows the role and the lines by heart. The gift in such a relationship is to recognize the Godliness in the adversarial role, to recognize the Godliness in one's own reaction of diminished vibration, and to allow the love that truly exists at the higher level between these individuals to surface and to grow. For, each one has been cast in the given role by choice. And each has the opportunity to transcend the drama and learn the lesson by choice.

What is being presented, then, is the chance to forfeit being "right" on a given issue in favor of recognizing circumstances as the non-issue that they truly are, when beings are aligned in Oneness. The karmic adversary becomes the catalyst for change when there is nonattachment to outcome on the parts of all concerned. And one is able to choose either to engage or simply to carry on peacefully on one's own path. One is able to recognize the completion of certain life theme interactions with key individuals when one can, in all honesty with oneself, recognize a heartfelt wish of well-being for the individual who played perhaps the most injurious role in one's lifetime.

This sentiment goes beyond the traditional concept of *forgiveness*. Generally, as commonly understood and applied, *forgiveness* is a gesture in which a being consciously releases future tethering to an issue by giving lip service to releasing blame for a past action. While in theory this effort appears to be well directed, in application this is a self-righteous practice that rarely produces the desired result. For the key issue: one's own stance on the issue in question, would not have been released in the process. Thus, the negative energy charge would have been retained at the cellular level, magnetizing to the individual a continuing barrage of experiences on the same theme, *forgiveness* or not.

The key to completing these patterns is not to *forgive* the other party their transgression, which keeps the energy polarized, but rather, to release in total detachment, any care one may still be carrying, whatsoever, about the outcome of *any* drama revolving around that issue. The gesture, then, becomes not one of *forgiveness*, which revolves around issues of blame or non-blame for a perceived wrongdoing, but rather one of total transcendence of one's attachment to outcome.

In this rarefied state, one is able to regard, with a full and loving heart, an individual playing his role, dutifully, and to move forward, unaffected one way or the other. In this way, there is no possible reinforcement of the vibrational charge surrounding the issue in question, and less likelihood that one will continue to witness repeat performances of that particular scene.

The transcendent being does not arrive at the place of sublime indifference overnight. It takes a bit of practice. But, as you begin to recognize the patterns in your day-to-day interactions with people, there will appear to be less and less conflict and more and more harmony. In these times of acceleration of all experience, you can anticipate reaching closure on many of your dominant life themes in the times soon to come. And you can anticipate the dawning of another octave of experience that gradually takes precedence, and becomes the dominant next phase in an ongoing journey toward recognition of your Oneness with All Creation.

chapter seven

The power of intention.
The energetic prescription for world peace.
The part every individual plays in the creation of global conflict.
Taking responsibility for the effect of every action upon the whole.

Right now is all there is. Right now is all there ever will be. Right now is what you have come into physical form to experience. And right now is the concept upon which your core understandings of the true nature of your reality are based. There is no past. All there is, is that which can be created. And creation, by definition, can only happen *right now*.

Your world, as your experience has shown it to be, is based on a system of action and reaction. Of cause and consequence. Of linear perceptions based upon beginnings and endings. In fact, none of these concepts *are* as your experience has shown them to be. Your perceptions are but a measuring device by which you can gauge the extent to which you are able to translate intent into form. For the sake of argument, let us eliminate form, for just a moment. What remains is pure intention. That is what *is*. That is the essence of Creation. That is the foundation upon which all else rests.

Your intention, in any given moment, sets the stage for the full manifestation of your experience. There are no random events.

Things do not just *happen* to anyone. Intention is the cohesive element that translates the conceptual into form. In these times of unprecedented acceleration of the vibration that manifests as your reality, the time lag between the inception of one's intent and its materialization as "form" or "event" is negligible. And the correlation between intent and manifestation will become obvious as the time lag that separates them continues to diminish. Ultimately, as your realm of experience *ascends* into higher ranges of vibration, manifestation will be instantaneous.

For some amongst you who resonate at the higher ends of the energy spectrum that encompasses your reality, the experience of instant manifestation is at hand. And with those capabilities goes the responsibility for the effects of one's intent not only upon one's own circumstances, but upon the reality experienced by all.

What is called for in these times of great change is a corresponding shift in conscious awareness. What is happening, to a greater or lesser extent, within each of you who bridges the gap in consciousness between the world of what was and that which is increasingly coming to be, is a systematic relinquishing of the obsolete patterns of response that would continue to manifest an outmoded reality that increasingly lacks relevance. Within each of you there is a radical shift in perception taking place. And each is undergoing a transformation of the ideals that form the basis of your responses to the moment-to-moment experiences in your life.

Situations where great importance had been placed in maintaining a particular stance are now perceived as less crucial. The need to be "right" in all instances, and to defend that perspective at all costs, suddenly gives way to the need for harmony and for a spontaneous perception of the perspective of the adversary. The need to triumph over another, regardless of the circumstance, is based upon the needs of ego. And this ego-centered state of separation is the one overriding factor that seeks to undermine the impetus toward unification in Oneness, toward which all energy throughout Creation is focused.

The process of relinquishing one's conditioned attachment to learned responses fostered by ego, has been a gradual one. Now, the momentum of accelerated vibration results in dramatic shifts in consciousness in all who are attuned to these changes. Interactions are more intense, and the emotions evoked are calculated to take the underlying point of the exercise to the extreme, such that interactions appear to be caricatures of behaviors that might be expected, ordinarily.

When the heat of the moment passes, one is left to wonder "what on earth that was all about." And one recognizes certain *ha* reactions to be out of proportion to the circumstances that triggered them. Ideally, that awareness calls up for scrutiny one's own participation in such dramas. And it offers a respite from the self-righteous needs of ego that might blind one to the truth underlying the dynamics in question. Ideally, the cost of having to be "right" is blatantly apparent when, in the winning, what may have been truly of value has been lost.

Extremes of emotion are to be expected, both within oneself and from those key players with whom one interacts. Be prepared for dramas in your day-to-day experience that are calculated to stimulate learned behaviors that are rooted in limitation and ego. Attitudes that may be harbored beneath the whitewash of denial must be unmasked and presented for your careful examination and transformation. You can expect opportunities to abound in your experience of these times, designed to accelerate a shift in consciousness that is vying to keep pace with your amplified abilities to manifest your reality.

The state of beingness toward which you now travel at unheard of speed is one in which the inception of your intent and its manifestation happens simultaneously. This level of capability would be incalculably dangerous in the hands of beings invested in a self-serving orientation. And the corresponding extremes of experience that manifest prior to the attainment of those levels are calculated to drive the point home, unquestionably, for those still rooted in resistance. For the shift in awareness will be experienced by all. Ultimately, the momentum toward the state of Oneness commands the harmonization of the intent of all. Energy that is out of sync with that momentum will feel the consequences of that discord and will be hard-pressed to keep pace with the parameters of the reality that is rapidly coming to be.

Self-protective mechanisms, such as rationalizations for behavior that would justify one's stance in a given episode, only serve to prolong the length of time that might be spent relinquishing one's need to control the outcome of certain kinds of interaction. Eventually, there is no longer the need to react to circumstances calculated to provoke a predictable response in a conditioned way. When one is able to let go of the need to remain *in command* and to emerge from an encounter in a position of dominance, the accompanying energetic *charge* is diminished and the intensity of the interaction de-escalates proportionally. Ultimately, one ceases to manifest such levels of conflict entirely, as the energy that magnetizes them would not be present.

This, in essence, is the energetic prescription for the "peace" to which so many on your planet pay lip service in these times. To truly *create* "peace" on a global scale, it is necessary to step back from the overview of global conflict and to perceive the interactions that precipitate it as what they truly are—manifestations of energy. To shift an environment in which discord reigns supreme and is unyielding, it is a futile effort to enter into a duel where bravado collides head-on with bravado. Hostility met with hostility simply breeds escalated hostility and reinforces the vibrational building blocks of the situation into ones that will continue to manifest more of the same.

To shift the energy underlying these ongoing global situations, it is necessary to address the energy that comprises them. Each participant, regardless of how inconsequential the involvement, adds a piece to the energetic equation. A mind-set of *dominance-at-all-costs*, breeds as its ongoing manifestation, the vibration of separation rooted in ego, which impedes the momentum of the entire human race in its journey toward Oneness with All Creation. The key to moving the stagnant energies of global conflict lies in the recognition of the need to shift the energies of the interpersonal dynamics of *all* participants.

It is the responsibility of every individual to become aware of the patterns of response that are calculated to sustain the diminished energies of separation. A response that is nonreactive to a provocative encounter serves to dissipate the energy charge and provide the conditions for harmonization of the mutual concerns of those in question.

By consistently reacting to conflict with the conscious intention *not* to "fuel the fire" by asserting your position and striving to emerge the "victor," you affect the energy of each encounter in the highest possible way. For, when presented with a noncombative response, the adversary is not provided with the energetic tools with which to further escalate conflict, thereby diffusing the energy *that* individual brings to the encounter. By taking command of a potential conflict by consciously sidestepping it energetically, each individual makes a contribution, which is experienced globally.

The whole is merely the sum of its parts. This is the basis for the entire thrust of the impetus toward reunification with All Creation that marks these times. Within the momentum that drives the unprecedented shift in consciousness so many are experiencing, is the opportunity to recognize that one truly *does* make a difference. With every word, with every gesture, with every choice, and with the underlying sentiments and beliefs one holds at the heart level, one adds a measure to the energy of the whole.

In truth *all* are responsible, energetically, for co-creating global conflict. And all are capable of making a measurable difference in the efforts toward world peace, by taking responsibility for the energy projected in every encounter with every fellow being with whom one shares the adventure known as "life."

It is with that mind-set in the forefront of your consciousness that the transcendent being within you moves forward in these times. When you are clear that the world-shattering situations taking place around the globe affect every life form with which you share the reality of existence here, you begin to realize, and to affect with that very awareness, the intricate web of interconnectedness of all of it.

It is far too easy to turn a blind eye to events happening a world away, and to delude yourself into believing that such situations do not directly affect you personally. The advent of instantaneous information, with which your dimension has now equipped itself, eliminates the excuse prior civilizations might have had for detachment from global responsibility for all events, regardless of where they are taking place. Your civilization does not now have the luxury of that excuse.

The inclination of most people to absolve themselves of responsibility for the world situation at large, which historically could be relegated to being uninformed, cannot be dismissed so easily in these times. For, each of you who lives and breathes here carries the full measure of the capacity to create—in the Now moment—the world as Divine intention conceived it to be.

You are on the very edge of a startling new frontier of experience in the days now dawning. You have stepped to the very edge of your capacity for Godliness in human form. And some have peered over the edge of that cliff and recognized their God-given abilities to co-create the world as it was conceived to be. Know that there are no limitations here, save those that you claim as your own. The *ascension* and the harmonization of all life in your realm is a simultaneous state-of-beingness which is ongoing and ever evolving. And it is touched by every breath taken, by every word spoken, and by every blessed stroke of your collective, materialized intent.

Let each such action be one that is inspired consciously, on your own part, and you will make a meaningful contribution. Let every gesture be reflective of your awareness of your own inter-connectedness with all life, and that creative act will carry the enhanced vibrational charge needed, collectively, to affect a shift in awareness for all.

Do not delude yourself into thinking that the world situation is "out of control." Quite the contrary; the situation is very much "under control." It is under the moment-to-moment control of the collective mind-set, which co-creates it and recreates it in the ever-evolving moment of Now. The adverse conditions with which much of your world is grappling in these times are not the victim-oriented results of random conditions. All of it is energy based. All of it has been created, energetically, by the unified force of the abilities of each and every being here. And every bit of it could be shifted, instantaneously, to conditions reflective of the ideal of All Creation, were the hearts of all focused in that intention. That result *can* be brought about. That result *will* be brought about. All that remains are the options of what will be experienced, and by whom, in the process of that shift.

The momentum toward unification in Oneness with All Creation is under way. The force of that momentum is a fact of life itself and cannot be impeded. For, the power of Love is quite literally unstoppable, exercising its capability to manifest fully and to create itself—its vibrational essence—in every conceivable expression of life.

What is optional are the exquisite heights of joy to which those aligned with Divine intent are destined to travel. What is optional are the traumas that will be co-created and experienced by those whose choices reflect their embodiment of separation from that momen-tum. What is optional is the sense of living limbo of those who are marginally aware of the reality of their ability to make a difference in these times, and whose reluctance to honor their instincts and defy consensus thinking keeps them frozen in the eternal past.

Life is moving forward, dancing with the wind, and harmo-nizing with the joy in the newborn breath of every life form on the planet. This is the dance of Creation that beckons to you in these times. This is the reality that you are capable of manifesting at this crossroads of time and space that you perceive as your world. And this is the only moment that will take you the full distance, and deliver you directly unto your destination. This moment. This very moment. Right Now.

chapter eight

Anticipating extremes of experience as
life-themes are brought to closure.

Daring to dream.

Facing the void.

Understanding the blind leap of faith.

Attaining the perspective of multidimensionality.

When a soul emerges into conscious awareness, the layers of experience, which have been carried forth through eons of incarnate reality, begin to dissipate the energetic charge that would have magnetized repeated examples of major life themes, were completion not imminent. As one approaches the fullness of the scope inherent in a given theme, the charge carried forth builds to a crescendo, providing particularly poignant episodes that epitomize the lesson in question, lest there be any doubt whatsoever regarding the underlying issues.

Do not be alarmed, as you become *aware* and the issues become obvious to you, when you find yourself immersed in extremes of discordant situations. It is you who called forth these dramas. Not consciously, of course, for in your own eyes you would probably be above such encounters entirely. But at a vibrational level, the powerful energetic charge still present within your energy field is capable of manifesting opportunities to explore those themes, despite the fact that you may have attained clarity and full understanding of the dynamics involved.

There is more required than one grand "Aha," as the light bulb of recognition bursts into the view of your conscious mind, to release fully the energetic remnants of the life theme. Do not feel, as these powerful episodes present themselves, that the experience is evidence of spiritual backsliding on your part. Quite the contrary. By virtue of the fact that you have manifested extremes of experience, despite being in a space of heart-centered clarity with the issue in question, you can feel confident that you are at completion with it. You will wish to respond in ways that will not re-escalate the energy charge that is being released in the process of drawing certain chapters to a close. Real awareness of the arduous process through which you have journeyed will allow you to respond with detachment and maximize your potential for bringing recurring dramas to closure.

With the advent of the acceleration of your ability to manifest your day-to-day experience, there is no longer the luxury of deluding yourself into believing that circumstances "just happen" randomly. There are no longer the excuses for ignoring *coincidences* that victim-consciousness provide. It becomes obvious, when the backlash is virtually instantaneous, that you have participated in a major way in the very creation of your own worst nightmares. That initial clarity sets the stage for an enlightened overview of the full epic. And you are able to see the threads that have become entwined in the tapestries of turmoil and triumph that illustrate your history.

From the perspective of the overview, one can enjoy the humor in the absurdity of some of it. And one can marvel at the antics and at one's own blindness to what now seems obvious and avoidable. When those types of circumstances can no longer "push your buttons," your own sidestepping of the energetic hooks helps to create conditions where the opportunities to do so cease to manifest. These times of completion are about setting the stage for new kinds of experience. When the energetic remnants of those dramas have been swept away, you will be ready and able to create a very different kind of adventure.

The reality you will be co-creating with the loving brothers and sisters with whom you share these times is one in which the sweetness of the highest possible outcome for all is manifested automatically. For all will know that it cannot be otherwise. In this state of spontaneous creation, one expects to experience the best-case scenario in all circumstances, and is rewarded with that as one's reality.

The question then becomes: What is it that one *wants* to experience as one's reality? It is less a question of what is *possible*, for under these conditions all things are possible. There are no limitations. One's reality manifests as a melding of will and desire—a bonding of intent and of one's joy and passion in the act of that creation. Life takes on an entirely new perspective, as one comes to understand life as a chronicle of one's heart's desire coming to fruition, and to experience its enjoyment as one's birthright.

The shift is subtle. And when you have made that shift, you may not be consciously aware that you have actually turned the corner until confronted by an awareness that the obstacles and impediments which had come to be taken for granted, are somehow no longer there. One ceases to anticipate those setbacks, and thus stops creating them. For what one expects to experience lays the groundwork for the manifestation of that experience, in one form or another. When one expects and anticipates the optimum outcome for all concerned, that outcome cannot help but be manifested as reality. Under the conditions of the world on whose very edge you stand poised, that state of the instantaneous materialization of elevated intent is the standard by which all experience will come to be measured.

Naturally, free will is very much at play in the new paradigm. One will be fully capable of manifesting disaster scenarios as well as triumphant ones. And one will become keenly aware of the power of one's thoughts, emotions, and focused intent. Instant manifestation of ill will or negative focus are the potential pitfalls in a world where you get exactly what you create energetically, virtually at once. And the wielding of this newfound power by some is a temptation that will be met by instantaneous reprisal, where the severity of the lesson would not easily be ignored or forgotten. In preparation for those conditions, you are equipping yourself, in these times, with a response mechanism designed to circumvent the pitfalls of ego-focused reaction.

As the vibration of your world continues to accelerate at unprecedented speed, the potential gift of instantaneous manifestation has been placed in the hands of those of you who serve as the forerunners of the times to come. One by one, as each of you comes to completion with your life-theme issues and adds a measure of elevated vibration to the energy of the whole, the conditions of the collective become standardized and are experienced by all.

Some will manifest their full magnificence and experience their attunement to the Oneness, in the transition. Some will succumb to their own stubborn refusal to yield to the momentum of life itself, yearning in unison for Oneness, and suffer the trials of separation under intensified conditions. No one will escape an awareness that monumental change is at hand. And no soul, however lost in denial, will be able to emerge from the times to come untouched by the knowledge that responsibility for one's reality rests with oneself. For all will recognize that reality as a vivid illustration of their own choices.

The choices that are made under the conditions of the new world of instantaneous manifestation will be choices made from conscious intent rather than being the reflexes rooted in happenstance, born of a diminished reality. When used as a tool for conscious manifestation of circumstances that reflect the highest good of the collective, the ability to manifest one's heart's desire in physical form becomes the means by which each individual, in the sanctity of his own consciousness, can harmonize his personal will with that of the whole.

When each and every being is clearly focused on the ramifications of his own actions upon the collective, that awareness is reflected exponentially throughout all of Creation, adding that measure of elevated perspective and harmonious intent to All That Is. Likewise, when one has harmonized with the heart-focus of the collective on universal well-being, the vibration of the elevated intent of the totality is reflected in what is manifested by each and every aspect of the whole. This is the ultimate expression of the popular saying that each being "makes a difference." Indeed, each of you does. Much more than you know.

The challenge, in the emerging state-of-beingness, is to attain balance between the perspective of the overview and the personal ramifications of one's choices. When choices are made from the perspective of personal or material gain at the expense of the collective, that vibration of *separation* sets into motion an energy configuration that contributes to the manifestation of circumstances that would reinforce one's sense of separation.

By opting for self-serving solutions, one creates the conditions, energetically, under which detrimental situations are experienced that reflect the underlying message of separateness. It could become easy, once one is keyed into such an energy spiral, to relive some of the old beliefs that might have manifested more gradually under former vibrational conditions. And one may lose sight of the underlying message in all choices in the new paradigm: either the reflection of one's alignment with the momentum of unification, or the reflection of one's adherence to the illusion of separation from Oneness.

Ultimately, one becomes clear in one's focus. And the options selected at each crossroads reflect choices whose ramifications result in the highest expression for all. When viewed from that perspective, there *is* truly no choice that would be of lesser benefit to the individual while simultaneously serving the universal highest good. Applying these principles now, by demonstrating your awareness of how you create your experience, it is possible to set into motion a new standard of conditioned response that reflects and manifests, consistently, the highest possible outcome of any interaction.

As each of you becomes aware of the true nature of your reality and how you set about to create the circumstances that memorialize your mind-set in a given moment, you are able to step back from the circumstances of your life and attain an overview. Ideally, that vision is a melding, not only of your history in a given area of experience, but of your aspirations and dreams of where you might be headed, were the highest possible outcome to manifest for you.

When you permit yourself the *luxury* of openly, unabashedly, fantasizing about what it is you truly yearn for, and dream of, you set into motion the energetic parameters for manifesting your heart's desire. Until you give free expression to the limitless vision you keep under wraps, you cannot, by definition, create it in your reality. When you operate your life from the mind-set of unworthiness to *have* your heart's desire—when the thrust of your energy is not daring to ask for what you truly want out of fear of disappointment—that disappointment is virtually guaranteed.

Were you to envision yourself in circumstances where your deepest longings were made manifest, without reservation and without compromise, you might begin to experience the radical shift in the circumstances of your life that would provide for you the very evidence that you do indeed create your life. Were you to dare to risk relinquishing the limitation-based thinking that keeps you anchored to the experience of disappointment in the areas that matter most to you, you might just experience a glimpse of liberation from those patterns. And were you to take the *blind leap* needed to catapult yourself out of your energetic rut entirely, you might find yourself able to circumvent a good measure of the repetition of events that are the norm in this process. That *blind leap* is one that is taken not within the confines of your mind, but is sourced within the depths of your heart of hearts. It is here in the very core of your energetic being that the connection awaits you that will, ultimately, carry you the full distance.

When you recognize the level of connectedness that you carry within your very own heart and experience the love that is harbored there for you, you will have taken the first tentative steps toward that leap. For the leap in faith comes not in one's denial, or one's repression, of the fear of "the void" that is virtually universal. The leap in faith comes of daring to *face* the void and know it for the manifestation of the illusion of separation that it, in fact, is. In order to transcend this, the ultimate fear—the fear that one is actually *alone* in this odyssey called life—it is necessary to surrender totally *to* that fear.

In order to know, experientially, the state of fearlessness that comes of aligning with one's Godself, it is necessary to undergo what might be considered to be a series of initiations. These manifestations, as experiences, of one's fear of the state of *disconnection*, are in fact illusory devices that you have created for yourself so that you might have the means of proving otherwise. By consciously choosing, in one's darkest hour, to reject the vision of hopelessness that appears inevitable, and to choose instead the knowingness that the outcome will reflect your highest possible good, you open the doorway within to the place of loving trust that will lead you home.

This *blind leap in faith* has been spoken of throughout time immemorial, and is known by every culture throughout your planetary history. Yet most address this reference with an air of mockery in light of the very real-seeming circumstances at hand. What is called for is not bravery and heroism in that "moment of truth," but total detachment. A level of surrender is called for that has released all attachment to outcome. This level of surrender is achieved when one stands on the very edge of one's gravest fear and knows, in that moment, that there is nothing to fear.

Embrace yourself, in these times, and acknowledge yourself for the extraordinary progress you are making, as a soul, in every waking moment. The very fact that you are drawn to reading these words attests to an openness on your part to aligning with the momentum of this multidimensional journey. Know that to have done so reflects great courage on your part. And that to continue to do so, despite the resistance of consensus thinking, puts you in the forefront of those destined to emerge in the new world relatively unscathed.

The opportunity to circumvent some of the mountains that most will manifest and choose to scale lies in your ability, in the moment at hand, to release the need to control the result or the dynamics of any circumstance in which one finds oneself. By consciously shifting one's intent to one of conscious *allowance* of the manifestation of the highest good of the collective, one enhances the opportunity to manifest the brightest possible outcome for oneself. In so doing, one is able to secure a state of beingness that is unencumbered by eons of trial and error and is free to explore the joys of the manifestation of Divine Will in alignment with one's own.

This is the blessed state of being toward which you strive in the present period. Yet, it is possible to manifest this state, effortlessly, merely by relinquishing the need to embody separateness, and embracing wholeheartedly the truth of the multidimensionality with which you have aligned your vision. What is meant is not that one would relinquish identity, for surely one is able to retain autonomy, but rather, that one would simultaneously embody one's knowingness of the full scope of one's beingness, while manifesting the persona, in physical form, that you know to be *you*. Thus, in the elevated stages of the transformation process, one would actually *be* the physical embodiment of the full multidimensional spectrum of beingness that is, in fact, *you*.

By opening to the reality of that heightened state of being, one would have the perceptions possible in the embodiment of each of a range of levels of identity, while retaining self-awareness as *you*. And the response mechanism would be that of the enlightened perspective made manifest. One would retain the knowingness that comes of incarnate experience, while sourcing the heightened knowingness that comes of true multidimensionality.

Each of you who is focused as a traveler on the path to Oneness is capable of functioning at these levels at any time. This is not a state that you will arrive at "someday," when you have leapt over a given number of hurdles. This is a state of beingness that is attainable in the present period and, in fact, is a state that most of you embody now, from time to time. Many have become aware of moments, where sensibilities are heightened, where the heart center is open and *connected*, and where one somehow is attuned to a level of wisdom and focus that goes beyond what one normally experiences.

In these isolated moments, one's vibration has elevated to the extent that one is able to embody the higher levels of awareness and manifest the responses that would be the norm under those conditions. Thus, even though one would not, in those moments, have access to the benefit of a full theoretical understanding of the underlying teachings, one would be able to *apply* those understandings instinctively in one's responses to interactions and occurrences.

Surely most who read these words have experienced moments where one has tapped into levels of clarity and perspective that are rarefied. And most have had experiences where one speaks with a level of wisdom that is at once profound, and yet simple. In that moment, there is the utmost clarity on the issues in question. And one wonders, in passing, "where the wisdom is coming from," for it transcends conscious mind. These isolated moments are a taste of the state of beingness toward which you journey. These are moments where you embody the elevated perspective of the enlightened aspect of your own being, with whom you are bonding in increments.

The process is not focused on a clearly demarcated "goal line" that you cross, once and for all, after a marathon run. This process is ongoing. There are quantum leaps in vibration and in the consciousness that accompanies it. And there are setbacks, as one is given opportunity upon opportunity to apply the understandings attained, until the concepts are internalized, not as newfound knowledge, but fully integrated as knowingness. As one is able to apply one's understandings consistently in one's day-to-day life, one is able to manifest the exquisite moments of clarity more and more consistently. Ultimately, the lucid levels of perception become the norm, and one's perspective stabilizes at the higher frequencies, permitting the more *enlightened* state of being to preside.

It is to be expected that moments of profound clarity are interspersed with episodes of diminished response where one's performance in a given interaction is less than elevated and reflective of the vibrational levels embodied in the moment. Do not fault yourself in these momentary setbacks. For, full integration of the principles upon which you are working at the deepest level is a gradual and ongoing process. The testing conditions with which you are living in these times allow the principles in question to be fully integrated. The application of the understandings is given a full range of opportunity to be expressed as life experience. And one is able to reach a place within where one can *feel* whether or not one is *attuned* at the higher frequencies and know when one is operating from the higher end of one's energy spectrum and when one is not.

With each choice made and in every encounter, one reinforces the levels at which one is able to perform in one's day-to-day life. As the principles are integrated into one's response mechanism and the *reflex* reactions of cultural conditioning are deleted, one emerges in a balanced, harmonious state that precludes the possibility of being drawn into encounters that would jeopardize those rarefied levels. The conscious sidestepping of questionable encounters and compromised environments help to reinforce one's heightened levels of attunement and one's ability to sustain those levels consistently. One becomes aware of a newfound self-protectiveness, stemming not from fear but from self-love. With it comes a recognition of one's right to honor and hold exalted the sanctity of that state of being.

One's priority becomes one in which the self is revered, and the maintenance of one's state of inner harmony outweighs any inclination to engage in encounters where conflict and discord would diminish that state. One becomes aware that the need to put forth one's viewpoint and to have it embraced by others is of less importance than maintaining the harmonious state within. A peaceful sense of allowance takes precedence and one finds oneself responding with what could be called "detached indifference," more often than not.

In this state, there is simply not the vested interest in certain issues that may once have been major "triggers" of emotional response throughout most of one's life. Now, such matters seem irrelevant. One takes on a distanced perspective with regard to the choices of others. And one realizes that meddling in the affairs of another has no place in this journey. Ultimately, one's choices are one's own. And while it is the cultural norm, for so many of you, to put forth your viewpoint on the actions and choices of others, this is an action that detracts from the focus on self which is of greatest importance in the times at hand.

You may feel compelled to share your more *enlightened* perspective with another, but know that when that perspective has not been requested and is clearly unwelcome, your wisdom will fall on deaf ears. Simply because you have attained clarity with regard to certain issues does not mean that others are ready to receive those insights. Each of you is on your own timetable. Each of you, essentially, is on your own unique journey. And even though many of you are making the journey hand in hand with another, the timing for the illumination of certain issues comes when the individual is ready to fully integrate those understandings, and not before. You can expect to encounter the "stonewall" response of others who are simply not able to see the simple perfection of the perspective that you have attained.

Resist the inclination to feel frustrated or disappointed when your newfound wisdom is not embraced by another with whom you are aligned on your journey. There is no place for expectation with regard to the vantage point of another being. Simply present your perspective with sincere and loving intent, as it applies to your *own* life experience. And if the conditions are such that the seed of your truth falls on the fertile soil of another's consciousness, then you will have served as the messenger, carrying forth the energetic catalyst, conceptually, that initiates the process of internalization within that being. Were the viewpoint presented from the standpoint of interfering in the free will or free choice of another, then the energetic charge carried in the message would have dissipated in the transference and would not be received or recognized as the pearl that it may well be.

It is in your highest interest to refrain from any attempts to debate and to hammer your point home when the subject of discussion is the life issues of another being, regardless of how convinced you may be of the elevated nature of your own perspective. It is not for you to judge or to call another's attention to what may appear to you to be a distorted or flawed perspective. Your responsibility is to retain that clarity with respect to your own process and your own life issues. That is all. Unless you are serving in these times as a teacher, and in that capacity your guidance has been sought by another, you are well advised to retain your internalized focus with regard to your "revelations," and to reserve your opinions for the situations where they are invited and welcome.

Your journey will carry you forth through the varied scenery of a radical new world, in the times to come. And at the same time, your newly elevated vantage point on the same old sights will add a dramatically different outlook that makes it appear as though you were seeing the world for the very first time. That world is changing. And you are changing with it more rapidly than you can imagine. The task at hand is to take care of your own emerging consciousness by applying focused awareness on the potential repercussions of every interaction and every energy exchange with another. In so doing, you make the highest possible contribution to the collective and to the intimate circle of fellow travelers who walk beside you on the road to Oneness.

chapter nine

The Plate of Life: An allegory.
Confronting resistance to change.
Coming to terms with obsolete priorities.
Recreating your life as a joyous reflection of who you really are.

This is the time to imagine what life might be like, if you were able to manifest what you really want. How would you orchestrate your life if there were no limit to what you were able to have or do? If you could start again at the very beginning, or anywhere in between, how would your story read? How would your journey end? That is a good place to begin.

Working backward now, from a vantage point of the end of your life, having created it as perfection, having accomplished all you sought to, having experienced all you hoped to, having tasted all you wished to, having manifested the highest possible expression of your own *dream* of physical reality—where would you be now? If you were taking your final breaths and watching an instant replay of all of it in your mind's eye, how would it feel to you? Would there be contentment? Would there be joy in the moments of the culmination of your life's story? Would there be any reluctance whatsoever to move on? Look at it.

This is the time to dream your dream as it can be. For all of it *can* be. What remains to be seen is what of it, from the realm of all possibilities, you will choose to experience. When presented with an enormous table laden with foodstuffs and delectable confections and one average size plate in hand, which selections do you put on that plate? All will not fit. And to sample more than a few savory bits would grow to be distasteful. Yet, all the choices are right there, awaiting you. All, potentially, have already manifested as possibility. Which, then, do you choose to experience consciously?

Naturally, the question arises: how many plates is one allowed to have?

In answer, there is no limit to the number of plates one may take and fill to brimming, if so desired. The rule is: only one plate may be taken on each visit to the table. And a fresh plate must be taken, should one desire to visit the table again.

You are not required to finish everything you have put on your plate. Perhaps, in anticipation, you have created a plate laden with fruit. After mouthful after mouthful of sweet, delectable fruit, the fruit begins to appear less appealing. After awhile, one may regret putting so much fruit on the plate and choose not to experience what remains. One would feel, in that moment, quite satisfied as far as fruit was concerned. Yet, there would be the sense that something was left to be desired. Somewhere, there still might be a craving for spice and an appetite for the adventure of the table. But, until the fruit plate was turned in, cleaned of its offerings or not, another fresh plate was not possible. And a bit of *time* would need to be allowed before one could digest all the fruit and be ready to appreciate the delights of a plate filled with spice.

This ritual can be performed endlessly. Any of an infinite number of combinations of possibilities can be placed on a clean plate, in the experience of visiting the table. Yet, eventually, one tires of the table. Eventually, one has tasted and satisfied oneself with so many variations on so many themes, that one does not feel the need to experience the table. One becomes aware that there is not the hunger for the selections on the table that once there was. In fact, one becomes aware that one is able to live quite happily without visiting the table at all. For the fullness of all the experiences at the table leaves one infinitely nourished, and one feels quite content to be still. Just to Be.

That is the stage of beingness that many of you are encountering in these times. Having tasted the indescribable joy of just *Being*, one feels less inclined, at a soul level, to spend yet another large chunk of *time* on yet another visit to the table. For, in between visits to the table, there would have been periods of resting and digesting, where varying levels of just being in the Stillness— the *Isness*—had been experienced. In fact, there you sit now, with quite a full plate, feeling less and less inclined to follow through with mouthful after mouthful of what you once imagined would be enjoyable.

Instead, you remember, on a level you cannot even identify, how absolutely wonderful it was when there was no plate at all—and no table. Somewhere within, you are able to recreate the conditions from that other *interim* state of being. And you choose, in isolated moments, to take a break from the brimming plate to just *Be*. Eventually, it becomes so obvious that the experience of *Isness* is so satisfying that *Isness* becomes one's priority, plate or no plate. When confronted with that realization, it is clear at a soul level that one may be complete with the table. And one understands that it is perfectly wonderful to just *Be* even though there is, technically, still a plate in hand.

Until one is at that point, however, there is still a spectacular table. And the truth remains, that one stands before the table, in every given moment, able to create and recreate the variations on the plate at will. One is not "stuck" with an unappetizing plate of leftovers, simply because one has tasted some of the selections on the plate. And one is not required to force oneself to consume what's left on that plate, simply out of habit. The opportunity to transform that picked over plate into one that is covered with fresh, tempting selections is always there. And that possibility is yours to exercise at all times, at will. For the plate is not one conceived in limitation. Its offerings are only as one perceives them to be. And as one rises to the fullness of one's ability to manifest one's reality, and to create what one truly wishes to experience, there is no limit to what one plate can offer.

The plate of life is a reflection of your choices, in every given moment. Whether the plate appears full or appears empty to others is irrelevant to the way in which it nourishes your state of beingness in any given moment. A pristine, empty plate could be perceived by some to be a reflection of deprivation and a cause for concern or compassion. Yet, to the one who holds that plate, its fresh emptiness is a reflection of one who has chosen to travel unencumbered. That plate's austere appearance may well be a reflection of an awareness of the riches of unmanifested experience of the world within that others cannot see in physical form.

To attain that level of beingness, one's plate, by definition, would have been cleared of superfluous choices. There would have been an awareness, in the process, that one cannot travel with ease, focused on the metaphysical, while bearing the burden of a heavily laden plate. And radical choices would have been made that would enable that individual to explore the unlimited possibilities of flying to the heights of human experience, without having to be concerned with balancing one. In these times, many have sought instinctively to simplify their experience, and stand ready to teach others, by example, to do the same.

Still others, who are in the interim stages of transformation, wrestle with the logistics of integrating their newfound awareness with commitments that have been made while creating a life of complexity. It is the ones who stand on the brink of spiritual breakthrough and have achieved, fleetingly, a connectedness with multidimensional aspects of themselves, who feel most poignantly the contradictions posed by bridging two worlds. In the days to come, these ones can anticipate a confrontation with their own inner knowingness regarding the direction in which they perceive their lives to be headed. And many will succumb to their own reluctance to dismantle the entanglements that have defined their existence thus far.

We do not wish to imply that it is in any way inferior to have manifested an accumulation of belongings on your journey. These are the trappings of an incarnate experience. Yet, it is important that one consider the price one may be paying, in terms of self-compromise, in order to maintain a lifestyle whose relevance may be obsolete. When the motives for material advantages were based in a mind-set of competitiveness, which was a manifestation of ego, the sense of satisfaction that had been anticipated and hoped for may not have been realized.

One is left, then, with the empty evidence of material gain that is devoid of the passion with which one came into form. It is that passion that seeks expression. For that is the driving force of creation which powers all life. When the zest for living and expressing and creating is missing from one's day-to-day activities, one has, essentially, disconnected from one's own Divine essence and from the interconnectedness of all life. The key to that connectedness lies not in whether or not one has a rich array of selections on one's plate of life, but in whether one is able to express and to experience one's joy of living through those choices.

Many who read these words have experienced the agonies of realizing that the scenario that they have spent most of their lifetime constructing no longer delivers the satisfaction that had been envisioned. Yet, there is so much investment in terms of time, effort, and resources in the maintenance of that lifestyle, that the prospect of change is daunting. When one's deepest needs as a spiritual being are repressed or are sacrificed to the maintenance of a surface lifestyle built on a foundation of material gain, the energy that seeks expression will set about to manifest that change, if those choices are not made consciously. When one has opened to the higher energies that are driving all of Creation toward Oneness, it is not possible to continue to manifest conditions of separation in one's outer world.

Should steps not be taken to shift the focus of one's life in such a way that the joy of living is made manifest, that energy of disconnection will set about a chain reaction whereby change is manifested despite one's best efforts to preserve the status quo. It is to be expected in these times that one's "house of cards" comes crashing down, quite unexpectedly, when one perceives oneself to be "stuck" in the stranglehold of obsolete commitments.

It is entirely possible to modify such an extreme scenario of energy transformation by tuning-in to the relevance of one's life choices to one's state of beingness, and taking action to consciously shift that focus in the early stages of the process. For, it will not be possible to avoid the changes that must be made energetically in order to keep pace with your spiritual evolution. You are becoming who you truly are, many of you in spite of yourselves—and despite your reluctance to defy consensus reality and to stand up and be counted. That too will come to pass, when the moment is right.

The work now at hand is to *arrive* at that moment. The task before you is the assessment of your circumstances and the modification of any and all aspects of your mode of creative expression, so that it becomes a joyous reflection of the higher energies with which you are aligned. It is the nature of the process to bring up for scrutiny the core issues that served as the very foundation of one's lifestyle. Recognition of the rudimentary belief structure and the priorities that underlie your conscious choices is a fundamental part of the restructuring process.

Fear of loss of what one perceives oneself to have built is a powerful impetus for the shifting of that energy. For, fear of anything whatsoever is a catalyst for the manifestation of that very outcome. In order to redirect the focus of one's intent so that it is aligned with the momentum of change inherent in life itself, it is necessary to be willing to let go of what no longer serves you energetically, and to make way for the manifestation of a radical new direction.

The belief structure you are setting about to realign is the vehicle that provides the momentum for your transformation in these times. The time is now for your honest scrutiny of those core beliefs, to determine whether you are still able to give mental credence to concepts on which you have based your life choices. Chances are, you have gone through the motions of accepting much of what society has ingrained in your consciousness. And, unquestioningly, you have emerged from the stupor of your day-to-day existence with an underlying litany that served to reinforce the standard of separation that is the norm in your culture.

The values with which you nurture your young are steeped in the very notions of striving and of exceeding the performance of others, which creates the energetic rift that divides you. One being's triumph, when it is at the expense of another's well being, is a recipe for disaster all the way around, in these times. The premise that would have the gain of one counterbalanced with loss by another is the very manifestation of duality that must be transcended if the harmony of Oneness is to be achieved. For in the circumstances to come, the efforts of all will, by definition, manifest for the good of all. It cannot be otherwise.

Those who persist in the myopic, ego-centered focus of the present will fall by the wayside as they encounter and integrate the higher frequencies. The thrust of the momentum toward the unification of all consciousness will not touch some and spare others. All will feel and manifest the consequences of aligning with or resisting the powerful energies of change. All will know, as they rise to the fullness of their potential as beings, or succumb to their stubborn refusal to acknowledge their connectedness, that the force they have encountered is undeniable. Some will call it God and will open with the fullness of their essence to the opportunity to integrate and become One with All That Is. And some will grumble and curse their deteriorated circumstances and blame others for their plight.

As the schism widens between those living in alignment and those living in separation from the energy of Oneness, it will not be possible to maintain a position of compromise. Ultimately, the choice must be made to respond to the energy that reaches out to include you in its loving embrace. Recognizing that invitation, within the depths of one's heart, is the beginning of the process. And as the smile of inner recognition spreads across your face, you know, without knowing how, that a passionate, never-ending journey has begun.

chapter ten

The ebb and flow of the tides of consciousness.
The power of nonattachment to outcome.
Timing the completion of core issues.
Riding the energies as a tool for manifestation
and karmic resolution.

The clarity you have attained thus far on your journey has served to bring you to this moment. Here, at this crossroads in time and space that you regard as "today," the consciousness of humanity stands poised, an in-breath of life, awaiting the inevitable out-breath to follow. And just as the rhythm of the breath is anticipated and experienced in harmony with the rest of your life functions as a fact of your physical existence, so too is the rhythm of your awareness—the ebb and flow of the tides of your emerging consciousness—in harmony with the in-breath and the out-breath of Creation.

The moments of clarity intensify, and then wane, over and over again. One experiences a spark of crystalline awareness and, in that exquisite moment, is convinced that clarity is there to stay. Yet, as one reaches to hold onto it, the illumination slips elusively past. And one is left to wonder whether one has actually awakened or is still wandering the back roads of the dream. In all likelihood, as the process of transformation intensifies, one is experiencing both states of being simultaneously.

The process of awakening is not one in which a definitive threshold is crossed and one is then *enlightened, transformed,* or *ascended.* There is much backsliding to be expected on this journey. And it is not unlikely to find yourself quite suddenly back at the beginning—in your own mind's eye—when you were just patting yourself on the back for having scaled some daunting precipice, thinking the summit was, at long last, in view. That is very much the nature of the experience.

Your own preoccupation with the concept of completion will keep that state of attainment ever elusive. Spiritual growth is not focused on a destination, but rather, on the journey itself. The realization of Oneness, which is the culmination of the process, is a state of beingness that you will embrace over and over again. And in the moments when that blessed state has slipped through your fingers yet again, know that you have not *lost* it, but rather have afforded yourself yet another opportunity to *find* it, within the core of your own being.

When you cease looking for the sense of connectedness and cease seeking answers outside of your own inner Source, the interim periods of separation, when your gravest doubts resurface, become fewer and farther between. Ultimately, you embody that knowingness. For, you are Oneness—in essence. And you have been so all along. When you make the transition from believing to knowing that basic truth, you are on your way to stabilizing the process of embodying that truth, such that you are fully aware of your interconnectedness with All Life at all times.

Know that the truth you seek is within you. The answers are there before the question has been fully formulated. You have manifested everything needed to have everything your heart desires right now. And there is absolutely nothing standing between you and the realization of your deepest longing to reunite in Oneness with All Creation. For, you are already there. Everything that is to happen has already happened. It Is—and continues to Be— eternally.

When your perception of the illusion of time/space you know as *reality*, is in harmony, energetically, with the momentum of the eternal *Now*, you experience what Is. When the energies wane, you experience the illusion, once more, of the elusive state of enlightenment just out of reach. Like the rhythms of the tides, this state of awareness washes up on the shores of your consciousness, nudging you into recognition of the knowingness harbored deep within. This knowingness does not wane with the rhythms of the transformation process, but is there within the depths of your being, eternally.

When the difference in these states of being has been experienced sufficiently to notice an emerging pattern, you are ready to begin to unravel the threads of the systems of belief that reinforce the illusion and keep it rooted there. When you have had the opportunity to taste the experience of Divine connectedness, to the extent that it is clearly identifiable and not perceived as a random occurrence, you are ready to embrace the process of peeling back the layers of limitation that reinforce the elusiveness of that experience. It is in the depths of that process that most who are knowingly in the throes of transformation find themselves.

One begins to draw a correlation between the moments of exquisite connectedness and the ease with which the events of one's life fall into place. Then, just as suddenly, one is blocked and stymied at every turn. One's will is thwarted. And it appears that, despite one's best efforts, nothing seems to go right. These are classic signs of the advanced stages of the journey. These are symptoms of a state of beingness in which one's attunement to the higher frequencies is stabilizing. And as one shifts one's focus from the attachments that keep one tied to material priorities, out of fear of loss, and embraces the inner-directedness and the sense of trust that transcends those concerns, one is able to let go. It is in the letting go of the limitations of the one that the limitlessness of the other may be realized.

For those who are attempting to juggle both states of being, as a way of hedging one's bets, the process takes longer. For those able to let go totally, in recognition of a connectedness that is undeniable, the shift can be instantaneous. Once that shift has been made, and one is clear as to how reality can be choreographed vibrationally, the foundations for transcending material limitations can be established. There is no question, when one is at this stage of awareness, that there is a correlation between the inception of thought and the realization of experience. And one becomes focused on the subtleties of harmonizing one's personal will with the rhythms of Creation.

When one's energies are attuned to the higher resonance, one is able to sense with ease the direction in which the current is moving, and one is able to be carried by the momentum of that energy and manifest outcomes that are harmonious. When one attempts to defy a situation by meeting adversity head-on, one disrupts the momentum and manifests results that are less desirable. Conflict can be circumvented simply by allowing it to pass without becoming ensnared in its grasp. One learns that the inclination to force one's personal will, when resistance is being encountered, can only result in an energetic nose-dive and the manifestation of circumstances calculated to create frustration. And one becomes less invested in forcing a result and more inclined to allow for the harmonization of one's own energies with the tides of Creation, to manifest the desired outcome.

Riding the wave of the energies is a skill that you will perfect as part of this process. Recognizing when you are in a state of connectedness is key to the timing of your responses to the circumstances as they present themselves to you. When your energies are at a low ebb and you are experiencing resistance, it is a time to pull inward and not to escalate adversity by directly confronting those circumstances. When you are floating upon an energy wave that is on an upsurge, this would be the time to initiate action.

In so doing, one sets one's desired result adrift in the current of the energies, and allows that momentum to carry one's heart's desire into manifestation. Nonattachment to outcome further enhances one's ability to realize an elevated result. When one's approach to living is one of trusting that the highest possible outcome will be forthcoming, that is one's experience of life. By resisting the inclination to allow fear-based conditioning to direct your choices, you reinforce your experience of riding the current in harmony.

Releasing the need to appear in control in one's own eyes and in the eyes of others is key to one's ability to progress through this stage of the transformation process. For there is no room for judgment here. Your own expectations with regard to your performance can severely restrict the pace at which you are able to progress through this phase and move on. An experience of adversity or a surge of intense emotion should not be cause for drawing the conclusion that one is off track. Allowing the energy to pass *through* one's field, and permitting the manifestations that are triggered to be unimpeded, accelerates the process of release.

Attachment to the expectation of an *enlightened* response from oneself to all circumstances restricts the possibility that a release of a negative energy charge may be achieved. When one constricts one's natural response mechanism by filtering one's emotional reactions with the mind, one inhibits the potential benefits in the releasing of energy charges still lingering around certain life issues. Permitting oneself the latitude to respond with authenticity serves to enhance one's ability to bring those issues to completion. Timing one's responses to these highly charged emotional triggers enables one to direct the release without restricting it, and thereby bring to fruition the highest possible outcome.

Similarly, the tendency to avoid certain situations and individuals as a way of circumventing conflict does not automatically guarantee one's unimpeded vibrational ascent. Ultimately, one's "buttons" *must* be pushed and the corresponding energy charge released, if one is to realize one's highest potential as a transcendent being in physical form. An energy charge that is allowed to remain will continue to draw to it repeated opportunities for release. Avoidance of the underlying issues and the maintenance of a calm veneer does not enhance one's progress. Quite the contrary.

Ideally, one is able to choose one's moment to work through core issues with key players in one's life drama. In so doing one is able to confront the issues at hand directly, while coming from a position of enhanced energy, and thereby making the highest possible vibrational contribution to the interchange. Karmic resolution of issues with key players in your life drama may be brought to completion under ideal circumstances and the optimum outcome achieved, when one is consciously aware of the potential in riding the waves of accelerating vibration. By monitoring one's own vibrational state of being before responding to an invitation to engage in conflict or conflict resolution, one is able to navigate through choppy waters precipitated by untold lifetimes of karmic history, and bring all concerned safely to shore.

Awareness of these choices is the key to all you would accomplish in this painstaking process. Tuning in to the ebb and flow of your own energies enables you to choose your moment and release the residual sparks of emotion in a way that is painless for all concerned. When the focus of your conscious awareness is directed toward that end, you are able to maintain the momentum of vibrational acceleration while releasing the self-limiting energy charges that are holding you back. By riding the wave of the energies with a clear and heart-centered focus, you become a lamplight to others who are caught in the tides of energy acceleration and are riding out the stormy seas of their own personal histories.

As you transcend the circumstances of your drama and come to embody the energy of Unity, your attunement to the higher frequencies guides you in guiding others who may be floundering by your side. Simply by being who you are, where you are, in this moment in time, and by sharing your truth and your own process honestly, you help the others with whom you share your journey. There is no need to whitewash your process for the benefit of others who may be inclined to be in judgment. There is no need to apologize for who you are and for the magnificence of your personal journey to Oneness. By being totally authentic in your humanness—your human frailties as well as your strengths, your self-perceived shortcomings as well as your triumphs, your darkest hour as well as your shining moments—you set the stage for becoming the shining example of triumph over adversity, with grace, that you truly are.

No one emerges from the journey of transformation without having weathered a storm or two and without being washed up on the shore, gasping for breath, now and then. That is the nature of the experience. It is foolhardy to think that you are expected to skim the surface of your journey untouched, and to emerge unscathed. That's not the way it works—when it works. For to realize the full potential of this journey, it is necessary that you be willing to immerse yourself in the treacherous waters of change, knowing that the ability to swim like a champion, under all possible conditions, is within you.

Let there be no doubt in this, nor fear, nor regret. The destination is pre-determined. And your course is set. You will arrive at that destination right on schedule. It cannot be otherwise. What is open is what you choose to create and to experience along the way. There is no point in deluding yourself into believing that you are not ready. For, it is far too late to wonder if it is safe to put your toe in the waters of transformation when you are already far from shore.

chapter eleven

Integrating the momentum of change as a population.
The catalyst for wars, famines, and natural disasters.
Deferring to your own truth over reality by consensus.

There is no set pattern to the way in which beings come into awareness. For some of you, the experience of awakening is instantaneous. And the necessary number of exposures to the truth of your own essence is minimal. For those ones, the experience itself is the proof needed to sustain the essence of the initial experience of *enlightenment*. For others, who have embodied that realization on countless occasions, the mind engages in the process, and the exquisitely simple essence of truth is obscured in a hail of questions, doubts, and mentalized concerns.

There is no judgment implied here. There is no method of awakening that is preferable to another. It is all *experience*. It is the journey you choose to give yourself, on your personal path to Oneness. It does not matter to Oneness whether you need to taste truth once or a thousand times before the Light goes on. This is a choice each being makes for himself. No two journeys are alike, and it is not anyone's place to presume that his or her path is the path of choice for another. All that can be shared is your own personal expe-

)f that path. For, all that can be taught is that which the student has chosen, at the deepest level, to learn.

Do not be inclined to fault yourself in becoming aware of the pace at which others may be traveling. Some may speed past, coming into instant realization. Still others, who walk by your side, continue to slip and flounder in puddles you have sidestepped— or crawled out of—long ago. It is not for you to assume an exalted stance simply because another has chosen repeat visits to the puddle in order to reinforce certain understandings. All of it is utterly perfect, just the way it is.

As you begin to sustain the rarefied perspective you have attained, it becomes obvious that you are not alone in your perceptions of what is so. For, the perspective you have assumed transcends that of the mind, which a lifetime of programming has conditioned to respond in certain ways. One takes on the vantage point of the overview, seeing several sides of a situation simultaneously. This *seeing* does not refer to *understanding*, which is a manifestation of *thought*, but rather, reflects *awareness*, which is simply the observing of what is so. That vantage point has no stake in outcome. For, it represents the detached, multidimensional perspective of your own extended state of being.

The higher octaves of your own beingness are not invested in the outcome of interactions in the "here and now" you perceive as your reality. They are able to add a measure of indifference to the energetic equation. And as you elevate vibrationally, you take on an augmented perspective and an added measure of detachment that allows for a level of objectivity only possible from a distance. While steeped in the emotion-charged dramas which are magnetized to you as part of your process, that elevated perspective is disengaged so long as ego remains engaged. For, in defending or asserting ego, you have committed to a perspective that is myopic and have placed the overview out of reach. Detaching from your investment in a particular viewpoint makes available the opportunity to see the multifaceted nature of all dramas. And it offers the potential gift in the recognition of a perspective that may not support the stance of a self still in the bondage of separation.

This level of *understanding* is not born of the process of thought. And it is not something that can be taught until the individual is ready to learn. This transcendent state of awareness comes automatically, when one is energetically attuned to shift into a higher gear of one's own consciousness. The higher level of awareness is no less *you* than you are. It is not a matter of becoming "someone else," for that someone else is you. And as your process evolves, you experience a quickening, wherein a knowingness crystallizes in such an impactful way that it is impressed indelibly upon your consciousness and becomes the only truth possible, at *that* level of awareness.

This is the nature of the process of reintegration, experientially, on the journey to Oneness. The awareness and the integration of heightened levels of *understanding* are the by-products of the process. And the end result will be achieved with or without your help. The reintegration of the fragmented aspects of your vibrational essence is a fact of human life. What is optional is the level of pain, disease, and discomfort one chooses to experience along the way.

When one clings to the trappings of a life that is a monument to separation, the dismantling process is a major undertaking and its manifestation in that individual's reality can be extremely uncomfortable. When there is surrender to the momentum of a process that is clearly "larger than life," one is able to ease through the transitions and experience the full magnitude of joy in one's realization of the heightened states of being.

These are the conditions and the choices before you now. For you *are* Oneness in every aspect of your essence. With every minute nuance of your being, you are the embodiment of the energetic equation of life itself. You are the physical expression of a momentum that yearns, in unison with all Creation, to reunite with All That Is. And that momentum is flowing in the direction in which it is flowing regardless of the thoughts, interference, or resistance of anyone—or everyone.

Should large numbers of individuals demonstrate resistance to the impetus toward Unity, the ramifications of that resistance will manifest for that group. When the collective vibration of a population of beings resonates at an impeded frequency, relative to the population at large, the group in question will experience extreme forms of energy release, which materialize as catastrophic occurrences. Energetically, this is the catalyst for wars, for famines, and for seismic occurrences and other "natural disasters." Some of these occurrences are, indeed, expressions of nature. But the impetus for them is provided, energetically, by the population itself.

There are no victims, although it would appear to some that certain individuals experience the results of energy release on behalf of the collective. For as an energetic collective, All are One. The thrust of the release would be the energy of the collective, and not necessarily the energy of the individuals affected by it. Thus, it is entirely possible for an individual who is focused in spiritual growth to experience the result of an energy release that is regionally precipitated. An individual's elevated vibration does not guarantee that that individual will be spared the experience of events triggered by the sum total vibration of the region at large.

The purging of large populations of individuals that had been foreseen for these times will, in all likelihood, *not* occur to the degree that had been anticipated. Much has transpired and the interjection of the free will of the collective has served to shift much of the catastrophic scenario that had been envisioned by seers over the course of the centuries leading up to these times of transformation. And yet, despite the monumental shift in consciousness of large segments of your population, the energetic purging of certain geographic locations seems inevitable.

The transformation of which we speak is not limited to individual human beings on planet Earth. It is a phenomenon that will touch every aspect of life itself, throughout Creation. All life forms will participate in the journey to Oneness. And all will be affected, energetically, by the choices and by the actions of all.

As an individual who is open, conscious, and focused in manifesting your loving intent, your obligation, first and foremost, is to yourself. The choices you make in these times reflect your highest desire for your own personal well-being. At the same time, your awareness of the momentum of the whole, which parallels your personal experience of transformation, will guide you in making choices that reflect that expanded awareness.

Yet, your personal well-being is not guaranteed by virtue of the fact that you are making conscious choices. You are affected, vibrationally, by the energies that surround you, in a multiplicity of ways. And the extent to which you integrate your awareness of the interplay of the energies in which you immerse yourself—and to which you allow yourself to be vulnerable—will determine much of what you will experience.

It is quite possible for an individual who is geographically well situated, who dwells in a harmonious environment, and who is open to the dynamics of change and to the emergence of the Divinity within, to manifest an exalted, joy-filled experience of transformation. It is equally possible that others, who compromise in their choices, either consciously or through lack of awareness, will manifest escalating degrees of difficulty as their energies are caught up in the complexities of the energies of the collective.

What you term "common sense" is definitely a factor with regard to where you choose to place yourself and with whom you choose to interact. Vibrationally, you diminish your own energies every time you engage in a *negative* encounter with another being. When you choose a *negative* environment in which to live, you subject yourself to constant exposure to energies that are pulling in the opposite direction to the one in which you are consciously headed, and you are affected by them.

If the environmental disturbance is too extensive to be transformed by interpersonal dynamics, there remains the choice to change your location to one that is harmonious. The choice to refrain from exposing yourself to *negative* environments is always there for you. Ideally, that choice will be made from a place of conscious awareness that the energies of the whole do affect you, regardless of how elevated you consider yourself to be.

We are all of One essence. And even though the momentum is one in which the actions of the collective affect each of the parts, and the choices of every individual affects the whole, there is an overriding impetus of Divine intent driving the process. Unity will come to be. And it is of little consequence, from the collective vantage point of All Creation, whether beings at a particular crossroads in time and space make the contribution of resistance or nonresistance to the energies of change. These powerful forces will carry you with them—flowing in the direction in which Life Itself is going and at the pace at which Life Itself is traveling—either way. Your perception of the journey, your personal experience of it, is what you are here to create.

All the rules are changing now. Your world, as you have been schooled to understand it, has already ceased to be. The cellular structure of every life form on your planet has been altered. The resonant vibration of every living thing has been augmented. And the attunement of all consciousness to heightened levels of existence has been achieved. As a race, the human population has opened itself to receive the gift of Grace. And even though precious few are aware of that shift, all are manifesting the result, in one form or another.

Some, who have recognized their newfound abilities to manifest reality as they would like it to be, have learned to pool their collective strengths and to create a force for change on behalf of all. These ones, who are small but growing in number, have set the pace for others in the "here and now," and continue to demonstrate by their own choices the possibilities available to all. These are the forerunners of a new paradigm. These are the pioneers whose lives herald a world whose rules are being written and continue to be rewritten in the moment.

The pace at which change is manifesting is an ongoing phenomenon. Life is not simply turning the page and writing itself a new overall script to which all must adhere indefinitely. The very foundations for the creation of your reality are, in fact, ever changing. In these times, that change is happening at a pace so rapid that it can be noted, not only in the cosmic overview of your history, or even by a *generation*, but in a single lifetime. Yours.

Your very life is a testimonial to change. And as you become consciously aware that the only thing that can be counted on is the realization that nothing can be counted on, you will shift from a mind-set of expectation to one of allowance. You cannot "control" anything, now. You are, in fact, totally "out of control." And these are the optimum conditions for maximizing the process of energy integration and for manifesting life experiences that you will find enjoyable. Resistance to the reality that things are not the way they were, when your schooling purportedly taught you the rules of the game, will only reinforce the difficulties you may choose to create for yourself. Openness to what your own experience has shown you is *real* is the best possible response to the conditions at hand.

It matters less what others may be saying, or what the so-called teachers of your times may be espousing as truth. Your own experience is the highest truth, for you. And it is *this* reality that, ideally, serves as your lamplight in the uncharted territory of these times. Each of you is a master in your own right. Each of you has sufficient life experience to serve as a reference point for what is so, for you. Conditioned deference to the leadership of others over the input of one's own experience can only inhibit the pace at which you travel on your journey. For, your life is a testimonial to your own choices and the insights you are able to glean from them. The habit of looking to others for a nod of approval does not serve to reinforce your autonomy as a self-realized being. It reflects and fosters dependency. There is but one truth on which you can depend, at—your own.

are possible now. In essence, the slate has been wiped .... new kind of world. One in which dreams can be realized in an instant. One in which the deities who walk amongst you can be recognized as your own emerging selves. It is a world where you are able to feel supported, happy, and successful in your endeavors. And one where the indescribable joy of being in sync with the momentum of limitlessness, is your birthright. These are the conditions at hand. Right here. Right now. Not someday. But in this very moment. The sacred journey of transformation has delivered you right to the doorstep. All that is optional is whether you choose to cross the threshold and experience it.

chapter twelve

The elusive dream that is reality.

This is the moment you have awaited since time immemorial. Your consciousness stands on the threshold of a radical shift for which you have been preparing for lifetimes. You sense that you are at a place of completion with your major life issues. You are able to identify the patterns and the themes that have surfaced again and again in the dramas of your daily life. And you sense, unquestionably, that something has shifted in the very depths of your being. The shift is subtle—barely perceptible—yet it is undeniable. The energy flows easily. And resistance is nowhere to be found.

You are a pioneer in uncharted territory, yet you are most assuredly not alone; for you experience the connectedness from within that could only be Divine. You are at a place of Oneness with All Creation. You have passed the point of no return on your sacred journey. And you have surrendered totally to the momentum that carries you, effortlessly. Your life has become a joyous celebration—a gift you have given to yourself. This is the moment.

This is the moment that you recognize what has been there all along. This is the state of being, eternally present in consciousness, that is crystallizing into form. You have given definition to your heart's desire. And now all that remains is your experience of it.

The elusive dream described above is, in fact, your reality. It has already happened. Now, all that remains, quite literally, is your experience of it. And perhaps you wonder, in this moment, how much longer the dream will remain just out of reach. The answer? As long as you wish it to be.

As long as you continue to tell yourself that you're almost there—almost, but not quite—you sustain the experience of the eternally unattainable dream. In fact, The Dream is happening in your reality, right now. And the way to be present in it is by being present in it—right now. You do not require anyone's assessment of your progress, or anyone's permission, to be instantaneously living The Dream. All that is required is to know that you are already there.

chapter thirteen

Embracing the Divine Moment: the acceleration
of the process of experiential compensation for "the past."
Recognizing the radical change in the ground rules
that govern physical reality.
Becoming "the rock" upon which all else rests.

Resistance to the changes that are transpiring within you will
necessitate prolonged repetitions of categories of experience
that, essentially, you have outgrown. As long as you cling to the
idea of the way "life is supposed to be," your life circumstances
will continue to reflect a perspective that sees itself at the effect of
circumstances beyond your control. That experiential evidence
contributes to the perpetuation of a mind-set that views itself as
a "victim." And around and around it goes, the experiences reinforcing the presumptions, and the presumptions setting the stage
for experience. Eventually, you tire of the injustice of it all. And
in some poignant moment of desperation, you will begin to dig
within yourself and to unearth the clues that, ultimately, will lead
you out of the wilderness.
    As you reach saturation point with the experience of disap-
pointment and suffering, you will have set the stage for the shift
in consciousness that can begin to create life anew. For, unbeknownst to you, the life you believe yourself to be living has not

remained a static condition. You have assimilated much in the way of amplified vibration that would have opened the doors to the higher perspective that *you*, as an elevated soul, understand and embody. Yet, still enmeshed in the complexities of your life script, you have done everything in your power to resist the radical change that those levels of energy are calculated to stimulate. And, most likely, you have continued to cling to the remnants of your self-styled life raft, as it begins to drift into the turbulent seas of change.

It is true that you were not prepared for these times—not in the way you expected to be. You were not taught to expect that suddenly, in mid-stream, your life would veer "off-course" and there you would be without a compass, or a map, or any of the other externalized crutches that you have taught yourself to rely upon. All that remains, are the clues that begin to emerge from within. And in shifting the weight of responsibility for navigating your way through these uncharted seas from what has been learned—to what has never been forgotten—you are, once again, on your way.

This time, however, the *way* has altered. It has all the familiar landmarks. But the landscape in which you find yourself is a shifting one. And you learn, instinctively, to float within the fluidity of its embrace. This is not the world of the preprogrammed automaton that goes through the motions of enacting his robotic routine, with predictable results. All that might have been predictable has been deleted from the program. And, in increments, you begin to experience a taste of the magnitude of the real power that is your true essence.

With a boost from the accelerating vibration of the world around you, you have been catapulted into new levels of experience—parallel and augmented levels of reality that enable you to transcend the nature of how you experience life. In essence, you have *ascended*. And how you adapt to the subtle differences in the nature of your new surroundings helps to determine the level of struggle you will continue to encounter as you acclimate yourself to conditions of unrelenting change.

As each level is encountered and each set of conditions is assimilated, vibrationally, you begin to refine and re-refine your perception of the nature of your reality and your place within it. And you recognize that you are invested in an ongoing process that has a distinct sense of where it is headed and has no need of your logical mind to steer the ship. With each profound level of vibrational augmentation you assimilate, understandings emerge as *knowingness* and you become quite comfortable with a process that begins to put the past, and the trials of transformation, in perspective.

These understandings are not in the form of facts with which you have been schooled, but rather, in the form of a vantage point that has always been within you. But, until these times of upheaval, these understandings were dormant, waiting for a frame of reference to give them relevance. Having transcended the conditions that kept you blinded in limited levels of perception, you are able to *see* what, until now, you could not. Your world and your place within it have shifted—ever so subtly at first. And you may not even notice, initially, that you are in fact somewhere else. And then, it happens again. And yet again. And slowly, you begin to understand the nature of what is truly happening within you— and in the world around you that reflects it.

Ascension is not a onetime hurdle that, once traversed, is an event relegated to the past. It is a never-ending process. You are experiencing its effects all the time. And it is a fact of Life Itself, whether or not you are comfortable with the idea of it. You have gifted yourself with the experience of *awakening* to the reality of your circumstances in order that you might be liberated from the prison of karmically induced conditions. Now, there is the opportunity to shift some of those patterns. And now there is a chance to rise above the conditions of experiential reprisal for choices made in levels of reality that you would consider to be "the past."

Now, you are able to flow with the momentum that unites All Creation. And with the help of the energies that flood your world, you have been gifted with the experience of a Divine moment—

one in which you have the chance to accelerate a process of experiential compensation that, under denser conditions, might have taken centuries. Or, in extreme cases, might have cast you into a holding pattern of ongoing adversity, indefinitely.

The call of the higher purpose of Divine Intent calls for a radical change in the ground rules that govern physical reality. And in order that All Life might partake of the opportunity to taste their innate Divinity and ultimately, to unite in Oneness, it was necessary that certain conditions be altered so that the energies of stagnation might be transcended by those who were ready to be free.

That is the nature of the experience of these times. That is the impetus underlying the shifting sands of your experience of life. That is the opportunity being extended to those who dare to risk all they *know* for the chance that all they *truly* know might be revealed—at all costs.

You have awakened in the middle of a never-ending dream. And your sense that you might still be dreaming has never left you. Yet now it doesn't seem to matter. For, you have had a flicker of illumination at center stage. And you have seen sure signs that the entire drama in which you experience your self-awareness can be altered at will. You have experienced evidence that in this particular dream, you are not "the hunted"—the innocent who lives at the mercy of the volatile whims of a hostile world. You have declared a time-out in the midst of all that chaos. And you have glimpsed yourself—safe in the sanctity of all that swirls around you.

In all likelihood, you haven't remained in that sacred center longer than a moment at best. But the realization registered nonetheless, that somewhere within the realm of possibility there was that indescribable sense of peace. And you recognized that state of beingness— for it is the nature of your own very essence. And this time, you will not be required to spend lifetimes trying to recapture the magnificence of that moment. You gave yourself that experience, in what you may suspect is some kind of dream-state, for you know that this time the sense of that connection would not be forgotten.

Ultimately, you will realize that you have not been dreaming. For, you are no longer asleep. The unrealness of the sense of separating from the circumstances that taunt you and thwart your will begins to establish for you a sense of separation from the illusion that you considered to be your life. You are not this nightmare. And whether or not you wish to continue acting it out becomes a question of choice. You have been given a split second glimpse of your own sacred essence as separate from "all that"—safe in the silence at the center of the cyclone—so that that choice might be identified as an option that can be acted upon at will.

You are not *in* this movie, unless you choose to perceive yourself to be. You are, in fact, *watching* it. And the seemingly unrelenting circumstances that have you in their grasp are, in fact, illusory devices that you have created to instill certain levels of awareness and understanding. Each blow to your pride, each disappointing outcome, is no more than an instrument of your own will, a symbolic *prop* with which you, as the consummate playwright, sought to mirror yourself. With the help of these powerful experiential symbols, you have scripted the opportunity to see yourself in action and to begin to recognize the moves and the lines you know by heart—and to see beyond it.

Ultimately, you will begin to notice the correlation between your unbridled intent and the shift in the circumstances you are able to draw into your life as experience. And there will be no doubt that you have begun to manifest a different caliber of experience—one that emanates from a space of inner trust and contentment, rather than from a churning core of fear and turmoil. The evidence of that fundamental transformation of the essence of the being within, is reflected back upon you everywhere you look. And there can be no doubt of the power of inner peace, made manifest, that has become your experience of physical reality.

The symbolic representations of the thought forms that float freely within your consciousness will continue to manifest, during this transitory stage. And the harmonious foundation, on which life has begun to rest, will continue to be peppered with episodes of adversity and discord. For your reality is a vivid representation of all that dwells, overtly as well as dormantly, within your consciousness. And until you have manifested the opportunities, as life experience, to draw the deep-seated energies that are harbored within you into release—and ultimately to closure—those energies will continue to emerge in the form of life experience.

Your consciousness is not a bland canvass, devoid of bias and passion, simply because you have been drawn deeply into your transformational journey and have conscious awareness of the symbolism represented by the images that unfold before you. You are still a product of your own unique essence, your conditioning, and the unresolved remnants of the dramas and traumas of your full incarnate history. All are still factors actively in play in drawing to you and in refining the resonance of your experiential reality. What will have shifted, as you continue to sift through the day-to-day details for the clues to life's mystery, is the background of inner harmony against which it all now unfolds.

The challenges, which manifest naturally in the lives of everyone, will continue to emerge in your reality as well. Yet, now these conflicts are not perceived as the earth-shattering catastrophes they may once have been. You have conditioned yourself to sidestep much of the provocation that you continue to magnetize into your energy field, and in so doing, you have begun, systematically, to dissipate the energies that habitually have drawn these kinds of circumstances to you. Slowly, you begin to become aware that the intensity of these interchanges has waned. And now, you are able to weather what might have appeared as a potential storm of major proportions, with barely a ripple upon the waters within.

You will have succeeded in structuring a renewed sense of inner trust, built in increments, upon a foundation of growing experiential evidence that, despite the accelerating momentum of the changes all around you, *you* have become "the rock" upon which all else rests. All the trappings of external security, upon which you once relied unquestioningly, have all been shaken or destroyed or abandoned. The relevance of much that was once considered irrefutable is now in question. The scripted role that you seized, in the idealized passion of youth, is now visibly flawed. In the aftermath of all the disillusionment—of the fragility of all that you presumed was etched in stone—you unearth your own eternal essence.

Despite evidence to the contrary, you are none the worse for wear for having lived through the symbolic earthquakes of your personal life dramas. If anything, your sense of resourcefulness has been strengthened. Your resiliency has been reinforced. And in the absence of much, if not all, of what you expected you would be able to bank on, something indestructible and timeless remained—your own sacred essence.

It is that very same essence that you have set about to excavate from within the core of your fears and your mentalized conditioning. Buried in the depths of your illusions, far beneath the distortions of all you were taught to believe, was a level of self that would remain untouched. It is that precious spark of your own Divinity that you sought to discover, safe within you, when all else failed—as you knew it would. You were the one who set it up that way.

When the shreds of the illusion with which you cloaked yourself had fallen to your feet and you were, at last, naked of pretense in your own eyes, you would—perhaps for the first time—be ready to see it.

Some of you have battled more inner resistance to the simple truth of who you really are than have others. And some have left the aftermath of a war-zone in your wake. Some of you knew that it would take little more than a tap on the shell of your crystalline awareness to break through to what shines from within you. Others of you were prepared to undergo a virtual holocaust within your consciousness— the resistance was that firmly entrenched. Ultimately, when all the mentalized devices for sustaining the illusion of separation have been disarmed—you surrender the fight.

at last, there is nothing left to lose, you are ready. For in the sacred space of humility, are you able to recognize and to embrace what has never been lost. That precious spark awaits you. It has given you clues to its whereabouts, all along the way—a little glimmer, now and then, just to keep you on track. But for some, it is only when you are absolutely convinced that you are hopelessly lost—when you simply do not know where to turn—that you turn within, and the real journey begins.

You have choreographed every move, so that you might be brought to this moment—regardless of what it took to get you here. Your unique dance is a reflection of your own interaction with that inner resistance. And it is that which has kept you bound to the illusion of the old paradigm and the gospel of limitation to which many of you were wedded. It required the wrenching experiences of disillusionment that you have weathered to break the bonds of some of those ties. For, the power of guilt and fear continued to nourish the unrelenting sense of helplessness with which many of you emerged into awareness in this reality. Transcending that conditioning is a feat not to be underestimated.

By virtue of the fact that you are reading these words and considering these concepts, you have surely emerged from a history of these kinds of trials. And you have reached the place in your journey where virtually everything you once held sacred has been scrutinized for relevance—and aborted. That is the plateau that must be reached before the real ascent can begin.

When you succeeded in stripping yourself of everything that supported the monumental piece of fiction you masterminded, and called reality, you became ready to begin to grasp a concept of reality, and your place within it, that is unquestionable. Now, you have embarked upon a life direction in which your inner sensing determines what is and is not so. And the power of the consensus understanding of what is real—and what is unreal—is known to be irrelevant, if it cannot be verified by how it feels *to you.*

It becomes less a question of what can be validated through analysis and lengthy journeys through the labyrinths of logic, than what your own heightened sensibilities confirm to you. And you begin to rely more on your own *inner truth*—and less on the road maps of a bygone world—to guide you through the uncharted territory before you.

These times represent an unprecedented crossroads for many. For, you have emerged in awareness at a place where many worlds intersect. Your perceptions, and the choices they prompt you to make, will help to determine just how rocky the climb ahead will be. Those of you who have reached a place of inner surrender to the majesty of what you have begun to experience—in your inner world—will encounter the "path of least resistance," which will lead you on the next leg of your journey. You will recognize it, inwardly, even though you may believe it to be "the great unknown." For the part of you that has opened, at long last, knows it well.

chapter fourteen

Bridging two worlds in one lifetime.
The development of heightened physical senses
and psychic abilities.
Perceiving and interacting with other life forms
indigenous to this reality.

Imagine for a moment that life as you know it is but a fragment
of the true nature of reality. Imagine that you have been given
a privileged glimpse into a world where the scope of what can be
created is limitless. Imagine that you have been empowered with
the ability to manifest anything and everything you wish, merely
by willing that it be so. Imagine that you are no longer at the mercy
of circumstances that are seemingly beyond your control, and that
life is the end result of your highest intent, in all instances. That
is, in fact, the nature of your reality. That is the potential with which
you have been empowered. Not in some future time and place, but
in the "here and now."

As the shifts in energies continue to accelerate and the momentum builds, the world you experience will shift accordingly. And
life as you know it will take on the refined characteristics of
realms of experience you would consider to be *other* than "here and
now." The norm for the creation of one's experience will differ from
what has been accepted in your world thus far in your lifetime. For

this lifetime marks an unprecedented shift in the nature of what is perceived as *reality*. And you who have chosen to incarnate during this period are truly pioneers who herald the world, as it will increasingly come to be.

You will not disappear from one set of circumstances and reappear in another. Your perceptions will be a refined expression of the reality you have created thus far and will continue to fine-tune as the process progresses. Ideally, those of you who have come into awareness of what is indeed transpiring in these times will succeed in circumventing some of the pitfalls in the shift toward instantaneous manifestation.

There will be ample time provided for the fine-tuning of the skills needed for manifesting the highest result, prior to the time when misapplication of those abilities would naturally result in disastrous consequences. Some of you now reading these words, whose amplified vibration would place you at accelerated levels of this process, are experiencing the poignant results of those abilities in advance of the population at large. And many are struggling with circumstances that are the result of those newly enhanced yet unrefined skills.

In the times to come, the population at large will collide head-on with its ability to harness the potential to create instantaneously with focused intent. Those who have not released the superfluous baggage of negativity prior to reaching those levels will have created circumstances that will undermine their ability to retain form at the higher levels. The shift will be sudden and dramatic in many instances. And there will be those who rise to the occasion and transform their lives in a seemingly miraculous way, virtually overnight. Others will succumb to their conditioned adherence to "rules" whose obsolescence becomes increasingly obvious to those whose awareness flows with the tides of change.

The weeding out process of who will be able to move forward in their present form will thus be accomplished—not by outside determination, but by one's own choices. Those who are not able to assimilate the heightened levels will have created circumstances which provide an exit from their present life script, and will be provided the opportunity, at the appropriate juncture, to reemerge in form at levels of manifestation that are more suitable. Those who are able to master the challenges characteristic of the higher dimensions toward which your world ascends, will begin to experience the ability to create their hearts desire as reality.

In this transitional period, most who populate your realm now bridge what are essentially two worlds. As their choices continue to refine their realm of experience, those choices will continue to determine who is able to retain form. Ultimately, when the energies stabilize, and the characteristics of two worlds merge as one "here and now," those who have relinquished their tethering to a world as it once was will be among the first to experience two worlds in one lifetime.

Many of you have begun to experience the characteristics of the world to come in the present period and have observed the subtleties of change in your day-to-day circumstances. The accelerated pace of that change leaves little room for doubt of the reality of what may once have been dismissed as figments of the imagination. Yes, these perceptions and skills are real. No, you have not lost your mind. But, in actuality, have begun to find it.

Abilities, which previously may have been considered to be reserved for "psychics" and seers, will be commonplace amongst the population at large. The ability to sense what is not perceptible to the five physical senses, as you have come to identify them, will be a natural and normal ability. These are skills with which all are gifted and which will be developed to greater or lesser extents amongst individuals.

One's vision will be enhanced to encompass the ability to *see* energy patterns and the ways in which energies flow amongst life forms in response to thought and emotion. As a result, communication will be facilitated in a way that cannot be camouflaged by word or deed. The clarity with which one is able to communicate under these conditions insures that one's intent cannot be misinterpreted. Ultimately, thought forms will take precedence over the use of verbal interaction as the communication method of choice, as is the custom in other realms of existence. Over the course of many generations to come the mode of communication amongst beings will shift from a dependency upon speech and written exchange to a culture skilled in nonverbal communication.

In the times to come, you will have relinquished a dependency upon the limitations that separate humankind, culturally, into isolated pockets of humanity, and will have taken the quantum leap into the realms of interaction that eliminate the barriers that now insure separation. In the quest of humankind toward the experience of Oneness, the universal implementation of the natural skills once considered to be reserved for "occult" practice will be a necessary and very basic step forward. In the transitional period, which will encompass many generations to come, you will begin to experience varying levels of these abilities.

Gradually, you will become aware of the ability to sense the colors that surround all life forms. You will see, quite easily, the vibrational patterns that will enable you to identify the underlying emotion and the intent of beings with whom you may have interaction. It will be increasingly difficult to disguise one's true motive or position on an issue with clever use of language. Honesty in one's expression will be a guaranteed by-product of the process. As one set of skills initially supplements the other, both forms of communication will work simultaneously and become the norm of human interaction. Ultimately, language will be replaced entirely by thought forms that offer the rich subtleties of exchange not now possible in your reality.

The five physical senses with which you have been equipped will take on enhanced levels of perception as the vibrational levels continue to accelerate. Food will bring exquisite levels of pleasure as one's sense of taste and smell allows for fuller expression. You will begin by noticing, perhaps only casually at first, that particular dining experiences are exceptionally enjoyable. You may choose to credit the skills of the chef with the outstanding cuisine. Yet, it quickly becomes apparent that the experience of dining has taken on heightened levels of pleasure consistently. And it becomes obvious that it is one's own senses that have become refined. As the levels continue to accelerate, the levels of pleasure possible increase accordingly. These categories of pleasure experiences serve to open for you the higher energy centers you refer to as chakras, and facilitate for you the higher levels of energy integration necessary for continued progress in the ascension process.

The sense of smell, with which you have been equipped, is a doorway to the higher consciousness toward which you strive, whether knowingly or not. The heightened ability to perceive the subtleties of fragrance will serve to open for you expanded avenues of expression and experience. The sensuous nature that is the natural human condition has been culturally inhibited over the course of countless generations, in what you consider to be your civilized world. In what you would deem more primitive cultures, human sensuality is an esteemed aspect of one's nature and one that is expressed openly and with great joy.

As one's senses take on heightened levels of perception, it will be difficult to repress the levels of pleasure possible from the simple act of smelling a flower, for example. The barriers of culture will begin to crumble, as the simple pleasures of existence become powerful focal points of life. The joy of being alive will come into full expression and will be universally undeniable. The priorities of striving for the sake of material gain will begin to erode as one's heightened sensibilities open one's consciousness to very different avenues of focus. And the complexities of present-day existence will give way to an emphasis on simplicity—and love.

Sound vibration will be recognized for its significance as a means of transmitting emotion and will be a key to the opening up of one's feeling nature. Sound therapies will emerge as fields of major importance in maintaining the physical well-being of the human form. Emotional health is the key to the maintenance of the physical form in an optimum state of vibrancy. The opening and clearing of blocked and repressed energy centers will be facilitated by consistent exposure to certain forms of *music*. Engulfing the senses in the rhythmic patterns of vibration afforded by selected types of music will serve to enhance one's ability to integrate the higher vibrations and accelerate the ascension process.

Using this vibrational gift will become a process through which one becomes attuned to one's own emotional response mechanism to determine which patterns of vibration will best serve to clear the various levels of blocked and stagnant energies now undermining the human condition. As one's sensitivities become enhanced as a result of energy integration, one becomes aware that certain patterns of sound stimulate the emotions accessed through particular chakras. The correlation becomes easily identifiable. And the field of music will emerge as the integration of an art form and a therapeutic science, in humankind's quest to perfect the health of the physical body.

By stimulating the experience of selected emotions, one is able to bring to the surface and to release stagnant energies that are the underlying cause of disease and ill health. Often these emotions lay dormant in the subtle bodies, having been carried forth through lifetimes of accumulated neglect. Beneath the surface of even the most consciously aware amongst you, are eons of experience that for cultural reasons have not been integrated into the energetic whole. It is not necessary to reexperience the context of the episodes that linger within you as energy, for the vibrational clearing prescribed does not require the understanding of the mind, but rather the knowingness of the feeling body.

It is not necessary to know, for example, that a sense of sadness that may be present was instilled by unresolved grief in a prior lifetime. The circumstances that precipitated the emotional blockage are irrelevant to the fact that there may be an underlying aura of sadness in the energy field of a particular individual.

One's curiosity may be peaked and there may indeed be a certain fascination to the discovery, through access to altered states of consciousness, of the details of other incarnations. But the point of the exercise would have been missed entirely if the common thread, experienced as emotion, were not identified and dealt with.

It is entirely possible to access and to release the layers of blocked and repressed emotion, accumulated over lifetimes, by becoming aware and sensitive to the categories of emotion being stimulated by experiences in *this* lifetime. When one allows oneself full expression of what is felt at the deepest levels of one's emotional body, one serves to clear those blockages and to open to the heightened sensitivities of which one is capable. Stimulation of the physical senses with conscious attunement to their correlation with particular categories of emotion, is a direct and highly effective way of clearing the energies that can inhibit progress achieved at other levels.

The enhancement of one's vibration is key to all one would wish to accomplish in this transitional time. Avoidance of any interaction that would be counter to that focus would be an action of choice. Tuning in to one's natural abilities to sense energies, it would be advisable to exercise selectivity as to where and with whom one interacts in one's day-to-day activities. Individuals whose energy resonates discordantly with you are likely to drain your vibrational levels during an interaction.

It becomes less important, as the transformational process accelerates, to be polite or to assert oneself regarding a perceived injustice, than to focus one's awareness defensively about the energetic pitfall inherent in a potential interaction. It will come to be perceived as preferable to avoid certain environments and individuals completely rather than to subject oneself to exposure to discordant energy. It is not your mission to try to convert others or to change any mode of beingness other than your own. When one monitors, with conscious awareness, the energy one brings to any situation, one makes the highest possible contribution to the well-being of all.

oneness

As your vibration continues to accelerate, you will become aware of subtle shifts in your perception of all that surrounds you, for everything in your world is comprised of energy. You will become keenly attuned to your surroundings and will feel the urge to place yourself in areas where the environment resonates with an augmented vibration. Honor those sensings. You are likely to feel compelled to spend large portions of your time in the haven provided by nature. And in so doing, you will discover that you have become sensitive to the subtleties of interaction with the other levels of consciousness that co-habit your realm.

It is entirely to be expected that you will become keenly aware of an entire realm of existence whose subtleties eluded you at the lower vibrational levels at which you emerged into consciousness in this lifetime. Now, as the worlds within your world come to overlap, the true realities will emerge in vivid and fascinating detail. In the sanctuaries of your forests you will discover the richness in the world of nature. Here a broad spectrum of consciousness comes to life, when one becomes vibrationally enhanced, and one discovers the natural ability to interact, in awareness and in thought, with life forms that once were considered to be inanimate.

Conscious awareness—what some consider to be *intelligence*— is inherent in every life form in your world. Some of you have already discovered the ability to see the energetic definitions—the auras—that surround the physical forms of all matter. Some are able to perceive, with surprising ease, the world of the nature spirits whose joy in being alive brings a fresh perspective to the experience you have come to regard as "life."

In time, you will be able to see, in a way that could be considered *physical*, life forms that were previously imperceptible to the physical senses of most humans. And those abilities will come to be regarded as *normal* by generations to come. There will be a cooperative air of live-and-let-live amongst all creatures in the crossroads in time and space you consider to be your world. And the natural harmony, with which this realm was blessed at its inception, will be restored once more.

That is the world toward which you journey, at unprecedented speed, in the present period. These are but some of the abilities which you can anticipate having available to you in your experience of aliveness in this physical incarnation. This is the adventure that awaits you as you venture forth from the prison of illusion you consider to be your reality. And a small taste of what awaits you when you let go of your tethering to the familiarity of the past and open to the possibilities to be experienced in the eternal "here and now."

chapter fifteen

The vibrational prescription for maintaining physical wellness in a rapidly shifting reality.

The fortitude of one's physical form is a subject of great importance and one on which many are focused in these times. The purification of one's physical form as the vehicle for ascension is one of the most crucial areas toward which one can direct focused intent, and one toward which we wish to direct your attention. Your form is a direct reflection of your vibratory levels at any given time, for the human body is merely the manifestation of energy as form.

To maintain the physical body in a state of optimum health, it is necessary to look beyond consensus wisdom based upon truths of the past. For, your limited physical world provides you with the clues of the scientifically verifiable, and this alone. The wisdom needed for these times is founded upon a world of spirit not accessible to the physical senses.

The form in which you venture forth on this sacred journey harbors within it what could be termed "cellular memory." In this vibrationally based encoding lies the keys to the physical and metaphysical transformation in which you are engaged. The "cellular memory" referred to here deals not merely with the linear history of past experience, carried forth as energy, which influences one's physical state. The encoding in question is carried to this time frame from what you would consider to be the future, and manifests at the encoded moment of the eternal "here and now." The molecular changes occurring in your physical form are triggered energetically both as a result of the manifestations of personal choice and the energetic changes occurring all around you.

The challenge now confronting you is to integrate the monumental cellular changes occurring within every being on the planet, with the reality of everyday living as you understand it to be. The ground rules of your realm are changing with every passing moment. And the pace of that transformation can leave you feeling marooned in an alien land if you are not prepared to surrender totally to the process and to accept that many things simply do not make sense. Not yet. As time adds experience to the equation, understandings will become obvious. And occurrences, which are clearly *real*, yet from a certain frame of reference may have been difficult to explain, will suddenly take on scope and structure and fit into the framework of a reality with newly established parameters.

In the interim period, in which you most assuredly find yourself at present, the approach of choice is to trust one's experience as one's truth, despite the fact that that experience often defies logic and the accepted ground rules of your world. Those rules are best relegated to a history that continues to shift in every waking moment, and will continue to do so for the duration of your journey in physical form. For physicality, by definition, is a condition structured to accommodate change.

Nothing has ever been constant in your world. But until this period in your history that change occurred so slowly, it was immeasurable and provided the false impression that the human condition was a static one. Now, as the energies that surround you accelerate with a momentum never before experienced in your world, what could be termed *human* is a being who has, in fact, been born anew.

Your present medical science will need to contend with these changes and will find itself increasingly challenged to solve the riddles programmed into your forms, as the interrelationship between the physical and the nonphysical aspects of life becomes undeniable. Medical personnel will increasingly defer to those now known as "healers," as technical knowledge is replaced by spiritual connectedness. True healing will be the inevitable result of addressing the non-physical infrastructure upon which life itself is based.

Techniques that are feeling-based will produce often-instantaneous results, where previously tried and true medical methods yield disappointment and a sense of futility. The population has, even now, begun to recognize the validity in the seemingly miraculous. It senses instinctively that the answers that are sought transcend what is available through traditional methods.

Vibrational medicine will replace the traditional techniques in present practice. And technical schooling will come to serve as a footnote to an emerging population of young beings gifted with healing abilities they oftentimes do not understand. There are others seeded amongst you who are skilled with healing abilities now considered rare amongst the population at large. And these ones, whose energetic connectedness has become apparent to them, will be guided in how to teach the techniques of purification to beings presently coming into form in far more complex physical bodies.

The purification of one's physical form is the single most significant activity upon which you may choose to focus your energies in the present period. For within your cellular structure you carry eons of vibrational imprinting calculated to keep you rooted, energetically, to a realm that is fast becoming a vibrational relic. In order to transcend that tethering, it is necessary to recognize that monumental changes are occurring within you and to allow those changes to occur unimpeded. It is counterproductive to the objective of all you would hope to achieve from this point forth to inhibit in any way *symptoms* that may occur as a natural by-product of the process of purification.

The amplified energies, with which you are surrounded as a natural part of living and breathing, have a purging effect upon the human cellular structure. There are aspects of your physical form that react to these stresses in ways that traditionally would have been classified as "illness." Yet, to alleviate those signs of cellular cleansing would, in all likelihood, result in insidious deterioration of one's physical well-being.

Maintaining oneself in physical and emotional balance is key to the longevity one would hope to achieve. Benign physical symptoms should be recognized as the signs of cleansing that they truly are and should be allowed to run their course unimpeded, despite the minor discomforts that may be experienced. Inhibiting such symptoms will, in virtually all cases, produce repeated episodes of the body's efforts to cleanse itself, with escalating degrees of discomfort.

The use of herbal medicines as practiced by certain indigenous cultures may have the effect of accelerating the cleansing process. The implementation of substances known to heighten the body's natural inclination to eliminate impurities from its structure is encouraged. Substances whose sole purpose is to mask symptoms and provide a false sense of well-being are counterproductive to the purification process and are therefore potentially dangerous. One is cautioned against concluding that insignificant physical symptoms are a sign that something is wrong. Quite the contrary. It is likely that such symptoms indicate the physical body's preparation for assimilating higher levels of energy and maintaining vibrant good health despite radically altered vibrational conditions.

The well-being of the physical body is interdependent upon many factors in the present period. Each of these variables works interactively with other energy forms, present in the cellular structure, to co-create the state of physical health. Certain teachers now on the cutting edge of energy medicine in your world are putting forth information that establishes with clarity the correlation between one's thoughts and emotions and the state of one's physical health.

While those teachings are certainly a milestone on the path, most of the information now being presented in this way still limits the scope of the subject to that which is measurable and experiential. The fullness of the creation of one's state of well-being must encompass the energetic programming one brings into this lifetime, as well as energy, in the form of experience, being magnetized into one's energy field by simultaneous aspects of self in realities that co-exist parallel to the one you recognize as your world.

These are concepts that may be difficult to grasp in a linear context, for their very definition defies the logic that is a foundation for the human condition at your level of existence. Nonetheless, it is necessary for one to be sensitive to the cues, recognizable as patterns of experience, in order to transcend the programming carried in one's cellular structure that would provide an automatic vibrational link to parallel life forms and consciousness that is, in essence, *you*.

It is entirely possible for a being to be making all the highest conscious choices with regard to physical wellness, and yet to be struggling, energetically, with adversity that manifests as impurity or illness. And while the cause of certain adverse conditions may rest or be partially influenced by circumstances beyond the physical, so too does the prescription for transcending those conditions rest upon one's ability to address the physical form from the standpoint of energy.

Parallel realities in which *you* co-create the world you experience in the "here and now" exert a strong influence, energetically, on what you consider to be this reality. The manifestation of experience, be it as an event or as a physical condition, is predetermined to some extent by the residual energy carried into the "here and now" by choices made in what you would consider the past, or indeed, the future. For all of it is actually happening, energetically, *now*.

Sensitivity to patterns of experience will help to isolate the core resonant energies that magnetize to them the vibration that manifests as particular physical conditions. When one addresses a condition energetically, either through the vehicle of thought, or by administering vibrationally focused therapy, one serves to dispel an element of the magnetizing charge that pre-disposes an individual to a particular condition.

Vibrational therapy, correctly practiced, is potentially the most significant breakthrough in the field of wellness in your present reality. For this approach is able to address what some term a "predisposition" to certain states of being. That predisposition is carried forth in one's cellular structure and manifests at the appropriate moment in one's lifetime, when accumulated vibrational toxins reach levels that result in physical symptoms. Raising one's vibration, as a conscious focus, can do much to alleviate conditions that one was predisposed to manifest, from one's very inception in this reality in physical form.

It is crucial that the layers of accumulated *karmic* toxins be released, energetically, as one's vibration continues to accelerate in these times. For, the physical vehicle in which you venture forth is now and will continue to be a reflection of all you have been and all you are yet to be, energetically. The choices made now exert a vibrational influence on the whole and help determine what is experienced on all levels.

In order to manifest physically at the levels toward which you travel, it is necessary to unburden the physical body of the eons of vibrational residue that you carry, inadvertently. It is not possible to sustain life at the higher levels if you are grounded by density in your cellular structure. It is necessary to *process* your energetic make up, in order to isolate the patterns of choice and response, physically, emotionally, and at the level of the core vibration some refer to as *spirit*. For all levels harmonize and resonate as the vibrational sum-totality that manifests as your experience.

When one is unbalanced in the energy carried at these interdependent levels, it is likely that the experiences one magnetizes may appear inappropriate. One is left to wonder why a seemingly elevated being, in the spiritual sense, might be manifesting emotional or physical adversity at extreme levels. It may well be that the individual carries residual emotional baggage, imprinted in the cellular structure, that draws to him a pattern of adversity, despite a level of spiritual development.

It is best to suspend judgment about the levels of progress made by others whose dramas may include you. For there are those amongst you who are walking contradictions, working through issues at the highest levels, and manifesting extreme scenarios that might be misinterpreted. Best to reserve judgment for your own process, and to tune inward for clues to the patterns that keep you in a spiral of experiential repetition that may have been transcended on other levels.

It is rare to encounter a being, in this stage of your transformational journey, who is balanced in his spiritual, physical, and emotional bodies. In most cases, the life issues that have surfaced as experience would have manifested as the result of energy imbalance, carried at the cellular level of one aspect that is not matched vibrationally at another. It is rare for an individual to harmonize the vibrational acceleration of all bodies at this stage of transformation. For a highly complex combination of factors combine to establish the levels at which the energies stabilize in each of these areas.

Once the purification process is initiated and conscious awareness of it has made purification a priority, one can expect to experience rapid acceleration in the areas where one has focused attention. It is to be expected that there is a sense of alternately progressing and backsliding, as key life issues are brought to the surface and dealt with. Like peeling back layers of the proverbial onion, the levels of accumulated toxins tied into key life themes are addressed and released, as one becomes aware of the patterns of experience that have invited repeat performances throughout one's lifetime. By allowing oneself to experience the depth of one's feelings on particular life themes, one is able to release, sequentially, a measure of the energy charge carried, and diminish the likelihood that extreme variations on given themes will manifest as life experience.

Ultimately, when one has probed the depths of certain categories of experience and has taken the time to address fully the toxic manifestations of the physical form, levels may be reached whereby balance is achieved. One then finds oneself at the leading edge of an energy wave as humanity surges forth in its ascent. When that stage is reached, one's perceptions begin to alter, initially in subtle ways, and one becomes aware of having a presence in more than one reality simultaneously.

It may be difficult for you to conceive of such a state of being from where you stand at this moment. Yet, it is likely that you will experience inklings of that stage of ascension as your process begins to intensify. Many are already having such experiences. And that state of beingness will be quite commonplace and will come to be considered the "norm" as the transformation of your realm continues to progress. The reality you once considered to be "carved in stone" would have, by then, given way to the subtleties of newfound perceptions. And it would have become obvious to all who remain in physical form that the *solid* foundations of your reality and physical evidences of matter are truly energetic thought forms that can be altered at will. At that point, life begins to take on a very different perspective.

When it becomes obvious that reality can be created by the subtle manipulation of the energies at each of a multitude of levels, entire fields of expertise begin to emerge, focused on balancing and maintaining categories of vibration. One discovers the abilities to create, at will, what one wishes to have manifest, and experiences the result as physical reality. The challenge becomes that of conscious awareness of the underlying impetus for certain actions. Purity of intent becomes a key factor in how successfully one is able to sustain one's levels and to achieve what one wishes to experience.

During these times of transition, you can expect to have glimpses into the world where these kinds of abilities are the norm. And you may note, with fascination, that there are certain days where everything seemingly goes "right." You can feel, in those moments, that you are "in the flow" with all that surrounds you. And quite literally, in those moments, you are.

When your energies are in harmony with the energies of your environment at large, you are, in fact, *manifesting* your intent and willing it into form. You are, in those moments, bridging the gap between the worlds and experiencing the higher levels as "here and now." For "here" is not a static place and "now" is not a static time. The reality you experience is a force field that is constantly in motion, ever shifting in response to the infinite combinations of subtleties that surround you.

You may perceive your world to be one that is fine-tuning itself in barely perceptible ways, and then, moments later, discover that things are radically different than you thought you remembered them to be. As you allow yourself to become immersed more deeply in the process, you will realize that there is but one factor that remains constant in what you perceive to be your reality. One awareness. The sense of beingness that is not separate from all that surrounds you, but recognizes itself as the consummate integration of all that is perceived and all that is perceiving it. That is the experience of Oneness toward which you journey. That is the experience that will be your reality sooner than you can imagine.

chapter sixteen

The sacred science of manifestation.
Transforming possibility into probability.
Overcoming karmic conditioning.
Manifestation as an emerging art form.
Building a foundation for mastery.

As you journey ever deeper into the transformation process, you will become intensely aware of the signals provided by your life circumstances and by your state of physical health as to your vibrational levels relative to all that surrounds you. It will be quite easy to determine where you stand in your own process, at any juncture, simply by becoming aware of the ease or the difficulty you experience in manifesting your heart's desire in your day-to-day life.

You will find that you have become the observer and the object of that awareness, simultaneously. And the process of assessing your state of beingness and modifying your choices accordingly will become an integral part of living. This approach is what many term "conscious." For, under the conditions now well under way, there is not the luxury of random action unsupported by focused intent. Every action, every thought, and every nuance of every choice each add their measure to the vibrational whole and contribute to the creation of the reality you experience as your life.

You will begin to feel pressed to assess your life direction again and again as the process intensifies. And you may find yourself feeling compelled to make radical changes in your life circumstances that would result in the severing of ties with situations that no longer serve your highest purpose, both professionally and interpersonally. It will become obvious to you that certain relationships and certain activities have become obsolete, in terms of your spiritual evolution. And it will continue to become clear to you that you cannot continue to justify perpetuating situations that leave you drained energetically.

You may already be keenly aware of the intensity of the influence of your surroundings and the individuals with whom you choose to interact, upon your state of being. For, the veils of separation have become very thin, and one experiences an intensified energy exchange with every being and every situation in which one chooses to engage. It is certainly in one's highest interest to be aware of the energetic environments in which one places oneself and to make conscious, focused choices accordingly.

It may be necessary for ties to be severed with affiliations that no longer resonate harmoniously. There are no rewards given for martyrdom on this journey. There is no advantage whatsoever in prolonging that which no longer serves your highest good. And there is no yardstick with which that determination can be made, beyond your own inner-knowingness. This is the time to become attuned to your life priorities and to selectively weed out the individuals and activities that are not uplifting.

You have no obligation whatsoever to carry others down the path on which you travel. Those who journey by your side must be energetically autonomous if the association is to be mutually advantageous. Those who continue to try to coerce you, against your natural inclinations, to accommodate their personal preferences, only serve to drain your energies and distract your focus. For the focus of this process is upon the highest expression of self. By honoring your own personal truth, and resisting the conditioned

inclination to compromise in the name of diplor
in serving the highest expression of the ener
which you are interconnected.

Becoming disciplined, in where and with wh.... ... .
interact, is highly recommended, with care that those choices
come not from subjective judgment of others, but rather, from focus
upon your own highest good. Until you develop the ability to be
vibrationally impermeable, you would be well advised to be aware
of the extent to which your energetic state of being is influenced
by everything and everyone that you encounter.

As the ability to hold one's energy stabilizes over time, it is likely
that the vulnerability that characterizes this stage of the transformational process will diminish. When one reaches those levels,
the natural sense of detachment that one adopts in the early stages
of this process, as a protective mechanism, gives way to a sense
of having merged, with conscious intent, with All That Is. For some,
the entire process is instantaneous. For others, focused on letting
go of layers of constraint, this stage of energetic vulnerability can
be prolonged and agonizing. One can continue to ride the vibrational roller-coaster throughout the transformation process. Or one
can choose to step off and seize control of a vibrational state of
being that one comes to realize is self-determined.

It takes some practice before you become acclimated with
the new levels and the techniques for harnessing your awareness
of the shifting energies as they occur in your daily life. You become
accustomed to sensing surges in energy and begin to recognize those
moments as opportunities to put forth, in the form of focused
thought or verbalized intent, what you wish to have manifest as
form. The ease with which results seemingly fall in your lap will
amaze you at first. And as you begin to become comfortable with
your newfound abilities, it will feel very natural indeed to be
choreographing the dance of your existence and watching the
performance virtually simultaneously.

One develops an instinctive sense of the timing of casting the net of one's consciousness upon the seas of opportunity. And the results that you manifest leave little room for doubt that the nature of your reality and the ground rules for optimum performance here have shifted radically. It is not the same world as it was when you were taught how to survive here, not so very long ago. The page has turned now. And a radical deviation from what you may once have believed was your life script is written in bold on a new page of reality that appears before you everywhere you look.

You may choose to cling, in denial, to what you have been told and what you have been taught. Or you may dare to recognize what is undeniable to your own senses and what is irrefutable as your own experience. And you may be amongst the first to know the wonders of a world in which you are truly a pioneer. The guidebooks have yet to be written. For those of you who have ventured forth on uncharted ground will have forged a trail, through your own experience of day-to-day living, that the others who follow in your footsteps will herald as gospel.

The truth you speak, as you share your life experience with the others who walk beside you during this extraordinary time of transition, will form the foundation of a reality that is both new and timeless. Your world will have shifted radically, from the standpoint of where, in the crossroads of time and space, you are acting out this particular drama. Yet, the abilities you have begun to manifest, and will increasingly come to do so, are commonplace in the realms of reality toward which your world evolves energetically.

The ascension experience, of which you are an integral part, is one that is in process eternally. It is the motion of Unity, questing toward the completion of its own heart's desire, delighting in the reuniting and the bonding with All that it Is and all that it continues to become. You are of that essence at every level throughout Creation. And in this lifetime, you have chosen to give yourself the experiences that carve the truth of the momentum of change, indelibly, in the stone of your consciousness. You have chosen to be present and to partake of the voyage. You have chosen to venture forth and confront the experience of the great unknown, in order that you might relay that knowingness to others who have yet to encounter the shifting tides of your reality.

You are amongst the forerunners of a new paradigm who will set the precedents upon which the ground rules of the new world will be based. You have identified yourself to yourself and have dared to stand alone in the Light of your inner truth, while others, still cloaked in the self-righteousness of consensus thinking, throw stones—as the very fabric of that reality unravels. And you have exercised the wisdom to stand firm in your truth and watch quietly as the cards are shuffled and reshuffled and the lives of others succumb to the shifting tides of change.

It is not a question of who is right and who is wrong. For each is convinced of the validity of his beliefs. And, as such, that is the reality and the parameters within which each individual operates. What will separate those who will thrive in the new energies from those who will perish is the framework for how one chooses to proceed in the face of the evidence presented. Those who cling tenaciously to a world as it once was will face increasing difficulty, despite playing by the "rules." Those who recognize that those rules are redefining themselves in the moment are best equipped to ride the currents in the direction in which they are headed.

The energy of nonjudgmental receptivity best equips you to translate pure awareness into action that is inspired, yet sensitive to the energies that will carry them to fruition. Developing an attunement to the energies as the surges peak and then wane helps you to harness the potential for manifestation and to avoid the low ebb in thought, word, and deed. Simply by being aware of the flow of the energies around you, and the ease with which you are able to sense a response to the creative *feelers* you send forth at the inception of a concept, you learn to merge energetically with the moment and become One with it.

The timing of one's response to a given set of circumstances can make a dramatic difference in the effectiveness of one's efforts. The ability to sense when to assert one's energies and when to withhold them is a powerful asset to be cultivated and developed. Knowing when to relinquish one's grasp on a situation and allow the energies to carry the potential inherent in the circumstances to fruition is a key to harnessing the power with which you have now been gifted.

It is not enough to recognize the potential in the ebb and flow of the energies as a means for timing one's own actions. One must be sensitive to the balance between action and nonaction as a tool for manifesting one's will. Oftentimes the action of choice is simply to do nothing at the appointed moment and to allow the elaborately interwoven variables surrounding a given issue to settle into place quite naturally. This is the difference between manifesting a result and allowing a result to manifest. Often the latter approach is the more effective and produces the most desirable outcome. Patience is a powerful skill. And you would be well advised to exercise it often while strengthening your ability to harmonize with the energies that surround you.

It is not always possible to harness a vibrational high point and the potential it offers for delivering a desired outcome. For even though your efforts might increase your chances of manifesting that result, the outcome of highest vibration has often been predetermined by factors that are beyond your conscious control. In the realm of possibility, all variables are present and vie vibrationally for the chance to manifest in the reality you experience. All are, in fact, materialized as form or experience, in the infinite field of possibilities that surrounds any issue or crossroads.

In the determination of which combination of variables will carry the highest electromagnetic charge, and thus materialize, karmic patterning plays a powerful role. Conditioned responses, preprogrammed by the life choices of all concerned on a given issue, weigh significantly in transforming possibility into probability. Much can be done to counterbalance the influence of such factors, yet they form the foundation of the creation of reality and cannot be discounted in your efforts to manifest a less likely result.

Do not feel that you have failed in your quest to amplify your vibration and respond in a conscious way simply because the result you most desire is not forthcoming instantaneously. It takes much time and practiced, controlled response to elicit a particular result and to offset the likelihood preprogrammed into certain preexisting variables.

As one progresses as a conscious practitioner of manifestation, the full scope of this fascinating art will come under careful scrutiny. And like any art form, the art of manifestation will invite mastery, as it does in other realities. One's very life circumstances become testimony to the skills one brings to this, the ultimate arena of creativity. For the medium is unlimited and the mode of expression embraces the perfection of the balance between heart and mind—between understanding the technical aspects of balancing and counterbalancing the energy and the passion one brings to the opportunity in question.

The canvas upon which the masterpiece is created holds inherent in it all the potential pitfalls called forth by related instances in what one would consider to be the past or the future. Each, in actuality, is happening in the "now" moment and carries the appropriate electromagnetic charge that adds its measure to the equation. One is able to influence the balance of this complex combination of factors and draw forth a less than likely result by becoming attuned to the energies of the moment, the environment, and one's own being, in timing an action or an expression of focused intent.

One can become exceptionally skilled at transforming conditioned responses, and overcome deep-seated factors that one might consider to be *karmic*, reversing patterns that have manifested for lifetimes. When such skills are successfully employed, one can diffuse the dominant electromagnetic charge surrounding a given issue and alter the range of probability on the issue in question. To do so consistently will be the hallmark of mastery and the foundation of the field of manifestation.

There will be many who approach manifestation as a science and yet others who regard it as the highest expression of art. In times to come, the melding of the two approaches will yield a generation of highly skilled practitioners who will set the standard for transcending form entirely. At the present crossroads in time and space you consider to be your reality, you are at the outer frontiers of that new world of possibility.

It will become common knowledge, quite soon, that each of you is creating the reality of your life experience. And the mindset you call "victim consciousness" will, by definition, be relegated to obsolescence. It will no longer be possible to blame another being or "circumstances beyond your control" for a given situation. For all experience will be recognized as self-determined, on a fascinating complexity of levels. And it will be necessary for every being to take responsibility for the part played by each in the co-creation of the reality of mutual experience. When it is no longer possible to deny one's own part in that creation, one is left little choice but to recognize the role one plays as *creator*, and to cross a major threshold in the journey to Oneness.

The new world, at whose brink you stand in the present moment, represents a transitory stage that integrates the world of physical form and the world of instantaneous manifestation. The care one is able to demonstrate in applying one's newfound skills will determine the degree of joy or frustration one is able to experience. And a by-product of the exercise is the knowledge that there is no one to thank or to blame for any of it except oneself.

In the present time frame, which represents a crossroads between two worlds, one is best counseled to be gentle with oneself. It will not enhance your situation in any way to blame yourself for what you realize is your own self-created condition. Likewise, it does not serve another for you to point out, self-righteously, observations and realizations culled from your own experience. The Ↄ another being may be wrestling with circumstances y transcended testifies to the fact that they are schooling themselves, experientially, on certain issues.

Real knowingness comes from life experience and that alone. One can certainly intellectualize the process and try to force understandings that have been introduced by others or read about in books. Yet, until the lesson is manifested as poignant life experience, the real mastery of the lesson, upon which transcendence is based, is not possible. It serves no one to point out, condescendingly, understandings that one was fortunate enough to have learned through painful experience. It is counterproductive to pay lip service to platitudes one has encountered mentally, and which are far from integrated as experience in one's own life.

There is no need for apology or for condemnation for life circumstances that might be considered to be beneath one's level of understanding on a given issue. The very fact that a traumatic episode has manifested in such a person's life script is a clear indication that that person is working on the mastery of a particular issue. Beings who are inclined to counsel others are cautioned to become aware of the subtleties of the approach employed. By providing theoretical truisms, or by meddling in the process of another, one nullifies the growth that might be possible in allowing the individual to experience those circumstances fully and to feel the emotions triggered by a given drama.

When encountering another who is enmeshed in a major drama and is teetering on the brink of a breakthrough in realization, it is best to lead that person, through carefully posed questions, toward discovering the answers within himself. In this way the lesson is driven home in a powerful way, and is not wasted and likely to be repeated, in order that the understandings be integrated as knowledge. Knowledge comes of having *lived* the lesson, not merely having intellectualized it theoretically. Be aware of your loving intentions, and be sure that you are not undermining the progress of another by preempting his process of integration with well-meaning advice.

You are here for you alone. And though you may delude yourself into thinking that you have transcended these times of transformation simply because certain metaphysical understandings have sparked a sense of recognition within you, the truth remains that your own process must be experiential if it is to form a strong foundation for the conditions to come. Honor your own process of transformation for the richness it is programmed to provide for you. And respect the magnificence of the processes of the beings who journey by your side, by allowing for the full expression of their humanness—and your own.

chapter seventeen

Diet for a new reality.
Maintaining wellness under conditions of accelerated vibration.
The significance of energy work.
The concept of cellular purification.

The higher levels of energy integration, of which you have had a small taste, will produce varying degrees of discomfort and symptoms in certain individuals that could be misinterpreted as illness. It is to be expected, as the levels are amplified and one's exposure to them intensifies, that the natural process of purification will take on new emphasis. It will become increasingly difficult to ignore evidence that radical changes are occurring in your physical body that, if left unaddressed, will manifest as poor health or a threat to the maintenance of life.

The forms in which you incarnated were designed to sustain the levels of density that were to be expected under the environmental conditions then standard in your realm. The levels of environmental pollutants now present in all the substances you allow to merge with you energetically—your air, food, and water—have added levels of density to your bodies that are so extreme as to have made the human being an endangered species in your reality.

When this foundation of impurity is compounded by vibrational levels designed to amplify and accelerate the natural purification process, the body is confronted with extreme levels of toxic refuse that it is not designed to process in the normal way. In many cases, your physical forms are already bogging down under the burden of the accelerated detoxification process being triggered by the amplified energies all around you. Under the new vibrational conditions, one can no longer sustain the levels of impurity that once were possible. The body's natural inclination to slough-off toxic debris is amplified to unprecedented levels, and as the energies continue to accelerate, will initiate the release of cellular waste at a rate that could result in a systemic breakdown, if one is not conscious of the process.

Focused awareness and conscious participation in the body's purification process is required to maintain the health of the physical body during the times of transformation now upon you. It is no longer possible to be lax in one's practices of nourishing the physical body and hope to sustain a state of health. The ingesting of substances that are toxic by way of chemical pollutants is best avoided. Substances that are physically addictive are counterproductive to the entire focus of maintaining a high vibration in these times.

The drinking of contaminated fluids, such as are available for public consumption in most areas of your world, is hazardous at best. Increased quantities of fluid intake are necessary for flushing through the accelerated levels of toxic waste being released into your physical body. It is important that pure spring water, or water that has been distilled, be ingested and that water that has been processed chemically, and is being offered as "drinking water," be avoided. Substances containing a high alcoholic content are not in harmony with sustaining a high vibration and are not recommended.

The milk of domestic animals can be considered a healthy part of the human diet only when it is uncontaminated by chemical pollutants and additives, and ingested in small quantities. Fruit juices that are processed in a natural way and are derived from unpolluted sources are recommended. There is no logic in consuming fruit products that are fed on contaminated water. One must become consciously aware of everything one consumes in these times, for each and every morsel becomes a vibrational part of your being and yet another potential toxin that the body could be burdened with processing.

The diet recommended for these times is one that is simple and uncontaminated by your "civilized" culture's efforts to enhance its food value, chemically. The food value in a diet of raw, unprocessed foods is unexcelled in its abilities to nourish the human body through the period of transformation now upon you. Animal products, for the most part, are not recommended in what is considered to be your "civilized" society, largely as a result of the contamination these creatures have endured and carry in their own cellular structure. By ingesting the flesh of one of these creatures, you succeed only in compounding an already toxic situation within your own physical body.

Your seas, for the most part, have been contaminated, and the creatures that dwell there have taken on a measure of that filth at a cellular level. Ones that function as scavengers and process the debris at the bottom of both fresh water and saltwater environments are not a recommended source of food for humans in these times. Water creatures that have been cultivated in unpolluted conditions may be considered as a source of food for those who feel the need for more protein in their diet. It is not necessary to consume large quantities of animal protein in these times and, ideally, sea creatures are not to be considered a staple of the human diet.

The flesh of land animals is not generally recommended for reasons of vibrational complexity that only adds to the difficulties with which the human form now contends. Domesticated animals who are raised as a food source and whose flesh is fouled with chemical additives are to be discouraged as a food option for human consumption. The eggs and by-products of these creatures are equally unsuitable for those focused on a healthy diet.

The maintenance of the vitality of the form in which you travel in these times is to be a major focus of your attention as the energies accelerate around you. The air you breathe becomes an integral part of every cell of your being and carries the corresponding measure of vibrational purity or impurity of the environment from which it derives. Once it becomes integrated within your cellular structure, it adds to the balance of density your body is struggling to unburden. It is recommended that one become consciously aware of the environment in which one has chosen to live and to make the decision to change location if fresh, clean air is not readily available.

One should be prepared to be ruthless, if necessary, with other considerations that may present themselves as variables in such a decision. For the very survival of the species is at stake. And breath is a vital key to the maintenance of life under the coming conditions. Areas that offer the simplicity of non-industrialization and non-urbanization are preferable to those that may offer more sophisticated cultural advantages.

One is encouraged to weigh carefully the relative merits of the options one may be considering for possible relocation, if the present environment is deemed unsuitable. Simple, sparsely populated environments where rain and fresh water are plentiful are highly recommended. Locations where fresh air is replenished naturally by rapid recirculation make ideal environments in which to dwell in these times. Areas cleansed by frequent rainfall offer strong advantages over locations that may be landlocked and suffer from conditions where the air is likely to be stagnant.

Weather patterns will intensify during the times to come and regions which are presently suffering from extremes of environmental adversity are likely to experience an intensifying of those conditions as the process accelerates. It is to be anticipated that extremes of weather become the norm for certain areas where the natural balance has been disrupted by pollutants and by other forms of vibrational adversity. It is likely that the planet itself, in its own need to detoxify, will provide the conditions of purification in areas that are most contaminated. One can anticipate extremes of weather to continue in areas that are highly populated and highly polluted, as a natural means of purifying the environment. These areas do not constitute locations of choice in the immediate future for those seeking to relocate to more suitable conditions.

The optimum setting in which to live out the times of transformation would be one in which the population is limited and the resources of nature are abundant. Such a choice may call for a total reanalysis of one's life focus. It may be in your best interests to seriously consider abandoning an inappropriate environment in favor of a location that offers more wholesome attributes, despite the economic sacrifices that may be called for in such a decision.

Your overall well-being is under the influence of powerful forces that act in intricate combinations to create physical health under rapidly changing conditions. The choices you make in the present period will strongly influence the conditions with which you will be contending in the near future. It is foolhardy to think that it is possible to maintain the status quo, in terms of what you might have believed at the outset would be your lifestyle, when the evidence of radical change in every aspect of existence is all around you.

It will take much courage, on the part of some of you who consider yourselves to have a great deal at stake, to make a radical deviation from your anticipated life script and forge an alternate plan. For what may appear ill advised when priorities are based on the amassment of material wealth, may well constitute the direction of highest choice when viewing the world from a conscious perspective.

By becoming aware and sensitive to the changes in your physical world and the unseen conditions that comprise it, you enable yourself to become liberated from the limitations that might otherwise imprison you in the past. It may be necessary to seize the opportunity to spring oneself from the grasp of conditioned expectations and to look carefully at the ramifications of choices that may have been made with blinders on. When you look carefully at the world as you are recognizing it to be, it is clear that the ground rules have changed in a life-altering way. And that it is entirely appropriate to make life choices that resonate with the momentum of that change.

Trust your inner sensing in determining the direction of choice, under the current conditions of transition, and be less concerned with the input of your logical mind, which may be conditioned to feed you factors that are fear based. Know that at the highest level you have made the choice to be present in the reality you consider to be the "here and now." And from the perspective of the highest expression of *you*, everything is in Divine order. In the present moment you may not understand the perfection in the circumstances in which you find yourself. Yet, from that heightened vantage point, it cannot be otherwise.

Use your logical mind to make the highest choices possible with regard to the care and nourishment of your physical body. And rely on your deep-seated inner knowingness to help you navigate the more challenging passages on the path. For here, facts give way to feelings. And the truth you carry within the depths of your being is accessible to you as the compass of your soul, there to provide direction and timeless wisdom through the challenges ahead. The skills needed to access that guidance are not learned, for you already know them. What is required is the courage to allow what has been programmed within you to surface, and to embrace what will be vibrationally unquestionable—as the answer to your prayers.

Know that in the present period you are being assisted at the highest level by aspects of your own being who have a vested interest in your physical survival. It is in the highest interests of all concerned that you thrive through the transitions to come, and that you emerge in strength and wholeness in the world to come. Your physical form will undergo changes in the interim period that will enable you to sustain life at other levels of existence and to have a presence, energetically, in realms where you may now be only marginally connected.

By focusing your attention on the maintenance of your form in a state of purification, you will maximize your chances of completing the process of full interconnectedness with kindred consciousness that is, in essence, *you* at other levels. Full conscious awareness at those levels will only be possible once you have attained full integration, at each of the energy points you refer to as chakras, within your energy field.

There are issues to be confronted and transcended at each of these points, for each is the manifestation, in physical form, of a multidimensional network of energy and of consciousness. By being aware of and receptive to the need of the energetic whole to clear these lines of interdimensional communication, you make the strongest possible contribution to the ascension of the full energetic spectrum of all that you are.

The process encompasses the microcosm of your reality and the microcosm of every nuance within that framework, and goes on to include the macrocosm of all that you are, which is, in essence, All That Is. All That Is cannot be all that it is without all that *you* are being present and interconnected in all ways. Great care is being taken at levels beyond your conscious awareness to ease you into this process so as not to disrupt the delicate energetic balance and the perfection that is your physical form.

Each of you has a unique set of variables with which to fit energetically into one realm. As the vibration of that realm ascends, the radical changes within your physical form, in its effort to adapt, add exponentially more factors to an already complex equation. Ultimately, it will not be possible for many to sustain a presence in physical form under present conditions. The rate of acceleration is such that retained density at the cellular level will result in a systemic breakdown in the bodies of all but the most conscious beings amongst you.

Those of you who count yourselves as candidates for transformation of your physical bodies in the times to come, are being carefully guided at a multitude of levels. It is pointless for you to expend great effort broadening your mentalized understanding of the ascension process without placing an equal emphasis on the condition of the vehicle through which you are able to participate.

There are many beings now amongst you who have developed the ability to conduct heightened electromagnetic frequencies through the vehicle of their physical forms. There are countless techniques for this practice, all unified by the effect upon the physical body of elevating the vibration at the cellular level and detoxifying, incrementally, the energies carried there. When the physical form is exposed to these amplified vibratory levels, the effect is manifested in the subtle bodies as well as in the physical body, and the result of the release of karmic as well as physical density is achieved.

There is no one method that takes precedence over another in this so called "healing" work, though vast differences occur in technique and in the result that might be forthcoming, under ideal conditions, when these skills are correctly practiced. The determining factor in assessing any of the energetically based healing modalities that are presently being practiced in your reality, is your own sense of the result that may or may not be forthcoming. It would be beneficial to all who wish to maximize their efforts to purify their physical bodies to investigate the available therapies, both from the standpoint of being a recipient and of becoming a practitioner. For the purifying effect of allowing these energies to pass through your energy field in the process of being transmitted to another cannot be underestimated and is a valuable by-product of what could otherwise be considered service to humanity.

Exposure of your physical form to the higher vibrational frequencies is highly recommended on a regular basis. For the ultimate effect will be the acceleration of the purification process, regardless of which school of energy work is chosen. Your own inner knowingness is the best barometer of whether or not a given method is effective and meaningful for you. By tuning-in to your sense of well-being, particularly in the area of your heart chakra, you will be able to determine quite easily whether or not a given modality or practitioner is one that offers you a path worth pursuing.

Ultimately, everyone who considers himself to be a full participant in this interdimensional effort is capable of carrying and transmitting high levels of therapeutic healing energy. And teachers abound in these times who are most willing to pass this knowledge on to you. Trust in your own abilities, at an intuitive level, to source the guidance and therapies that are best suited to your circumstances.

Your core vibration is one you have carried into this lifetime. This is an identifying configuration that marks *who* you are. And this vibration will not be dissipated or altered by exposure to energies being transmitted by another. One's core resonant vibration can only be enhanced, or accelerated in this way. One becomes more of what one already is through every aspect of the cleansing and purification process. And as one peels away the layers of accumulated vibrational density and debris that are carried within the energetic forms of every being in your reality, one is able to glimpse the true nature of humanness and experience what is possible within the context of physicality.

The key to maximizing the process of energy assimilation is the state of your focused intent with regard to that energy. Were you to approach the experience from the standpoint of wishing to *take on* the energy of another, that mind-set would, in essence, nullify the beneficial effects possible from exposure to the energies. For one does not adopt the energy of another when this work is correctly practiced. Through exposure to the amplified vibration that is passing *through* another being, the vibratory levels of one's own essence is enhanced.

It is advantageous to approach the practice of receiving energy through the vehicle of another with the intention of having the result be the release of physical and nonphysical density, rather than the intention being that of affecting particular physical symptoms. The alleviation of symptoms may well be the result of the work, but is not to be the focus of the intention of the receiver or of the provider, if optimum benefit is to be realized. Ultimately, when one engages in energy work on a regular basis, significant levels of toxic release will have a cumulative effect and can be expected to result in a renewed sense of physical well-being. One cannot hope to achieve such levels of wellness, under the coming conditions, with sporadic attempts at such practices.

The maintenance of physical health under conditions of accelerated vibration requires adaptation and the revision of one's priorities. It will no longer be possible to maintain optimum standards of health with physical means alone. The conditions with which you contend on a daily basis require that basic practices, focused on maintaining health, be supplemented with energy practices focused on cleansing the subtle bodies of residual density. Ultimately, the physical form will reflect the sum-total vibration of all aspects of your energy body, as the result of your efforts.

This form you inhabit is the vehicle in which you will journey to the higher levels of existence that await you. To create the vibrancy that you would wish to experience in these times, it is necessary for you to begin to regard your form as one that transcends physicality. In fact, the physicality of your form is the manifestation of levels of vibration at corresponding levels of perception. *All of it is energy*. The tangible body is best served by regarding it as the result of your efforts rather than the focus of them. For, were one to focus upon the limited physical reflection of a totality which is energy based, the results would be equally limited, and the hoped for result of vibrant good health would fall far short of what is possible.

You can anticipate the experience of the symptoms of illness when undergoing an intensive program of energetic healing. Do not assume that the work is ineffective if your physical condition worsens directly following embarking upon a purification regimen. The very symptoms that would indicate illness to those conditioned in physical focus are, in fact, an indication of *cleansing*, when viewed as energy. Toxic release is your evidence that purging is taking place and that your energy field is being relieved of a burden that was carried in a particular region of your cellular structure.

Likewise, when exposed to high levels of vibration, the toxins harbored in the emotional bodies of your form are released. This process can be expected to replicate the experience of the repressed emotion, often at profound degrees of intensity. One might be inclined to conclude that one were emotionally unbalanced based on episodes of emotional release, which, in all likelihood, will follow exposure to high levels of healing energy. In fact, such an experience would indicate that balance was restored and that certain layers of repressed emotion, which is energetic density held at the level of the emotional body, had been released.

As the process intensifies, one approaches the depths of the karmic burden carried emotionally, and begins to peel back the layers of patterning that have colored one's experience and one's responses through lifetime after lifetime. As you begin to emerge from this transitional phase, you will experience a sense of liberation from the constraints of emotional conditioning with which you have contended all your life. It becomes obvious, in your responses to provocation and emotional stimuli, that the reflex of emotional response has been transcended and that you are no longer operating at the mercy of the feelings that once dominated your experience.

Letting go of the negatively charged energies surrounding life issues, when stimulated energetically through healing practices, is a way to maximize the effects of those therapies and to begin to break the vibrational chain that would continue to magnetize to you experiences of a similar vibration. Resist the inclination to hold back during these episodes of profound emotional release. For the responses that have been triggered are symptomatic of untold levels of history carried within you. And as each successive level is revealed and released, you are quite likely to begin to experience a sense of liberation from lifetimes of emotional imprisonment. Standard provocative cues cease to produce the standard emotional reflex action. And at long last, the chain is broken that held you in a spiral of emotional conditioning.

What you can expect to experience is a sense of detachment from the emotions themselves and from the kinds of circumstances that once triggered them. You begin to perceive yourself as coasting over the surface of scenarios that once hooked you into endless repeat performances of agonizing dramas. And a subtle sense of indifference is your cue that the energy has shifted within you and that you are free to choreograph the dance of your experience as you choose to have it be.

It is to be encouraged that you take the time to delve deeply into the residual emotional patterning that is coloring your experience in this time of transformation and that you engage in activities designed to stimulate the cellular memories harbored in your emotional body. For beneath the illusion of calm in even the most controlled exterior, is a well-layered structure of density that must be released if you are to transcend the levels of vibration to come. It is best not to judge yourself in the course of this process. Expectations of having made a certain degree of progress can conceal conditioning harbored deep within and serve to undermine the very progress that you may assume had been attained.

Know that this is an ongoing process. The testing conditions and the patterning they are calculated to provoke are cyclical. Do not assume that you have somehow graduated and transcended your humanness simply because you have attained certain levels of conscious awareness and have done certain amounts of focused work on the refinement of your emerging transcendent identity. That mind-set is rooted in denial, regardless of how elevated you may feel you have become. And its implementation is a recipe for emotional backsliding into habitual patterns that may have been considered history. Expect that you will be presented with circumstances that are opportunities to exercise your emotional body and help insure that it remain free of the densities with which you once may have been programmed.

Energy work as an ongoing practice is a recommended part of the lifestyle of those with focused awareness of the ascension process. Like regular exercise and a healthy diet, a lifestyle rich in therapeutic energy practices contributes to the maintenance of physical wellness throughout the many stages of transformation. It is recommended that one consider seriously the advantages in becoming an energy practitioner, at some level, so that one is able to give as well as to receive the benefits of healing energy. This is a gift with which all are blessed. And it is incorrect to think that certain beings are somehow *special* because they are able to radiate healing energies from the hands or other energy centers. These ones have merely taken the time to master those skills and have opened themselves to receiving the inherent benefit of making these energies available to others.

It is also very much a part of one's suggested fitness regime to avail oneself of therapeutic energies that one generates oneself. The same skills that are directed toward the physical bodies of others can be applied to one's own physical form with beneficial results. It is not necessary to assume that healing energy work is something that can only be received from another individual. Each and every being is fully equipped with everything necessary to radiate healing energy and to avail oneself of it. With these skills, one is no longer tied to certain areas where such talents are readily available. And full self-sufficiency is entirely possible and may be a path of choice for many in the times soon to come.

These times provide an opportunity to prepare for all that will transpire energetically in your world. And these times are ripe for equipping yourself with the skills and the understandings that will form a foundation for the momentum of ascension. In the present period, those of you who stand on the leading edge of that wave may experience the backlash of the amplified energies now surging all around you with an intensity that is startling. Awareness of the process and your place within it best equips each of you to respond with grace to the ramifications of the transformation process. And it provides you with the ability to ride the wave and to experience the wonders of the world that awaits you.

chapter eighteen

Bringing relationships to completion
and walking away with loving detachment.
Breaking addictions to others.
The significance of summary life experiences.
Allowing others to live or to die in freedom.

Disproportionate emphasis on little things that occur begins to bring into perspective the priorities you have placed upon certain areas of your life, once the process of transformation is fully under way. You will begin to become aware of your own reactions to incidents and recognize your own overreaction to certain types of scenarios. Your own emotional response is your cue to tune in to categories of emotion that you harbor, well hidden within your energy field. Your reactions have little to do with the individuals or the situations in question. These vehicles for your own growth have been strategically scripted into your drama as catalysts for directing your awareness to the deeper issues still held energetically within you.

When you become aware of recurring scenarios that trigger strong emotional responses, take the time to distance yourself from the scene in question and look carefully at what may be symbolized by those circumstances. For, until you begin to do so, you will continue to manifest scene after scene of the recurring theme

he situations that most feel like a thorn in your side pose the greatest potential breakthroughs for you in terms of conditioned responses that keep you stuck, playing out the same scenes over and over again. To free yourself from ongoing patterns of repetition on given themes, it is necessary to attain a level of detachment.

The measure of importance you attribute to a particular theme is directly proportionate to the degree of repetition you can anticipate as your life experience. To transcend that pattern and break the cycle, it is necessary to surrender to the process and cease resisting what is being presented. Confrontation and attempts to force one's own will upon such circumstances are a sure recipe for more of the same. When you continue to manifest adversity, despite having theoretical understandings of the nature of creating your reality, it is time to dig for the underlying common thread that ties the entire history of such experiences into a cohesive volume through which real insight may be gleaned.

The key to liberating oneself from the bondage posed by certain life themes is to remove oneself energetically from the scenario, in totality. So long as you continue to have an emotional investment in the potential outcome of a confrontation, you are engaged energetically. When you remove yourself from the drama and walk away, you contribute in the most significant possible way to the completion of that theme. For nonattachment to all things material is not limited to material *things*, but encompasses every possible *situation* in which you are mentally and emotionally invested.

A sense of receptivity, combined with an openness to the opportunities presented, is the state of being that will manifest for you the circumstances that best reflect your true heart's desire. For, that which you have wished for at the highest level is often there before you, and drifts by unnoticed simply because your energies were focused upon the manipulation of circumstances where the energy did not flow with ease. One cannot hope to transcend physicality and simultaneously remain bound to it. It is not possible, in these times, to force a favorable result that is not forthcoming with ease, and attempts to do so only prolong the time needed to transcend that conditioning.

The concept of nonattachment to the outcome is the key to becoming free from the tethering to the recurring dream or nightmare, which may well be your life at present. For, the situations you are creating in these times are poignant examples of those themes, calculated to get your attention despite the level of discomfort that may be invoked in the process. So long as you are emotionally invested in that outcome, you have laid the groundwork for your continued imprisonment.

Attachment to certain individuals, who you may have cast in your life script, is yet another category of tethering that must be examined in these times. Certain beings are there for you in order that particular issues come to the forefront of your awareness and play out as dramatizations of those themes. These individuals are there to sing a particular song. When you are complete with those issues, the song is no longer necessary. Prolonged contact with such beings only subjects you to unnecessary repetitions of discordant tunes.

One should be prepared to weed out of one's script those players whose purpose has been served by the shared history that has been co-created. It is likely, at the levels of transcendence at which you have arrived, that neither of you is served by prolonging the pattern of interaction. Recognize when you are continuing to participate in interactions merely out of habit and when the relationship is still viable and mutually nourishing.

. Addiction to another being is a common occurrence in these times. You may find that it takes a good bit of courage to let go of the familiar companionship of certain individuals. Yet, when the interaction is fraught with adversity, it should be blatantly obvious to you that the potential benefit in the connection has been outlived. Harmony is the key word in all relationships in which you would wish to engage. When that harmony is not forthcoming despite your best efforts to manifest it, one is best served by walking away from that relationship, severing ties, and doing so without animosity—merely with detachment. For, the potential benefit in terminating any relationship is nullified if one leaves the stage in a fanfare of emotional charge. The object of the exercise is to diffuse the situation with that individual, energetically. And that objective is surely not served by engaging in a poignant end scene that only fans the fire rather than puts it out, vibrationally.

True indifference is not a state of being that can be faked, although many of you will go that route, initially. For, indifference does not mean that there is not caring for the other being. It represents your unwillingness to remain ensnared in a particular energetic pattern. It represents nonattachment to the drama in which you have been mutually engaged. And it materializes your recognition of the mutual benefit of noninteraction. Indifference, as many would misinterpret it, terminates the relationship without nullifying the charge energetically.

Feigning indifference, while silently seething inside over resentments that are unresolved does not free you from the pattern in question. It merely sets the stage for further enactments, possibly with other players. So long as you carry the vibration of resentment for wrongdoings you feel have been perpetrated upon you, you have set the stage for a repeat performance. When one is truly liberated from this cycle, one is able to experience the drama fully without becoming ensnared emotionally. Caustic words and actions would not register as pain inflicted, but would merely be recognized as words and actions. Judgment as to their merit or lack thereof would be suspended.

Acceptance, unconditionally, of whatever has been presented, without the need to try to change it, and without the need to fit it into the context of ones own system of values, constitutes the recipe for release from whatever contractual arrangement may have been in place with certain beings. One is not required to carry anyone on his or her back energetically, in these times. And those who would try to hold you in a pattern of interaction against your will, only serve to prolong for themselves the life themes and the control issues they are conditioned to enacting. Whether or not they continue to enact their dramas with you or with others is the option you have been presented in recognizing the pattern and the obsolescence of particular relationships.

When one is able to sever ties without severing the love and caring that may well still be present for the individual in question, one is able to truly transcend the need to continue playing out that scene, either with that person or with others. Walking away with loving detachment is the lesson here to be mastered. And liberating oneself, out of love of self, is the gift to be graciously received.

The lessons to be learned in the process of bringing relationships to completion are a major portion of the work you are capable of accomplishing in these times. Overcoming your resistance to the mundane aspects of severing your interconnectedness with certain beings is the challenge of this process. For, the conditioning is established, in most who are dealing with this issue, to bend to the emotional lure of familiar patterns and to become drawn into the drama that formed the central theme of that relationship.

It is only by transcending the emotion associated with that drama that one is able to detach from the circumstances in question. In order to do so, it is necessary to be able to identify the underlying themes governing certain episodes and to probe the depths of your understanding to reveal the complex web of interconnected issues that helped create them.

Once you are able to grasp what is actually happening in these encounters, a measure of the energetic charge carried in the drama is dispelled. And with the glimmer of understanding, a measure of detachment is achieved. After several poignant episodes that often occur simultaneously or in quick succession, you emerge with a sense of release from the grasp in which you have been held.

One becomes aware, often quite suddenly, that the energy has shifted. And issues that once were major triggers for battle somehow pass by without a ripple upon the waters of your consciousness. One becomes aware of a sense of acceptance of certain patterns of occurrence, and of the futility of trying to impose one's will upon them. As one by one the recurring situations become diffused, the need to continue manifesting those circumstances diminishes, and the compulsion to continue to interact with the beings that traditionally prompted them is dissipated in a natural way.

Generous periods of alone time are recommended during the reconstruction phase that follows. One becomes aware of a need from within for a distancing from the circumstances in which one may have been enmeshed. And a radical change in one's situation is to be expected. It takes a period of time to integrate the understandings, once a major shift in awareness has been accomplished. And it is recommended that one refrain from replacing the obsolete set of distractions with a new one, in the initial period.

One will surely become aware that a prescription for solitude has been received, and of the scarcity of options for replacing old connections with similar new ones. And one begins to find profound comfort in the stillness and in the sanctity of one's own process. The necessity for interaction with other beings is regarded as a lesser priority, and the format for the reconstruction of one's circumstances is established.

Dissecting oneself out of one's life conditioning is a painstaking process that can be expected to take months or even years to complete. Do not fault yourself if you realize that you are still responding to familiar signals. Recognition of the patterns and the themes is a major part of this work and must precede extracting oneself from their grasp. Finding the common threads woven amongst your life issues is merely the beginning of the process. You should not expect to be able to simply walk away from a lifetime of living theater and not be compelled to speak the lines you know by heart.

Eventually, you will exit the stage. And when you do, it will be with grace, and much joy, at *your* recognition of the magnificence of your performance. Your part will have been mastered. And you will be able to retire the role with ease. For, by then, you will have applied the life lessons to every aspect of your emerging selfhood. You will have recognized, with profound gratitude, the importance of that training in the formation of who you have become.

In this transitional period, give yourself the latitude to explore your process fully. This is not a race to the finish line that is completed with an eye to the process of others who may be undergoing similar experiences. There is no need to compare yourself with anyone, in terms of the progress you may be making. For, each of you is on a highly personal timetable. Allow yourself the luxury of fully exploring the richness of your own personal journey, culling from the details the precious grains of understanding with which you will nourish your emerging self.

The path each of you travels is unique. And though there may be similarities in the patterns, the subtleties of each individual's process are a unique experiential fingerprint. There is no value judgment to be superimposed here, either by oneself or by another. For the merit is in the magnificence of the journey itself, not in the speed in arriving at the destination.

Once you have emerged from this stage of your transformation process, you will be able to reconstruct your lifestyle. Many of you will choose to discard the trappings of the life you lived before. And your priorities will take on a radically different emphasis. Your focus on material acquisitions and materially-based security will have given way to a perspective that places value on the level to which one perceives oneself to be free of all constraints. One is less concerned with mundane issues of amassing comforts than with the ease with which one is able to manifest the scenarios through which one can enact one's sense of life purpose.

A level of trust in the perfection of the process is vital for attaining a state of inner-directedness that is free of restriction. There is, quite literally, no limit to what can be created under the coming conditions, by those who have set down the burdens under which so many stagger in the present period. Trust in your own ability to manifest precisely the opportunities that will bring about a sense of completion for you. And have the courage to let go of conditioned patterns and structure that would limit your ability to participate fully in the reconstruction of your life's focus.

When the need for security is rooted in fear, the very circumstances, which would constitute that security, may well dematerialize and give rise to a sense of security that rests on a foundation of love, built from within. For, the only real security in these times is the unmistakable sense of well-being that is experienced when you are in harmony with the flow of the higher frequencies. When you resonate with the accelerated vibration that permeates your world, you experience a sense of profound connectedness to everyone and everything. And you know, at a level that transcends mind, that you are safe, secure, and on track.

The details of how things will work out are perceived as less important than the sense of being in harmony with your own highest purpose. For, once you have aligned yourself with the momentum of the accelerating frequencies, you are in the flow with your life direction. And the stage of the process in which you find yourself is a reflection of your integration of your understandings of that process with the relevant life circumstances that come up for review.

Being in the moment with this process is key to all that you would hope to achieve in this time frame. It is not necessary for you to concern yourself with how things will come together—simply be in a state of trusting receptivity. Circumstances will unfold, sequentially, in ways that may well be unexpected, when you are willing to allow synchronicity to work to your highest advantage. Allow your situation to unfold, and observe the perfection in the process.

The completion of life issues is a fascinating exercise, when you allow the process to direct you, rather than trying to direct the process. And a willingness to relinquish the "need to know" will work to your advantage, regardless of how difficult it may appear to you to do so. For, the understandings to be gleaned are not available on demand, but rise to the forefront of your awareness effortlessly when the process is permitted to unfold in a natural way. The effort you might expend in trying to second-guess a complex outcome, could well be spared were you to surrender to the moment in which you find yourself and to the perfection of the sequence of events as they come to be.

Know that the orientation from which you have derived your experience of life will shift dramatically in the times now at hand. This is true not merely for those who have identified with the shifting tides of this period in your history, but for all beings in physical form. There are those who will undergo the radical changes to which we refer, without the benefit of the overview that would put the upheaval into perspective. These ones, who comprise the population at large, will be dealing with levels of change in their life scripts for which there is no precedent. And many will have difficulty in dealing with the demolition of the foundations upon which they have structured their lives. Much fear will be triggered in the process. And it is to be expected that violence and the hardships that result from panic will be widespread in the times soon to come.

It is important that you retain the perspective of the overview when presented with world events that reflect a reversion to fear on the part of the general population. It is not necessary to intervene in the scripts of others undergoing such trials, although you may surely choose to do so. For, the higher purpose would not be served merely by helping to alter the circumstances in the trials of others, without providing the understandings that give those circumstances relevance.

When one intervenes in the crisis of another in these times, one only helps to create the basis for a reenactment of the drama in question for that individual. The circumstances themselves are no more than an invitation. When the circumstances are poignant, the invitation is compelling and the tendency to overlook the lesson is progressively less likely. Were one to go through the motions of dealing with the drama, without recognizing the symbolism from which it springs, a repeat performance is virtually guaranteed.

In some cases, the blindness of the individual to the nature of the process is such that the scenarios created are life threatening and the chances of transcending the challenges at that point are slim. Know that in such instances, the individual in question has created those circumstances at a soul level, in order to punctuate the point of a particular life theme. It may well be in the highest interests of the individual in question to allow the drama to play out to a seemingly disastrous conclusion. For, that being, as a soul, will be able to reconstruct the life history after departure from physical form, and perceive the common threads from a heightened perspective.

Know that many will be making such choices. And many will choose seemingly violent exits from this lifetime in order to have experienced an example of a life issue that cannot be ignored. These summary experiences are profound opportunities for the beings in question to bring to a conclusion life themes they would not be able to master in a less dramatic way.

The opportunity for those of you who will bear witness to such events is to be able to honor the perfection in the process of another and to resist the temptation to intervene and attempt to *save* someone from what he is trying to achieve as a soul. It may appear that to do so would be heartless, in profound circumstances. Yet, to refrain from saving another from his perfectly created lesson would be the higher gift. For, the preservation of physical form is surely not the ultimate basis for action in all cases. It may well be that certain individuals may have sufficiently backed themselves into a corner, experientially, and the potential suffering posed by retaining physical form would far outweigh the advantages of life-saving heroics.

The challenge for you who have a heart connection with such a being, is to recognize the gift in the culmination of that being's process. And to know that that individual's highest purpose may well be served by allowing the process to play out to its natural conclusion. For the concept of *nonattachment to the material* is not limited to possessions, but applies to life itself. The lesson for you in such dramas is to be able to let go of your attachment to the physical life of another and to know that *life*, in the higher sense, transcends the identity that may be choosing to relinquish form.

Those of you who are confronting the challenges of life threatening scenarios in these times, whether on the part of others or within your own life script, have given yourselves a powerful gift. For, to confront death and to perceive it as the portal that it truly is, enables you to transcend the limitation of attachment to form, and to grasp the eternal wisdom that is possible in the act of letting go.

Many will be given that opportunity in these times of profound change. Many will choose to relinquish form and reap the under- standings that come with that act of surrender. And many will stand beside them in unconditional, loving acceptance of the wisdom in such a choice. Be empowered by the role you have chosen to play in such dramas. And credit yourself with self-acknowledgment for the wisdom and the strength required to allow another being to live—or to die—in freedom.

chapter nineteen

The experience of interdimensional ascension.
Bouncing between realities:
Shifting the focus of one's awareness amongst
simultaneous levels of reality.
The "extinction" and emergence of new forms of
plant, animal, and mineral life.

Never before in the history of your world has there been a time of transformation such as this. These times mark the completion of a cycle whose ramifications are felt throughout Creation. What is transpiring in the "here and now" of your experience is no more or less intense than the shifts being integrated by beings in other dimensions. For, All Creation is engulfed in the momentum of change. And all are grappling with the repercussions of the integration of accelerated vibration—and experiencing the wonders of a new world of perception—on an individual basis

In your world, these times mark the end of an era that has been characterized by unprecedented change. In a relatively short period of time, the human race on planet Earth has gone from the level of material subsistence to a level of sophisticated technological advancement that refines and re-refines itself with each waking breath. At the same time, your innate sensitivity and awareness of the reality of the world beyond the material has come to the forefront of the consciousness of humankind, irrespective of differences in culture.

There is a spontaneous experience of awakening transpiring throughout the "here and now" of your world. And for those privileged to be living in populations where awareness of these changes is acknowledged openly, there is much camaraderie and support available. For others in more repressed cultural environments, the experience of energy assimilation is a more personal one. Individuals going through these times under such conditions are experiencing the major shifts in awareness in ways that are profound and empowering, many of them unaware that all are undergoing these experiences.

For these ones, the opportunities for transcendence of limitations imposed by their indigenous cultural traditions, are unsurpassed. Each has been permitted to collide head-on with his own system of beliefs and has been given a firsthand glimpse into the process of the manifestation of the reality he experiences. Each has been given the tools to draw the identical conclusions, despite the "rules" of the consensus reality of his culture. And each has emerged from exposure to the blatant demonstrations of cause and effect that mark his recent history with a sense of responsibility that is inevitable.

The victim consciousness that marks your world is quickly being replaced by the realization that there is a connection between one's mind-set and what one manifests as experience. And this shift is universal, throughout your reality, regardless of whether the awareness is spurred by cultural openness to such concepts or by spontaneous awakenings on a highly personal level, triggered by one's own life experience.

There is no question in anyone's mind that unprecedented change is at hand. The question in the minds of so many is *why* and *toward what end* this momentum propels you. It is not necessary to understand the process, much less the overview on a grander scale, in order to integrate its effects on a personal level. It is of great interest to many in your particular culture, whose awareness has been stimulated, to probe the mechanics of the process. But the end result is the same, regardless of whether or not one has awakened to the "bigger picture."

Spontaneous recall of related incidents in one's life history occurs for everyone, and leads to the identification of a common thread that ties the collection of entwined experiences into a cohesive unit. People have the experience of stumbling onto the answers without even having begun to seek them. And for these ones there is less complication in the process of accepting the unmistakable truths presented, than for those whose minds are conditioned by skepticism.

One's own experience is far more significant *proof* of what is so than platitudes of logic that one has learned to parrot, and against which one's reality is often measured. The nature of these changes transcends your so-called logic. For, it is based on a blueprint of Divine intent that is unquestionable. Do not expect the inevitable conclusions you will draw from your experiences to "make sense." Often, they will not. Not at first. But slowly, all of it will emerge as crystalline clarity when you surrender lifetimes of learned conditioning to the unmistakable truth of what you *feel*.

What has been termed *inner-knowingness* is being kindled within the consciousness of every being throughout your world. And as each of you instinctively begins to attune to the higher resonance of that awareness, the *answers* that were once elusive emerge from within. Suddenly, you know the answers without even having formulated the question. For, you will have tapped into profound levels of deeper understandings that were unavailable to your conscious mind at diminished levels of vibration.

Once your frequency stabilizes at the higher levels, you will come into conscious awareness of levels of understanding that were not formally *learned*. Concepts take on a clarity and a breadth of vision that cannot be justified by linear logic. And you become aware that you have emerged as a very different kind of being, for reasons you cannot explain.

There is no need to explain anything to anyone. For, each is on his own timetable in this process and is not capable of understanding another's reality until his own life experience is able to parallel it. Each will come into awareness of the new levels at precisely the right moment for that awareness to crystallize. Until that moment, many will intellectualize the process and draw partially correct conclusions from incomplete evidence. For these individuals, that will be their process. And some backsliding will be the natural result of that pattern of integration.

There is no room for judgment in this process. For each of you is here for your own journey and not for the timing of another's. Resist the temptation to be seduced by your own ego in its need for validation. For, the truth you seek lies not upon the path of another, but within your own personal process of emergence. Allow yourself the latitude to experience that process fully and to explore the ripple effect particular revelations may have on illuminating the history you have amassed. All must be assimilated and the corresponding limitations released, in order to emerge fully functional as a participant at the next level.

The perfection of the timing of your own particular journey will become apparent as the *synchronicity* that triggers your most significant breakthroughs has the opportunity to play out. Permit yourself the luxury of savoring this experience of transformation. It is not one to be rushed, though many will try. For, the end result will manifest in its own time in a very natural way, when you allow the process to direct you and you cease trying to direct the process.

As the levels of repressed energy are released sequentially and each subsequent layer is stimulated and allowed to be brought to the surface for scrutiny, you will recognize the perfection in the timing of major experiences. Events occur in a particular order, the realizations garnered by the one forming the foundation for the resolution of the next. As the layers of experience are permitted to unfold, the underlying energy pattern is able to be dispelled through recreation of the corresponding emotional catalyst.

You are not backsliding in your process simply because you are once again rehashing issues that were presumed to have been

resolved. You are, in fact, progressing perfectly \
process to reveal to you the last remnants of en
experienced as emotion, and you allow yourself to
of the energetic charge it has been called forth \
sion of such sensations will only necessitate a repeat occurrence of
the same core theme, which must be completed fully before the next
layer can be brought to the surface as a life experience. In this way,
the major themes of this lifetime, and often the energetic remnants
from other lifetimes as well, can be brought to completion.

Occurrences of profound intensity are often necessary to represent the true culmination of a life's work on a particular theme. For, the density held on a cellular level cannot be carried forth to the levels of reality toward which you are moving. All will have to be brought to completion before the full spectrum of the motion of ascension can be manifested as form.

Those who are unable to grapple with the intensity of the episodes that may be created in this process may well opt out of the process entirely and relinquish their physical forms during the times soon to come. These individuals will be presented the opportunity to recreate themselves, energetically, at the newly defined vibrational levels at which they entered this lifetime. In those new forms, they will be empowered to manifest life experiences that will enable them to continue to work on issues left unresolved in this lifetime. The realm in which such beings will reemerge will be that shared by consciousness that has succeeded in ascending from diminished realms of reality presently defined by varying degrees of density.

There is no one specific *place* in which certain beings are presently manifested, prior to ascending to the level in which you emerged at birth. For the layers of possible realities are infinite and would be *personalized* to mirror the level of density with which that consciousness experiences self-recognition. Likewise, the levels to which you may choose to ascend will parallel the composition, energetically, at which you are able to materialize as form. Thus, the reality at which you emerge as materialized consciousness is one that is customized to resonate to your energetic sum-totality.

For those beings whose life lessons have been brought to fruition, quantum leaps in the caliber of experience possible can be expected. For others who have chosen to give themselves more time to resolve core issues, the levels in which they will reemerge as consciousness will parallel the one in which they find themselves at present.

The motion is ongoing. There is no start or stop to the process. There is no particular "day of reckoning" at which one either moves forward or is held behind. There is no "judgment day." There is no success or failure. The process merely *Is*. The motion of ascension is perpetual motion. And the process has been ongoing since the beginning of Creation. In these times the pace of that motion has accelerated. And physical beings are confronted with the reality that the forms they inhabit are challenged to sustain physicality at the augmented levels to which the environment in which they live has ascended.

There is simultaneous presence of every being at countless levels. And it is as natural as the flutter of an eyelid, to emerge with consciousness at the next lighter level of density, once the work has been achieved. One's awareness of the transition may not be apparent until it becomes blatantly obvious that the rules of "the game" have been radically altered. Ultimately, one realizes that one is not now present in the same world as one once was.

Under these conditions the changes are far too dramatic and the time frame in question too condensed for the ascension transition to be *seamless*, as would typically be the case. In fact, for those beings who are actively on the path of life theme resolution, one is technically *ascending* all the time. And the reality one perceives as the "here and now" is an ever shifting personalized reflection of one's vibrational state.

The level of resistance one experiences at the various *categories* of vibration you would consider to be your "dimensions," would be a mirroring of one's own density resonance in juxtaposition with that reality at large. Thus, one being is simultaneously experiencing the full gamut of possibilities and the full range of ease or difficulty at manifesting their heart's desire, or their highest thought for themselves, at an infinite number of levels. The focus upon a particular scenario and one's perception of *that* reality as the "here and now" is determined by one's ability to deal with the life lessons being presented at a given level of awareness. One is able, then, to *tune in* sequentially to a range of possible realities and to perceive that collective body of experience as one cohesive unit. In fact, one is technically bouncing between realities all the time, depending upon one's state of beingness in the "now moment."

When one's awareness, as a materialized presence, has bridged the gap between major categories of vibration, known as "dimensions," the crossing over is more dramatic and the transition more obvious. What could be perceived as *backsliding* experientially is, in fact, evidence of a major crossing over into realms of experience wherein one is then of greater density, relative to the environment at large. Interdimensional ascension is marked by dramatic and poignant experiences of difficulty where seemingly only days or weeks earlier, life was moving forward with an ease that had never before been experienced.

This phenomenon of the manifestation of one's efforts flowing smoothly, followed by one's efforts seemingly encountering resistance, is characteristic of ascension having occurred. For those of you who are experiencing a virtual roller-coaster of occurrences representing extremes of ease and difficulty, that very state would be indicative of jumping levels of reality in rapid-fire succession. These *symptoms* would indicate an individual who is completing life work on many levels simultaneously and is experiencing ascension at a radically accelerated pace.

As one nears the threshold that separates dimensions in the ascension process, chapters are often closed so quickly that one is virtually catapulted from the heights of one dimension to emergence at "entry level" realities in the next. It is important that one is prepared to cope with the ramifications of that dramatic shift. It is likely, without clarity regarding the nature of the process, that one may misinterpret the signs of such a shift and to conclude that one had somehow *failed* in one's progress. There is no possibility of failure on this journey. There are merely variations in perception of what *is*. And it becomes increasingly apparent that you are creating all of it.

It is in the highest interests of all of you who stand poised on the brink of the interdimensional shift, to come to terms with the power you, in fact, have to create your experience. The extent to which you are able to finely hone those skills will spare you that measure of difficulty once the shift has occurred. For, at the next major category of reality, manifestation is comparatively instantaneous. Slips in one's application of the principles one has mastered can be painful and costly. It is necessary to become accustomed to the manifested ramifications of one's thoughts and one's speech as experience, prior to making the shift into the next dimension.

As that threshold is approached, your experience begins to take on the characteristics of the higher dimension. The time lag between the inception of thought and its manifestation is minimal from the perspective of your awareness at present. Encountering an outcome that would not have been consciously wished for serves to punctuate for you the power you hold in thought, word, and deed. Ideally, you will train yourself carefully to monitor your thoughts and actions so as to avoid creating for yourself unwanted outcomes. And ample opportunity is afforded you at this juncture to fine-tune those skills.

Ultimately, as you cross over the threshold that delineates dimensions, your experience of manifestation will become far more poignant. And verbalizing ideas that are not intended at a heart level will have dramatic results, often to the detriment of all concerned. These times and the opportunity for awareness that they offer are provided in order to be fully conscious of your capabilities before having them put to the test of instantaneous manifestation. Your experience will parallel your willingness to surrender to the process and to go in the direction that life is leading you. Those who resist the changes that are programmed into your script energetically will prolong the time it takes to reach completion with the process.

At the same time as each of you approaches the threshold of interdimensional ascension, the planet itself is approaching a similar shift on a multitude of levels. As the vibrational frequency accelerates throughout the energy field of the Earth, the nature of the reality to be experienced, simply by standing still and not progressing at all, would be marked by radical change. The planet itself is undergoing unprecedented changes in its energetic composition. And the life that is able to be sustained at each of the various levels would be affected accordingly.

One becomes aware of species that have become extinct throughout your history. These life forms have not ceased to exist at all, but merely have chosen to remain at the levels of vibrational frequency to which they are naturally suited. As the energy levels in the reality you perceive as your "here and now" accelerate, many of those life forms are challenged to sustain life at the higher levels and their populations diminish. Ultimately, they are no longer found to be living in realms where once they thrived. For they have reemerged as *new* life forms in ascending dimensions to which they have *descended*, and with which they are vibrationally compatible.

Likewise, one will become aware of *new* species of plants and animal life that are adapted energetically to the new conditions of your ascending reality. These life forms have migrated from dimensions in which they are no longer able to sustain life, into realities that have ascended into their energy spectrum. These *new* specimens will continue to be *discovered* in your "here and now" as the energies of the Earth continue to accelerate and stabilize.

Minerals that are thought to be *new* or deriving from *outer-space* are little more than life forms that have chosen to materialize in realities with which they are vibrationally compatible. They are dramatic evidence, not so much of "interplanetary travel," which is a physical construct, but of the ability of every life form in existence to seek out and to materialize in a vibrationally appropriate environment. Such mineral discoveries will initially be presumed to be *rare* because they have not been previously encountered by beings who ascended from vibrationally diminished environments. In fact, these particular categories of mineral-life may well be prevalent in the conditions to which the Earth and your own conscious awareness have thus far ascended. And many people will be puzzled and astonished that no one seemed to be aware of their existence previously.

Such will be the subtle evidences that will emerge as physical confirmation of a phenomenon that defies linear logic. Many will argue with what will become increasingly obvious as the process intensifies, insisting that such theories cannot be scientifically proven. Indeed, they cannot. Not by the methods developed within your lifetime, based on truths that are fast becoming obsolete. The state of your world and the life forms that are now struggling to maintain physicality within it, are living proof that radical change is at hand.

The mechanics of the process will be understood by relatively few amongst you. Yet, many will successfully make the shift. For, they would have demonstrated the courage to honor their own instinctive knowingness and resisted the temptation to defer to authorities who remain stalwartly tethered to an outmoded structure. These so-called authorities will pose a major challenge to the progress many could make. And the test of self-knowledge will be implemented in defiance of much that may now be considered gospel within your scientific and philosophical communities. The opportunity presented, under the present and coming conditions of transition, is to recognize for oneself what is so. And to honor that truth, even in the face of adversity.

The spirit of adventure has captured the imaginations of many amongst you who recognize yourselves to be true pioneers on the border of uncharted territory. For you, the need to cling to the familiar has given way to an indisputable sense of being very much on track, despite evidence to the contrary. And as the intensity of the experience builds and culminates in the shift to come, your surefootedness, based on your own experience, will override the need for external reference points. The time for developing and strengthening that inner-balance is now, so that you may stand up and be counted in the "here and now" to come.

chapter twenty

Becoming your own frame of reference.

Perceiving a reality all assume is shared.

Orchestrating the way the world responds to you.

How alternate aspects of identity affect your moods.

The nature of remembered experience.

The higher self.

Massive changes taking place within your cellular structure are causing symptoms that many find puzzling under the conditions of profound change taking place in your world. Each of you is experiencing evidence of the ascension process in every aspect of your daily lives. And even though there may be a firm theoretical understanding of the basis for these phenomena, your conditioning as a being schooled in consensus thinking brings you to question, again and again, what your own experience has shown you.

There is no reliable frame of reference to draw on for some of what you may experience. For, life as you know it has taken a radical divergence from what you have been programmed to expect. You are being presented with conditions of an uncharted territory within the context of your own linear awareness.

Your concept of reality will have shifted countless times in the course of coming to this place in your unfoldment. Others who surround you will have reflected some degree of affirmation of the validity of these changes. Yet, now you find yourself questioning much of the ground you have covered. Even though many others are undergoing similar upheavals in their own lives, it is part and parcel of the process to drift back, yet again, into the seas of doubt.

You will experience this momentary sense of backsliding over and over again, as you begin to harness the surge in the energies that drives you to peer over the edge of all you have come to know and believe. Your priorities will have shifted so radically in this heightened phase of your transformation process that the choices presented are often between your own vantage point and that of another. You come to understand that there are truly no generalizations to be made about the nature of your own journey. And you will come to own and to cherish your own perceptions, regardless of whether there is contradictory information coming from other sources.

This is the time to cease looking to your left and to your right to be sure that the others with whom you assume you are sharing this experience of transformation are still beside you. In likelihood, they are not. They will have followed their own divergent paths, reinforced by their own experiences. The guidebooks penned by those who have, themselves, made this journey, can map the way for you just so far. For, each can only document his/her own personal experience. No one can begin to outline what will come to pass for you.

This is the time to relinquish the need to reach out for validation, once and for all. This is the time to cease looking to the so-called wisdom of another incarnate being, as a comforting pat on the head, to assure you that you're still on track. You know you're on track. Or you know that you are not. And no confirmation from another seeker can hope to help you, in the ways that truly matter, when you question, yet again, the foundation of your own truth.

The heightened stages of the journey of ascension are as varied as there are seekers making these transformational leaps. Each of you brings to the present moment, a unique package of circumstances, personal history, and a varying degree of openness to the phenomenon of change. Each is contending with a complexity of variables that will determine the degree of struggle with which you birth yourself into each heightened level of awareness.

Some, who appear to be lagging behind steeped in resistance to these changes, may suddenly, in a blinding flash of awareness, make the quantum leaps before your very eyes. Others, who would appear to have grasped the nature of what is transpiring, may linger endlessly, hashing and rehashing issues that had long since appeared to have been resolved. Neither of these stereotypes is a yardstick against which you would wish to measure your own progress, for none of you will even approximate the journey of another.

You will wish to look to yourself as your own frame of reference, without the inclination to impose your realizations upon another. There are so very many amongst you who are attaining degrees of understanding rarely encountered at your present level of awareness. And while you are far from alone in your experience of these times, in the same breath, you are more alone than you have ever been before.

No one needs to hold your hand through the progressive stages that lie ahead from this point forth. Nor would you wish them to. For this experience is not enlightenment-by-consensus. No amount of camaraderie will spare you the daunting moments of risk-taking that happen within your own inner depths, as the higher realizations are revealed to you. No beloved friend or companion can accompany you where you have chosen, at the deepest level, to go. This is a journey that is made in solitude. You have chosen to experience it in this way, as have all that have made this journey through time immemorial.

When you return in consciousness and make your appearance in this reality once more, it will be from a perspective that has altered. You will view yourself in a different way, although, from outward appearances, you will remain as you had been. Your perspective will have taken on the heightened coloration of the higher realms to which you will have become attuned, while many who perceive you will be looking at life through the same lens as they did before. And you will realize that everything has changed—and nothing has changed—at the same time.

The differences that can be perceived amongst layers of overlapping reality will be solely attributable to the lens through which one is able to view it. And passionate debates may ensue, as to what is and is not so, with players who have chosen to remain motionless, vibrationally, yet remain fully present in your world. These ones serve to anchor a vibrational reference point through which you are able to contrast your own levels of emerging awareness. No amount of elevated understanding, conveyed on your part, will convince these ones that change is the order of the day. For them, the risks are too great. And you stand as a threat to all that, to them, is safe and sure—and holy.

To them, you—who may well have experienced a firsthand encounter with the Divinity within—are the blasphemer. From their perspective, it is you—who may, fleetingly, have tasted the transcendence of linear identity—that is rooted in ego for having such a thought. To them, you are the one who doesn't belong in this world anymore—a world that they cannot see and could not begin to imagine. Yet, you can see it. You have begun to truly see it, perhaps for the first time.

These blatant discrepancies in the perception of a reality all assume is shared point to the possibility that this is a reality that is not shared at all. And a survey, even amongst kindred beings that are closely aligned to your way of thinking, would confirm that the only one who is present in this reality—is you. Yet, few are prepared to consider such a prospect.

The fact is, however, that the reality in which you experience self-awareness in this moment is a fluid phenomenon. It is subject to the ever-present, ever-shifting momentum of the infinite vibrational variables that comprise it. The version of that limitless kaleidoscope of possibility, accessible to your own limited vantage point, is there for your eyes only. Others may be looking at *life* through the same ethers, yet they will not be perceiving the world in the way you do. How could they? They are not you. And it is you who is creating all of it—as are they.

Allow each other the grace of the perfection of his/her life-vision, regardless of whether, from your perspective, that view is tainted. Neither of you is "wrong." Each of you is "right"—based on the reality each is capable of perceiving. And, in the collective, all are "right." For all perspectives co-exist simultaneously, none canceling out the other, regardless of the level of conflict represented. That is the nature of this Creation. All of it simply Is. What of it you wish to sample is the option that is eternally present. And those options hold less and less allure as you progress on this journey.

The tantalizing excitements that may once have formed the focus of your life begin to seem hollow and pointless and reveal themselves as avenues to ego-gratification. They are the reference points in a world that is based upon pleasuring the self and cultivating the favor of others. They are goals that may once have seemed attainable through the application of a lifetime of toil and shrewd strategy. Yet, once attained, all appear shallow and empty. There is not one amongst you, who has harvested the fullness of material "success," who was utterly gratified by it. There always was something missing. And so, you chose to come back to chase that elusive *something*, yet again—a different prize that was, in the end, equally empty.

At this stage in your journey, you have stepped back from your investment in attaining any of those *brass rings*. And from the overview of blessed detachment, you can see the world around you, swirling on a myriad carousels, reaching for, yearning for, striving for, cheating for, stealing for, killing for—whatever it is they've pinpointed as the focus of their attention. All of them are hooked on attaining the elusive *something* that is eternally out of reach— that elusive *something* that most continue to perceive as being "out there," somewhere. Perhaps you have come to recognize that *it* isn't "out there" at all.

Perhaps you have reached a point, as you read these words, where you have recognized the futility in all of it. And, as you continue to watch the world around you skirting the perimeter of its hopes and dreams, you recognize that you are not really a part of that game, anymore. It was fun. It was rich. It may even have been interesting, in parts. But mostly, it wasn't. Mostly, it was disappointing—not just for you personally, but for virtually all of you. That's the name of this game. That's what keeps you coming back to try your luck, yet again.

Ultimately, you reach a point where the prizes in the carnival no longer hold any appeal. That's when you begin seeking that elusive *something* somewhere else entirely. You know, without a doubt, that *it* isn't *out there* anywhere. It is within.

Many of you walk amongst the masses, knowing that you are focused in a different way than are most. Having sampled much of what *life* has to offer, you have declined its invitation to partake of more. Many have walked away from all that is familiar and predictable on a path that others do not understand—a path that, to the casual observer, is leading nowhere. Such paths abound in your reality, intersecting with the more heavily trafficked thoroughfares of the material world.

You need not disappear upon a mountaintop to pursue the calling of your heart—not unless you choose to. The highways and byways of this world all potentially lead to the key crossroads where you may explore the richness of another kind of scenery entirely, right there in your own backyard. And you will come to recognize that your own rarefied vision of reality holds a powerful resonance amongst the more mundane imagery that surrounds you.

Even though you can often feel that the trail you blaze through your very own neighborhood is regarded with skepticism and mockery, it has not gone unnoticed. Those of you who have chosen to experience your awakening amongst the masses are planting the seeds of that heightened perspective in plain view, right where the world needs them most. Even though others may not be able to see their world from your vantage point, they will have observed you. The lives of those you touch, even in passing, or teach by example, as you follow your own inner path in their presence, will be transformed by it.

As the nuances of your life's variations continue to play out, according to your choices, you begin to be able to direct what will be experienced and when.

When the hoped for result is not forthcoming easily, you have learned to sidestep the circumstances and go within, calming the turbulent inner seas that may be manifesting as discord in your outer world. You have learned to dematerialize one set of circumstances and substitute another variation on the same theme, simply by modifying your own inner state of beingness. You have become adept at jumping between realities, marveling at the sudden improvement of a situation, or groaning as your bubble bursts, yet again. You have become a master of the art of ascension, and most of you have not even been aware of it.

The ever-shifting imagery of experiential possibility presents itself for your scrutiny one circumstance at a time. The players and stage sets you have scripted are there, regardless of what lines are spoken by whom. Those things remain essentially the same and provide the element of continuity that makes *life* appear as a static set of linear circumstances. What changes are your own interactions with the variables within it. The nature of those choices determines which set of possibilities will manifest in your reality in a given moment and be recognized by you as having *happened*. The fact is, however, it has all happened. It all continues to happen, in a world of realities that are layered one within the next—all of them, right here.

As you call forth a given set of circumstances with the unique formula imprinted within your energy field, other parallel circumstances are stimulated into readiness. These alternative realities are

ng in the wings on the stage of infinite possibility, poised
nal cues calculated to carry them forth into mani-
..station. You alone determine which set of circumstances you will
recognize as experience, based upon your choices, in any given
moment. You alone determine the extent of the ease or difficulty you
encounter in bringing your dreams to fruition. And just as you alone
determine the way you respond to the stimuli the world provides, it
is you alone who orchestrates the way the world responds to you.

Your own energy field is the catalyst that determines, to a large
extent, the response you are able to elicit on the part of others. In any
circumstance, all variations are viable possible realities, capable of
being called forth into manifestation with the corresponding
vibrational formula. The actions and reactions of others are no
exception to this basic principle. When you project your energies
upon the palate of the ethers, others are guided to respond accordingly, whether knowingly or not. And you are able to modify the
outcome of virtually any interaction simply by becoming attuned
to the energies you bring to it.

Yours is a world unique to you alone. It is a custom-made set
of variables that reflect the nuances of your choices set in juxtaposition with the resonance of the environment in which you
have chosen to enact them. And even though you may share
parallel circumstances with many of the beings that populate the
theater of your awareness, yours is a drama that plays out before
an audience of one. It is you alone who encounters the world in
precisely the way you do. And it is you alone who determines how
long you will continue to watch the same predictable performances.

The players who populate your life script are present for you,
regardless of which choices you make or which combination of
possible realities manifest as life experience. They are called forth
to interact with you at the level in which you experience self-
awareness in any given moment. And their responses are governed
by the collective resonance upon which a particular stage is set in
a reality custom-made for *you*.

When you have amplified your own energy field to a sufficient extent, you are then able to shift your awareness and to participate in an alternate set of collective circumstances that more appropriately reflects your vibrational resonance. What presents itself upon the screen of your awareness, then, is a heightened variation on the identity you consider to be *you*. The others with whom you find yourself interacting are the very same players with whom you might have enacted a given scene in a more diminished environment. They are present, in your custom-made reality, as the manifestation of their own vibrational composition, and they then interact accordingly with the augmented set of variables you have called forth.

Likewise, from the perspective of the others who populate your inner circle, each of their worlds is custom-made for *their* eyes only. Your presence is called forth to interact with them at the levels at which *they* experience self-awareness. Your responses are influenced, vibrationally, in each of their worlds in much the same way as theirs are in yours. In this way, multiple variations on the same scene actually *happen*, yet each of you perceives it from your own unique vantage point.

As each of you *creates* alternate variations on the identity of others, with whom to interact at your own custom-made levels of awareness, these alternate aspects of consciousness and the circumstances they encounter combine to influence the energy fields of each of you. For that reason, it is altogether possible and often likely that your mood shifts, quite suddenly, in ways you find hard to explain.

An adverse reaction on the part of an alternate aspect of self, playing a role in a diminished environment, adds a sour note to the resonance of the collective *you* identity. Suddenly, you find that you are in a "bad mood" for what seems like no reason at all. Likewise, when you find yourself feeling elated, harmonious, and exhilarated for seemingly no reason, chances are you are experiencing the result of the augmented resonance of an alternate aspect of self that is enacting a command performance in the heightened reality of another.

As these interwoven fragments of your identity each add their resonance to the collective *you*, each of you struggles to remain centered and balanced at the focal point of awareness you regard as *your life*. You are largely unaware of the complexity of the composite that, in actuality, is co-creating your experience of reality.

Each time you venture into an interaction with another whose vibration is diminished and not aligned with your own, know that in doing so, you are simultaneously enacting the identical scene in his/her vibrational reality as well. An aspect of you becomes present in his custom-made world to interact with that unique set of variables. The result of his/her variation on the interaction between you may be far different from the scene you experience on your own turf. Yet, you carry a piece of that interaction within you, and without even knowing why, you suddenly are feeling less upbeat than you might have felt only moments before.

Those of you who are inclined to engage in sparring matches with others, out of a compulsion to appear "right" in your own eyes, often come away from what appears to be a victory feeling the energy of defeat, without understanding why. Those of you who remain in abusive relationships long after the adversity may have been resolved, are left to wonder why the energy of fear and mistrust lingers. Those of you who continue to experience chronic depression are often simply at the effect of the adversities encountered by parallel aspects of self in the vibrationally diminished realities of others.

Many of you are "moody" and subject to unexpected fluctuations in the way you feel that have little or no relation to the circumstances of your life. Chances are, you are feeling the influence of the multiple layers of vibrational input being provided by the countless levels of reality in which you, in actuality, are present. As you come to understand the dynamics of how your feelings, your environment, and your choices merge within you and are reflected as life experience, you begin to become selective as to where and with whom you continue to interact.

Ultimately, you walk away from discord of any kind, knowing that the price is too high, regardless of the trophy that beckons to you. Ultimately, you tune in carefully to your own sense of inner balance to guide you to the people and the situations that nourish you, vibrationally, and to alert you to the ones that do not. Ultimately, you begin to consolidate your fragmented identity by choosing carefully the circumstances in which you place yourself and selectively weeding out the parallel realities of others.

As each of you ascends into the heightened circumstances of more augmented levels of reality, your perception of the common thread that weaves amongst them, as variations of remembered experience, alters accordingly. Where, previously, an aspect of self might have participated in an elevated variation of an interaction in a guest appearance in the reality of another, those circumstances are taken up on the thread of memory when one ascends to those levels oneself. Thus, what is *remembered* is, in fact, the variation on the theme in question at the level in which one actually participated, when that level is reached oneself.

Diminished variations of interactions that once may have commanded the focus of one's awareness defer to the more heightened variation on the theme in question, as the fragmented aspects of self merge into the ascending composite of collective consciousness. What is *remembered* and believed to have *happened* is no more than an aspect of a multifaceted circumstance, with a heightened electromagnetic charge, that is perceived when one's awareness ascends into the range of that frequency.

In fact, you have actually experienced a mind-boggling number of variations on any given theme. Each of those fragments of vibrational possibility touched you, every step of the way, and helped to co-create the pinpoint of awareness you consider to be *you*. In actuality, you are infinitely more complex than you would dare to imagine.

Within the scope of each of you is an aspect of self that has mastered the challenges that still continue to confound you. That aspect of self is, in itself, merely a pinpoint of awareness within an infinite lineage, all of which are, in fact, *you*. Within the collective of your identity, that heightened variation on your life theme pushes and prods you, vibrationally, to fine-tune the issues you have come to master. That aspect of your identity, which lovingly and patiently takes on the vibrational repercussions of all your triumphs and disasters, is known to some as your *higher self*. It is this level of experiential mastery that walks amongst you, within the world of physical reality, in the persona of some who have come as spiritual teachers in these times.

There are some amongst you, who volunteered to remain in the world of physical reality to serve as the reference points that help those who are awakening to bridge the gap between your present levels of awareness and the dimensional realities toward which you continue to travel, as consciousness. These beings, who are regarded by many as *saints* and *spiritual masters*, are simply aspects of consciousness, experiencing themselves in physical form, within the diminished levels of reality you experience as your world.

There are comparable aspects of each of you, waiting patiently, in worlds you now visit only in your dreams. These aspects of self, ultimately, will encompass the collective of your linear experience, as you continue to merge in Oneness with all the fragmented aspects of who you know yourself to be. It is these aspects of your consciousness that reach out to you in dream-state and in the depths of your meditations. It is these *angels* who have come to remind you of who you really are, in the moments you are most apt to forget.

These aspects of your own Self, who nudge you into subtle levels of heightened awareness, are here to remind you of who you really Are. At times, they merge their energies with yours and give you a momentary glimpse of a reality you have perhaps only begun to imagine—not as a physical vision, but as a *feeling*.

This is the reason so many of you have begun to experience exalted moments of Divine connectedness, sometimes quite unexpectedly. This is what is actually happening when you begin to feel your energies shift and an exquisite sense of joy fills you, if only fleetingly, during moments of prayer, or deep contemplation, or within the sanctity of nature, or the embrace of silence and solitude. This is what you are feeling when you know you have been touched by something indescribably beautiful—and sacred—and you know you have not imagined it.

These momentary glimpses into the nature of the higher realms are experiential gifts to you who are awakening to the truth of who you Are. For, what you have come to these times to experience is not merely an intellectual grasp of the nature of the process. It is not simply a collection of metaphysical concepts around which you can attempt to wrap your mind. What there is to have is the taste of it, the profound *feeling* of it, the incredibly magnificent *experience* of it—the experience of knowing you have been touched by Divinity—that is a signpost on the road to Oneness.

oneness

chapter twenty-one

Attaining true freedom from attachment.
How you undermine your own best intentions, vibrationally.
Integrating parallel aspects of self into
the composite of your identity.

Many will venture forth in the times at hand, marginally aware of the magnitude of the changes that are transpiring within the cellular structure of those who are able to sustain physical form. And these beings will be living testimony to the difficulties and challenges posed by partial understanding of the nature of these changes. Many will pay lip service to the concept of ascension without fully understanding that the very essence of the concept demands that one take full responsibility for every aspect of one's life. Those who approach these times and the conditions of intensifying vibration with passive acceptance of the theoretical principles alone, will only lengthen the duration of the transitional period.

A common distortion of the concept of ascension would be to assume, passively, that ascension within a given time frame is a guaranteed outcome regardless of personal choices. Nothing could be further from the truth. This time frame and this particular transition, above and beyond any in your personal history, requires total immersion in the process to complete the exercise under optimum conditions. Those who approach these times with the assumption that they will be swept along effortlessly in the momentum at hand, are undermining the potential progress they could be achieving, and creating for themselves prolonged conditions of adversity.

Ultimately, all *will* make the transition and ascend interdimensionally. But there is no guarantee that this will occur in this lifetime—or even the next—on an individual basis. There is no guarantee that one will make the shift in the company of kindred companions who share your understandings of these times. For the process itself is conceived in timelessness. And the only schedule at hand is the one custom-made for you by your own choices.

Those who have defaulted in their efforts to interact with the energies and affect optimum change will have the experience of watching life seemingly pass them by. They will not understand why the lives of others appear to be transformed, while their circumstances continue to stagnate. For the journey demands active participation. There are no free rides to the destination that lies ahead.

Your own willingness to interact with the prompts that materialize for you in the form of life experience serves to determine how much repetition is required to create crystalline awareness for you of the nature of your personal process. Avoiding the issues being triggered by life circumstances only necessitates even stronger variations on a given theme. Once the common thread has been identified and attachment to forcing a result has been released, it is no longer necessary, or technically possible, to continue to experience examples of that theme. The energy charge responsible for creating those conditions would have been released and would not be present to magnetize that kind of experience.

As you peel back the layers of conditioning that serve to create your experience of life, you serve to lighten the levels of density that keep you tethered to diminished levels of reality. And, having made great strides in that respect, it often comes as a shock to discover that you appear to be back in the same movie that you presumed had been completed.

It is indeed possible that *you* had completed the lesson in question and had triumphed over the conditioned reflexes that habitually ensnared you throughout the experience of this lifetime. Yet, one factor has been added to the equation. *You* are, in all likelihood, not the same *you* as you were. You have evolved into a more complex variation of the theme you consider to be *you*. For, as you rise to the fullness of your perspective on the overview of your life, and ascend to subtle variations in level as you approach the interdimensional threshold, you will have integrated parallel aspects of your energetic sum-totality into the focus that you consider to be *you*.

All aspects of your selfhood must be energetically present in order for the interdimensional shift to occur, and all must be integrated, sequentially, in that effort. Aspects of self who are living what would be considered to be simultaneous lifetimes, focused on subtle variations on your life theme, are able to merge with you energetically once certain levels of clarity are reached. Often there may be minor variations in vibration amongst those aspects of self. And residual energetic charges carried by any aspect of the composite are capable of creating the conditions, energetically, for a repetition of old scenarios.

It is not necessarily an indication of a lack of work on your own part to suddenly be faced with old baggage on a new leg of the journey. It is a likely indication of a continuing pattern of completion in which you have integrated parallel aspects of self into the energetic whole. The reemergence of testing conditions can be an indication of the reinforcement of lessons that have, indeed, been mastered. The ease with which such scenarios are sidestepped serves as your indication of the growth you have achieved in key areas of your life's work. And your growing sense of comfort with the issues that have traditionally been the most unsettling is your indication of the escalating degree of complexity of the focus of consciousness you consider to be *you*.

There is no need, once the process is under way, to retrace your steps and rehash old dramas in an effort to cull-out key under-standings that have been identified. Know that the sense of peace that you now experience with themes that were once your undo-ing is your barometer of the level of completion you have attained. Awareness of the overriding life lessons sets the stage for an air of detachment to be cultivated with regard to those issues. And once distancing from the energetic *hooks* programmed into such scenarios has been attained, one is able to adopt a sense of amusement when predictable *hooks* appear and beckon to you to engage. For at that stage, the drama itself is essentially diffused by virtue of the overview attained. And from that vantage point, the episode can be seen as the symbolic representation of the life theme that it truly is.

Your cue to the stabilization of the energies surrounding certain issues and the successful integration of your multifaceted aspects of self, would be the nonemergence of predictable dramas in your life script. Ultimately, when the energy charge has been released completely, you can anticipate experiencing a profound sense of well-being that permeates your life. Suddenly, there is a rarified perspective on all that transpires and an overriding sense of detachment from the details of the dramas of daily life. From that vantage point, the outcomes of classic conflicts are unimportant, and that stance reinforces your ability to sustain the sense of freedom that you will have begun to experience.

True *freedom from attachment* is more than merely a mind-set and words that it has become fashionable to mouth in certain circles. Freedom is the ultimate goal toward which you are striving, as you process the final stages of your life's work. And the degree to which it is attained is measurable by the level of comfort or discomfort you manifest as life experience. A life script crammed full of complexity and challenge is indicative of an individual who is still very much in the grasp of life circumstances, albeit of his or her own creation.

Liberation from conditioned adherence to patterns of response is only possible when one ceases to be affected by the outcome of interpersonal encounters. When one releases attachment to outcome, one liberates oneself from the stranglehold that type of encounter has on one's life and from one's tendency toward the manifestation of adverse results.

The state of being into which one evolves, as one bridges the gap between dimensions, is one in which simplicity is prized over achievement for achievement's sake. One begins to question the work ethic with which one was conditioned in this lifetime, which reinforces the concept of "success at all costs." Such an outlook is based upon a dependency on the feedback of others, rather than a sense of well-being that emanates from within. As such, looking external to *Source* helped condition you to expect to sacrifice your heart's desire in an effort to please others.

The disharmony created by working at cross purposes with your own inner truth sets the stage for the energetic sabotage of your own best efforts. The more you *try* to manifest a result through your manipulation of the physical elements of your equation, the further you distance yourself, vibrationally, from the natural sense of balance that would manifest those very results.

The key to maximizing the effort you do put forth toward achieving a designated end lies not in how cleverly you assess what would be required to bring an effort to fruition, but rather in the level to which you are able to detach from the need to mastermind the process. The energy underlying that effort is not affected by how thoroughly you troubleshoot and anticipate the pitfalls that could undermine your result. Those efforts merely necessitate the creation of parallel pitfalls that would be magnetized to your effort, energetically. And you will, no doubt, find it extremely frustrating to have your plans undermined, repeatedly, despite the thoroughness of your preparations for success.

What often has not been addressed in such cases is the energy, in the form of emotion, which accompanies the effort. When one approaches any effort to manifest a given result, the intent under-t sets the stage for bringing it through to fruition. pproach is that of joyous anticipation of the natu-)ne's efforts, the manifestation occurs with ease and the process is uneventful. However, when one approaches an effort anticipating difficulty, and projects one's intent to circumvent it by mentally focusing on all the things that could go wrong, one sets the stage for those very kinds of difficulties to occur. It cannot be otherwise, for your mental focus creates your reality.

The degree of adversity you attempt to second-guess determines the amount of resistance you manifest to achieving your goal. Approaching the effort with the assumption that the highest possible result is automatically forthcoming sets the stage for your efforts to be well rewarded. The shift is subtle, but the result is powerful. For, it is based on loving trust of self to come through with the desired result, rather than an underlying fear of sabotage.

One creates with ease what is approached with the energy of joy. When one delights in the act of creation and brings the energy of joy to the effort itself, the result is blessed with the vibrational foundation upon which manifestation is based. When the focus of one's efforts is built upon a foundation of resentment, those efforts carry the vibration that will magnetize to them the resistance that will undermine them.

When one performs one's work with an attitude of hating the job, the stage is set for the manifestation of situations that make that job seem even more unpleasant. By shifting one's energy, even in subtle ways, the overall work environment can be transformed into one in which the efforts of all are well rewarded. And the level of satisfaction one anticipates as a result of those efforts produces that very result.

Victim consciousness takes many forms. One is often unaware of the subtle variations on this theme and the insidious ways it can undermine hopes and dreams. Approaching any effort with the assumption that outside factors are waiting in the wings to quash it sets the stage for that result to manifest. The anticipation of possible setbacks is based on an underlying fear of being out of control. Occurrences do not just happen. Everything is created energetically—by you. And the power to reverse an adverse history of disappointment is your birthright.

Fear of scarcity is a common factor that undermines the best efforts of many who habitually experience a thwarting of those efforts. Abundance is an option that has been programmed into the experience of life. The assumption that there is not enough or that there can never be enough, despite one's cleverness and fortitude, virtually guarantees that result. Whereas, the assumption that there will naturally be enough—be it time, money, resources, or whatever is perceived to be required to meet one's needs—produces that very abundance. You were placed here, in this time/space continuum, by your very own highest intent, equipped with all the resources necessary to create a life of joy and of plenty. Loving trust of oneself to provide what is needed helps to create the circumstances through which that result is virtually guaranteed.

These times are marked by radical reversals in the patterns that have been established in all areas of one's life. As one begins to grasp the ramifications of the concept of self-empowerment as it relates to the creation of one's reality, one is able to take responsibility for all of it. The need to justify one's actions in terms of the expectations of others begins to take a back seat to the priorities that emanate from within. And honoring one's own inner truth with regard to what is needed and desired takes precedence over cultural conditioning and the expectations and demands of others. Your obligation on this journey is ultimately to the recognition and implementation of your own true choices. And the loving intent with which you infuse all choices establishes the basis for the gratification of your heart's desire.

The patience with which you grace yourself during this process will go a long way toward modifying the discomfort many will experience. For time and practice is needed to integrate the new understandings and shift conditioned patterns of response.

Once you recognize the subtleties of the process of mastering the world as you are creating it to be, the delight in creating your reality as you would like it to be begins to be instilled.

These times are about embracing the power with which you have been blessed and relinquishing the remnants of limitation and fear that result in separation from self. The wholeness toward which you strive energetically fuels the impetus toward radical change that marks this phase of this lifetime. Recognizing the patterns of self-defeating response and releasing those tendencies is the task at hand. For there is truly no limit to what can be created and experienced in this lifetime. And no limit to the joy to be experienced when one unites in Oneness with oneself.

chapter twenty-two

Sidestepping the triggers that provoke
predictable patterns of response.

Defusing the poignancy of the adversarial relationship.

Stimulating the karmic resolution of emotion
at parallel levels of awareness.

Recognizing the Divinity that unites all experience.

The opportunity to transcend the patterns of experience you have acted out presents itself when you reach a place within where you are no longer attached to having to be *right* in the eyes of another. When you are able to let go of the need for ego validation on the issues that help define the history of this lifetime, you have taken the tentative first steps toward liberation from those patterns.

It is important that you remain aware that you have not been alone in these interactions. The experiential partners, who have been working out the details of these conflicts with you for lifetimes, also have a stake in the potential for the transcendence of these issues. Agreements remain in place for each of you to continue to participate in these patterns of interaction until there is resolution for all concerned.

Thus, it is entirely possible for you to continue to be drawn into dramas with certain individuals, despite the fact that you may have reached a place of completion with the issues in question. You

oted a shift in the intensity of certain kinds of experiences, as the energies that magnetize them diminish. Yet, within the energy field of your experiential partner, all the components for the full throttle of discord may still be present.

The invitation to engage in conflict with certain individuals may continue for some time to come, as each of you brings to resolution the opposing aspects of an issue in which you are mutually invested. While you may well find yourself playing out yet another episode in a serial drama, your own sense of the energies will have shifted. You will feel far less invested in meeting your adversary chin-to-chin, and more inclined to sidestep the classic triggers that once served to provoke you into predictable patterns of response.

Your partner is, in essence, dueling with an experiential surrogate in your form, as he brings to resolution his own poignant life theme issues. For, vibrationally, you will no longer be functioning as a catalyst that might escalate the energies in question. Having diffused your own residual energy charge on the issue at hand, you can only add the vibration of indifference to the equation.

Agreements of this kind will continue to manifest life theme dramas that draw your participation, so long as one member of an experiential partnership continues to manifest conflict around certain issues. By continuing to honor your agreements to be present and play your part in a given drama, you serve to help all concerned to bring a history of predictable conflicts to closure.

You are linked, karmically, with certain individuals for the purpose of facilitating such patterns of resolution. Even though you might wish to disengage your energies altogether and simply walk away, you are likely to find that it's not that easy. For, beneath the most insidious patterns of adversity that have surfaced between certain players in your drama, is a foundation of great love. Were that not the case, it would have been impossible for each of you to have continued to serve each other's growth in this way, in lifetime after lifetime.

Now that the augmented energies of these times of transformation are supporting your own impetus to move forward, each invitation to engage in battle with a familiar partner brings with it the potential gift of the recognition of a timeless soul mate. As you continue to release, from your own side, the vibrational ties that would perpetuate certain categories of interaction, you allow the love that genuinely exists between you to emerge and help shift the dynamics of your history.

Ultimately, each of you will be able to release the other, unconditionally, and to move forward in new categories of experience. Once your own passion surrounding certain issues has waned, it becomes easy to project the nonprovocative responses that invite a similar sense detachment on the part of a traditional adversary. You will find that the episodes that surface between you are fewer and farther between, as the energies that invite them continue to dissipate. For, without the vibrational foundation for a potential interaction, there is no basis with which to call it into manifestation. Certain relationships simply begin to "drift apart" as your attention and your energies are drawn elsewhere.

You will find that you begin to look back upon some of these most caustic relationships without the predictable anguish that once was triggered at the mere thought of that individual. For, the *sense* of the seething rage, or the profound hurt, or the unbridled terror that the actual interactions once manifested within you and that had been retained, vibrationally, would now have been released. And the passing thought that might once have been a sufficient catalyst to stimulate those unresolved emotions to the surface, now is not.

Now, you will notice that you can think about that individual, or some of the actual incidents you co-created, without feeling anything at all. The scenes are simply pictures in your mind that no longer seem to provoke or interest you. Individuals, who once dominated your every waking moment and haunted your awareness in dream state, have somehow faded into obscurity. And you are left to wonder about the validity of some of the major episodes of this lifetime.

It is important to understand that your present state of transcendence does not serve to invalidate the poignancy of the journey that was necessary to take you there. What you experienced is no less real, or relevant as a reference point in your history, simply because you are no longer focused on the full intensity of those issues. The opportunity in having brought those categories of emotion to resolution is to remember, vividly, the richness of that level of experience—and at the same time to know that you are no longer there.

One state of being does not cancel out the relevance of the other as a stepping-stone toward where you, as a manifestation of conscious awareness, wish to be headed. The purpose in coming into form at those levels of density was to provide yourself with the fullness of the emotional experience necessary to draw parallel levels of awareness into a corresponding state of resolution. In this way, you were able to open the doors to the possibility of the integration of all aspects of your consciousness that resonate to those emotional issues. Had you not co-created some of the incidents that brought those profound levels of emotion to the surface, you would not have had the catalyst in hand with which to release the density that has held you in certain patterns of experience for lifetimes.

So, from your newfound perspective, you may well be able to look back upon certain incidents and consider them to have been avoidable. But, in truth, had they not manifested to the extent that they did, you would not be where you are right now. You did not attain this rarefied perspective by chance. It was only by your willingness to probe the depths of your emotional responses, in tandem with the others who hashed it out with you by agreement, that each of you had the possibility of bringing the agony of some of those themes to completion.

You have served each other well—you who have facilitated in lancing the boil of another's repressed emotions. The memories may not be altogether pleasant, but then, they weren't meant to be. And the authenticity of those memories will remain with you, devoid of their emotional *charge*, so that you might have a frame of reference within which to place yourself, as you move forward toward other kinds of experience.

From the perspective of your experiential partner, your actions were just as objectionable as his appear to you. Each of you is simply looking at a common focal point through a different lens. Neither of you was "right" or "wrong." Neither of you was the villain nor the victim, regardless of what transpired. Each of you participated in the enactment of a drama, knowingly playing the part you were scripted to play, in order that a certain end might be attained, vibrationally. What transpired was one of many ways that end might have been achieved. And much vibrational backsliding was facilitated along the way, while in lifetime after lifetime each of you struggled to "get it right."

By trial and error, you, as a team, worked out the details of your contractual karmic agreements. You honored each other—and violated each other unmercifully—as each of you gave full expression to the manifestation of pride and ego. The role was played both ways, as each was given a turn to experience the effects of his own actions. In that way, the full spectrum of each category of emotion was permitted to manifest as life experience for each of you. For, no one who stands at the threshold of completing this work, here in the physical world, has opted out of any part of it.

Somewhere in the experiential history of all of you, there are memories of having inflicted the very wounds on another that you yourself have found so painful. And somewhere in the timeless past of the multidimensional presence that you have brought forth to today, is a character cast in precisely the role you now find most offensive—most likely a role reversed with the same partner.

As you now bring these categories of experience to culmination, it is interesting to begin to consider the vantage point of the perpetrator of your most poignant battles and to realize that th shoe could, just as easily, have been on the other foot. You might just as well have been the one playing the other role. And, chances are, you were—more times than you would like to imagine. For, that is the nature of the imagery of physical experience and what really brings it into form. All of it is conceived in balance. And the full spectrum of action and reaction is necessary in order to achieve it, vibrationally.

You have come to this moment of potential karmic resolution in order to recognize, from a place of nonjudgment, the essence of both roles in any interaction with another being, and to know that there is Divinity in all of it. Each of you fosters the emergence of the other into a state that transcends the need to perpetuate conditions that are calculated to hold you here at diminished levels of awareness.

Each of you, as consciousness, volunteered to go back into the arenas of turmoil, as an emotionally bound piece of *fragmented* consciousness, and explore some of the infinite possible variations on the theme of separation from who you really are. So long as you continued to manifest your ego investment in taking what transpired at face value, you served to reinforce the parameters for repeating that kind of experience.

The piece of you that separated from your own Divine essence, somewhere along the way, has been hashing out the vibrational manifestations of that self-perpetuating spiral, ever since. Now, it is time to shift that pattern. For the calling of Divine intent has been heard throughout Creation. It is time to put down your swords and your shields—and go home.

The image you hold of yourself as an autonomous being, separated from your fellowmen—and from a Divinity that you simultaneously worship and fear—will be revealed to you as the illusion it truly is. You are not the focal point of awareness you believe yourself to be. You are simply a facet in a light-spectrum—a fragment of a focal point—a split second flash of awareness in a whole that is infinite and eternal. You have deluded yourself into believing that you were *the main-event* for so long that you have amassed a volume of incarnate history, of epic proportions, to support that conclusion. And you reference a world around you that is calculated to reinforce those perceptions.

Far from view, yet ever present, is a level of awareness that transcends, in its overview of your personal history, the details with which you define your identity. That level of awareness, conceived in balance, has transcended the need to play any of the roles, or to experience the levels of conflict and resolution upon which you continue to focus, as you work out the final details of your sojourn into humanness. It is that level of awareness that watches patiently as the first inkling of your true multidimensionality takes root. And that level of awareness, of which you are a fundamental part, waits to include you in the loving embrace of all it understands *itself* to be.

In this way the process of ascension is ongoing. At each level of escalating vibration and complexity are aspects of your own being, each lost in the illusion of its own particular vantage point; each oblivious to the momentum that unites all aspects of the whole. That singularity of focus is characteristic of physical embodiment and a necessary part of the experience. Your adventure in the form of this particular identity, and the ones that may follow, could not hope to be carried out from the vantage-point of the overview. In order for the experience to be authentic, you will once again agree to experience the perception of the fragment of consciousness— regardless of its growing, multidimensional complexity.

As you continue to awaken within the structure of this particular illusion, you will integrate the final nuances of an entire category of incarnate experience. You will be drawing conclusions based on levels of understanding that are characteristic of the higher levels of awareness. As you progress ever deeper into this process of emergence, you will begin to be able to grasp the significance of the experiences you have lived through, over and over again, for centuries.

It is necessary, now, as you stand at the threshold of another kind of world, that you be able to see clearly the path you have traveled in order to get there. It is necessary that you be able to glimpse the limitlessness of your true identity from within the confines of physicality, as a foundation for the categories of experience to come. For, only then are you able to weave the threads that unite all you have been and done in a way that allows your release from those patterns. Were a reprieve from the myopic perspective of the fragmented consciousness *not* programmed into this pivotal point in your journey, you would be relegated to continue to repeat those patterns and unable to make the shift in awareness interdimensionally.

That is the nature of the transition at whose very edge you now stand. The last remnants of the core issues of this lifetime have been stimulated to the surface of your awareness for your scrutiny. And your recognition of the habitual patterns of interaction with others, who may continue to tempt you into the arenas of combat, now helps you to distance yourself, vibrationally, from those kinds of encounters.

Ultimately, you come to recognize yourself as the traveler you have come to embody. For you no longer dwell in the depths of the illusion that has dominated your emotional scenery for the duration of this lifetime. As you continue to pay the occasional visit to these levels of experience, it is as one would to a neighborhood of long ago. You no longer feel rooted there. And the emotional investment in continuing to hash out the mundane details of karmic agreements no longer holds any attraction.

These kinds of encounters have a familiar flavor to them—in that you have tasted them before. Yet, they no longer resonate with the bitterness that might once have provoked you into a self-righteous reaction. Now there is, more likely than not, a feeling of indifference at the sound of a familiar cue. For the one who is responding to it has transcended the limitations of your incarnate identity and perceives all *you* encounter from the vantage-point of the overview.

It is that aspect of self who is able to process incidents that continue to arise in the moment and to draw an instant correlation to parallel circumstances in "the past." You have connected with this heightened level of perspective through the very paths of emotion that once might have led you into battle. Now the battlefield within has been cleared of the karmic debris accumulated throughout the history you share with the others who assist you in bringing this chapter to completion. And, ultimately, each of you is able to view old familiar scenery from a newfound vantage point of transcendence.

The pathways of the emotions you have worked so hard to stabilize are those upon which your consciousness will travel in connecting you with heightened levels of awareness. For it is your emotional foundation that unites all aspects of the consciousness that make up your multidimensional identity. That foundation, once cleared of the ego based need to respond to provocation, serves as the pathway upon which all aspects of your multidimensional self unite in Oneness, and recognize that common bond as one that is shared with All Creation.

chapter twenty-three

Adapting to the escalating momentum of change.
Integrating parallel aspects of self
into the composite that is 'you.'
Experiencing the perceptions
of augmented levels of reality.

For many who are reading these words, the information contained in these teachings will be new and life changing. For others, it will be a confirmation of what has been learned experientially and what is known, at a deeper level, to be so. This knowingness does not emanate from the mind, where conceptual understandings and information are stored and then retrieved. Rather, the understandings upon which you draw in making your life choices reflect life experience and form the foundation of your *inner truth*. The building of that body of experience is the process at hand.

One is able to embrace a concept intellectually, when it is presented in this way, and recognize it to be truth. Yet, until one has the experiential knowingness that comes of having run the understanding through the filter of life and living, it is necessary that there be an element of trust. Trust that you have encountered a particular piece of information at precisely the right moment, and trust that it will surely be followed by an episode in your life script that will serve to reinforce that concept.

When one is working with information that constitutes major shifts in one's life perspective, it is to be expected that repeated episodes on that theme will manifest as experience. In this way one is able to build a base upon which a radical shift in one's world-view can rest. These are not understandings that can be instilled overnight. One can anticipate being exposed to a concept and to then experience several examples of that concept in rapid succession. In this way, the conceptual understandings of the world at whose edge you now stand can be reinforced. And ultimately, one is able to *know* rather than to *believe*.

Much that is new and different awaits you. And the criteria upon which your perceptions of these phenomena are based cannot be limited to the structure of a world that you have left behind. Your circumstances will shift in subtle ways as the days to come approach. And you will be swept along effortlessly in the momentum of that shift if you allow for the possibility that the keyword of the times at hand is "change." The foundation for life as you now know it to be is a fluid one. And the rules underlying the world you are co-creating are evolving in the ever-changing moment of *now*.

You who embody these changes in human physical form will bear witness to several worlds in one lifetime. It will serve you well to adopt a perspective that allows the unprecedented to become the norm. And you will come to trust in the perfection of a process that often serves a taste of the feast to come, well in advance of the main event. You can anticipate having the opportunity to bear witness to occurrences that would ordinarily be dismissed as figments of the imagination, in the present-day world of *reality by consensus*.

Those of you who are leading the wave of what is to come will not be afforded the luxury of eons of recorded history as a reference point. Each of you will be blazing your own trail through unknown territory, as you create a world to come that is custom-made to your specifications. You will be assisted in making the best use of your newfound skills by trusting in the validity of your perceptions and in your very real ability to create the reality you experience.

As you become a practiced artisan in crafting your life experience, you will garner the experiential reinforcement of the understandings upon which that art is based. Ultimately, your life script will be less of the hit-and-miss history of leaping ahead and backsliding that many have experienced as part of the transformation process. You will be able, after a given number of episodes, to recognize the common thread with which you now begin to weave an entirely new tapestry of experience. And you begin to delight in the recognition of your ability to alter the outcome of certain situations by directing your attention to the quality of the energy with which you approach them.

One becomes very clear that the consequences of one's thoughts and actions manifest as one's experience when that result is virtually instantaneous. There will no longer be the luxury of hiding in the well of victim-consciousness. For those depths have been relegated to a world now past, where the device of *time* provided for the deception of one's linear sensibilities. In the world you now have begun to embrace, your choices manifest so quickly that there is little room for doubt as to the role you have played in your own undoing or triumph. And there is less inclination to leave matters to *chance*. Ultimately, one embodies the impetus to harness one's own creative force field and to direct that power to the higher good of the collective.

One becomes aware, as this process unfolds, that there is less and less interest in striving toward one's own betterment. The attainment of material success symbols comes to be perceived as meaningless and holds little allure. And one steadily comes to be drawn to activities in which one feels one can make a difference for the world. Those who are rooted in patterns that are survival based will be afforded the opportunity to remain in realms where that focus presides, while others will shift their awareness, subtlely, to other levels of percep-

no value judgment intended here as to who chooses to g___ ___elf added layers of life experience with which to reap key understandings, and who is sufficiently complete in certain arenas to move on to other kinds of life's work. For, all experience is transpiring in the eternal moment of *Now* and, in essence, is occurring simultaneously. All possibilities exist. And the possibilities one chooses to experience produce a ripple effect throughout Creation and are reflected *energetically* in the *lives* of the infinite variations of experience that you consider to be *you*.

By making the highest possible choices in any given moment—those choices that emanate from heart—one makes the optimum vibrational contribution to the energetic collective of *you*. By foregoing the temptation to dive in and deliver justice oneself, one sidesteps the pitfalls that would set up parameters for an energetic nose-dive and the manifestation of the experience of adversity.

There is no need, once the initial experience of awareness is realized, to modify one's responses in an attempt to direct the process. One needs merely to maintain a state of openness to the energies, and to allow life to unfold in a natural way. Parallel opportunities present themselves simultaneously, within the life dramas of the collective of your identity, to make choices that reflect your attunement to heart centeredness. By making conscious choices, rather than acting on the reflex responses of a past orientation, you make the highest possible contribution to the energetic collective of *you* and to the manifestation of the highest results possible.

In this way, your conscious choices contribute toward shifting the patterns of other aspects of *you*, who may be experiencing varying degrees of *stuckness* on parallel issues. Energetically, these parallel selves experience a subtle shift in awareness at these moments. And oftentimes they are inclined to modify a reaction that would have been the result of ego focused conditioning to one more indicative of detachment. In this same way, your own response mechanism has been nudged into awareness by aspects of *you* who wait patiently in the wings for your higher awareness to take command. Your own transformation has been prompted energetically by the choices of parallel aspects of *you* who have been the forerunners of the process.

Each time you are presented with the opportunity to make an *enlightened* choice, know that the results of that choice will be felt, vibrationally, throughout all Creation. Likewise, when you feel the inclination to make a reactive choice, know that it is entirely possible that the urge to do so has been prompted, vibrationally, by a parallel aspect of self, caught in the grasp of discordant energies. Your awareness of the dynamics of this process provides you with the tools to shift that pattern and to redirect the energies. By consciously recognizing the instances of diminished vibration when they present themselves, one is able to surmount the instinctive inclination to fall back into habitual patterns of response and to reinforce those conditions energetically.

Perhaps you have begun to wonder about the parallel aspects of self, and to question the influence *they* have over the events of your life. Know that *they* are not other beings, but are aspects of your own consciousness who are experiencing alternative choices that you have foregone. Energetically, the parameters exist for the potential manifestation of all choices for which there is a vibrational basis. When you make a positive contribution to the energetic whole, you exercise the highest possible influence over the vibrational pool from which all experience is drawn. As the energies of the collective accelerate, certain categories of experience are ruled out. Thus, the reality you experience as *your life* is a reflection of your personal choices in juxtaposition with the vibrational balance of the collective consciousness of the *you* identity.

The variations at this level are subtle ones, as you are striving as a being to resolve life issues on multiple levels simultaneously. As these conflicts are resolved and balance is achieved vibrationally, the integration of the fragmented aspects of self is facilitated. At that point, it is no longer possible for one aspect of your being to exert an energetic influence over another, for *you* would then be unified with regard to that issue. In this way, you will be bringing to resolution each of the major issues with which you have been grappling throughout this lifetime. As one by one you unite with the fragmented aspects of self that represent conflicting standpoints on your major life issues, you elevate, in increments, the perspective of the one with primary *focus*—the one you consider to be *you*.

This is the work at hand, for those who have conscious awareness of the ascension process. Attention in word and in deed to all that transpires within the experience you call *your life* will expedite for you the time it takes to reach completion with this often painstaking phase in your personal transformation. Gathering up the fragmented pieces of your own essence is a crucial part of the journey you have undertaken. And it constitutes a necessary stage that must be surmounted so that you are able to make the major interdimensional shifts to come. It is not possible to make those shifts until all aspects of your being are unified. And it is to be expected, as one nears completion with the process, that areas still caught in the grasp of denial will be magnified as experience so as to prompt resolution.

The issues that you are most reluctant to face and to which you are most resistant are those that you can expect to see in exaggerated detail in these times. As the energies build to a crescendo around key life themes, you can anticipate dramatic examples of those issues to present themselves as life experience. The opportunity inherent in those kinds of episodes is to embrace the issue that cowers, cloaked in denial. When you own that aspect of your being and lovingly invite that characteristic to take its place at the head of your table, you succeed in closing the gap to the attainment of Oneness within your own being. For, it is the embracing of your vulnerabilities rather than their rejection that provides the key to the completion of this stage of your journey.

When the pieces of your puzzle interlock energetically, you can anticipate the experience of dramatic physical phenomena that should serve to punctuate for you the point underlying the drama. It is entirely to be expected that one manifests or dematerializes physical objects in the moment of that unification. For as the two realities merge, the oftentimes repellent energies collide dramatically and can result in the momentary appearance of aspects of one reality in the other. The material evidence from the energetically diminished level will be unable to sustain form at the new higher range, and will just as suddenly appear to vanish as if by magic.

One can anticipate such energetic merges to be accompanied by sound or light phenomena that manifest as a result of the colliding energies. When one assists in the process with focused declarations of one's intention to embrace the denied aspect of self, the phenomena accompanying the ascension of the diminished reality can be poignant, and the experience unforgettable. When one becomes aware of the nature of the process, such incidents can be perceived as fascinating rather than frightening. And one is able to regard with bemusement the extraordinary turns that life has taken.

Once the fragmented aspects of self have been united, one regards the world through the higher vantage point of the unified collective. And the initial incidence of the plummeting of the energies of the reality in *focus* can be understood to be the energetic reverberations of the unification process. As the energies stabilize, one is able to view one's life circumstances from the perspective of balance, with regard to the issue in question. And, as one-by-one these major categories of life experience are brought to resolution, one begins to experience life from a rarefied perspective that is free of conflict.

Suddenly, opportunities appear effortlessly. And one ceases to anticipate resistance to one's hopes and dreams and thus stops creating it energetically. One begins to assume that everything will go smoothly and that potentially difficult or complex scenarios will work out perfectly. And, therefore, they do. One begins to enjoy the process of learning to harness the power of creation, and one is increasingly able to sail smoothly through the scenarios of one's life. The resistance that one may have been accustomed to is suddenly not manifesting in one's life script, for one has ceased creating it. A brand new kind of life experience begins to be predominant.

As one approaches the major shift between dimensions that is to come, it is to be anticipated that a period of *smooth sailing* will be experienced. This is a reflection of one's state as a unified being and heralds one's preparedness for the conditions of instantaneous manifestation that characterize life at the next dimensional level. In the present period, most who read these words can expect to begin to experience a radical turnaround in the quality of the life experiences manifested on a daily basis. For the energies from the realm toward which you ascend act as a catalyst for you, prodding you toward higher choices and more optimal outcomes of your interactions with your fellow beings.

The aspect of self that seeks to integrate you, as a unified being, into *its* energy field is reaching for you energetically in subtle ways that are barely perceptible. Yet the ramifications of those vibrational connections contribute to the momentum of what is a universal motion. All of Creation is reaching out for the experience of Unity within the context of the identity of each of you. Each is adding a spark of Light energy to the whole. And each is feeling the tug and the impetus to become something more. This is not an experience in which any being is isolated, although all are manifesting it on an individual basis. The process is universal. All of you are going on this journey individually—together. And each is assisted by higher dimensional aspects of self in doing so.

Your own openness to concepts that you once might have considered *radical* attests to the fact that there is a monumental process of transformation under way within you. The impetus for these changes manifest from within, yet are the result of energy enhancement initiated at a higher level. When you respond to these energetic prods, you open the door to higher levels of energy to be assimilated within your field. In this way, you are being supported and supplemented, vibrationally, through the process.

The ebb and flow effect of the giving and the receiving of energy amongst the aspects of *self* manifests in ways that range from the barely perceptible to the dramatic. The motion is a fluid one and accounts for the instability of the state of your emotions and your sense of well-being. Even the state of your physical health reflects the state of flux of your energy field in these times of transformation.

Resist the temptation to jump to the conclusion that something is radically wrong with you if you are feeling out of balance on occasion. These kinds of waves of energy are to be expected, particularly when major emotional release work has been consciously undertaken. Expect that the energies will stabilize and reach a common ground, if allowed to follow their own natural momentum. Your own willingness to be in the moment with the process and to suspend judgment of your own journey will assist you in moving through the moments of discomfort and to arrive, sure-footedly, on higher ground.

The time required to complete this stage of the journey varies from individual to individual. But once you are in the process in earnest, you can expect the momentum to accelerate in increments, and your discomfort with the nature of the process to diminish accordingly. Once you have undertaken to participate consciously in your own transformation, it is no longer likely to revert to obsolete behavior patterns. For it will be blatantly obvious that the learned modes of response and belief have little relevance to the work at hand. One is able to be fully present without the need to defend one's choices to anyone. Those who are aligned to your process are right beside you in theirs. The others, who cast stones out of ignorance, are on their own journey and are moving at a different pace.

It serves no one to invalidate the process of those who are choosing to remain stuck in habitual patterns. You will teach them best by example. Be in the integrity of your process and do not seek to convert those who are not naturally inclined to follow your chosen path. Your journey will not go unnoticed, merely unacknowledged. For it will be difficult for many to release a lifetime of conditioning. Yet, they may well be applauding your courage in silence, knowing that they would not dare to do the same. Be patient and loving with these ones, who are often family members, and know that all will arrive at their destination at the perfect time for them to do so, for the seed will have been planted.

Several lifetimes, in linear terms, may transpire before some beings manifest the impetus for making those shifts in consciousness themselves. It does not matter, from the perspective of the "bigger picture," whether one experiences interdimensional ascension in this physical lifetime or in another. For, linear time, as you know it, does not factor into the process. All will be achieved within the scope of what you refer to as *eternity*. From that standpoint, there are no deadlines to be met. All is progressing precisely as it is progressing, in a momentum that is unstoppable.

chapter twenty-four

The significance of the experience of duality.
The purpose of the journey into the depths of humanness.
The gift of experiences of adversity as a foundation
for the experience of Oneness.

The inclination to place the concept of God in an exalted position within the framework of a personal philosophy is at the
root of all that holds one back in one's experience of God. For God
is not within you to be worshipped, or feared, or even to be
understood, but rather, to be experienced and known. The very
act of the exultation of the Divine creates a delineation between
that Divine presence and oneself—a state of separation that
constitutes a barrier to the very connection that one most fervently
wishes to realize.

The God within all life does not seek to be placed on a
pedestal, but hopes to be discovered as the source of one's own
essence. The God to whom you pray and from whom you beg mercy
or miracles is no more capable of manifesting the answer to your
prayers than you are. The only difference between you and God
is that God knows it—and you don't.

Our purpose in coming here to tell you the truth of the nature
of Creation is not to provide you with the basis for yet another

religion to which you can serve up your power. It is surely not to equip the charismatic amongst you with the tools to command the devotion and resources of your fellow beings. And it is surely not our purpose to create a new set of parameters for humankind to wield as evidence of a God who would remain in an exalted position to each of you. For the God that speaks to you now, in this moment, is Oneness—the Oneness that dwells *within* each of you.

Man has created God in an image that we are not here to "live up to." For to embody the exalted concept of the Divine, to the exclusion of all else, would limit the scope of all that Oneness is. For Oneness is you. All of you. The qualities that you strive most diligently to transcend are no less characteristic of what Oneness is than your *highest* thought or action. For what Oneness is, simply Is. There is no judgment. There is no higher or lower. All is Oneness.

The delineation and compartmentalization of the concept of God is the training you have come here to transcend. You have not come here to weigh the relative merits of one body of self-righteous dogma over another. You have come into form in these times to liberate yourself from the human tendency to do so. You have come to taste the experience of your own connectedness to All That Is. Not for the purpose of *knowing* God, but rather, for the purpose of knowing yourself.

We speak to you now, not as the "God" whom you would perceive to be separate from all that you are. But rather as Oneness—the Oneness that is the very essence of each of you.

As you fine-tune your ability to manifest your experience as you would wish it to be, you are taking command of your identity as a creative being. A being who is able to create, to manifest, to materialize, and to dematerialize is a being that is exercising mastery over the limitations imposed by ideas of separation. When one is in conscious alignment with the sum-totality of one's connectedness to All That Is, there is no limit to what can be experienced or created in physical form. The question for those who have perfected these skills is whether one wishes to expend one's energies manifesting the mundane into form or whether one feels sufficiently complete with that experience to cease having to do so.

Ultimately, as one harmonizes with the higher energies and merges with the aspects of self at those levels, one realizes that one's focus has shifted. The transition happens in a very natural way. And often, one is not even aware that such a transformation has occurred. Rather, one becomes aware of subtle differences in emphasis and with one's perception of one's life direction. One is often compelled to cast off the constraints imposed by a life structure built upon a foundation of striving for material gain, and to redirect one's energies to the manifestation of the experience of harmony for all beings.

The opportunity, once one has tasted the heightened sensibilities characteristic of ascending to accelerated levels of reality, is not to emerge from that experience of *knowing* with a "holier than thou" outlook with regard to one's fellow beings. The opportunity inherent in one's own realization of Oneness is to know that such experiences are happening to everyone, quite literally. The factor that determines who is able to integrate the experience as a catalyst for transformation and who is not is the degree to which one's perceptions are invalidated by denial.

Those who are sufficiently free within themselves to embrace their transformational moment and cast aside a lifetime of culturally induced beliefs are those whose lives transform in ways that seem miraculous. These are the ones who often become the teachers of the masses. For, they can teach the trials of transformation from the standpoint of having lived through the most poignant shifts in consciousness, rather than simply having intellectualized those concepts theoretically. Each of you has chosen to choreograph particular challenges into your personal life drama in order to reach the transformational realizations experientially. And it is important that judgment be suspended as to the path some may have chosen as a means of reaching a transcendent state of being.

Many will choose to punctuate their journeys with experiences that might be considered to be radical deviations from a spiritually focused path. Such individuals should not be presumed to be offtrack, but rather, given the latitude to create their own perfect route to the attainment of higher wisdom. For some of you, that journey necessitates experiences of plummeting to the depths of humanness in order to prepare a foundation for comprehending and appreciating the heights to come. And these beings are not to be considered in any way less God-like in their core essence than those amongst you whose journeys have been less dramatic.

Each of you has a particular focus that has been preselected as the highest path to your chosen destination. And each of you is diligently enacting those choices. The degree to which the repetition of these themes is necessary is the option with which most of you struggle in these times, and the obstacle all of you are destined to surmount—each in your own time.

The experience of Oneness is not a destination toward which you strive in your journey toward self-mastery, but rather the essence of the journey itself. For Oneness is your experience of beingness in this present moment. And Oneness is the experience to be encountered at the very next stage of your development. Oneness is every exalted plateau encountered and every stumbling block that trips you and leaves you disheartened and wallowing in the depths of despair. Oneness is the full gamut of your journey into humanness. For, this experience is what you have come into form to have.

Be not so quick to judge yourself or others who stumble beside you on your sacred journey. It is naïve to assume that a simple, obstacle-free path is a symptom of spiritual advancement. Oftentimes, a more challenging route has been chosen, purposefully, as a means of providing the rich depths of understanding that would not be possible through a life script that merely skimmed the surface of the human condition.

So, by all means, experience your experience. Live your life fully. Feel your feelings deeply. And know that the highest expression of your experience of aliveness is in knowing that all of it is your own creation. For in that acceptance of total responsibility for the condition you consider to be *your life* is the key to the realization that your life is so much more than that. In acknowledging that you are the creator of your existence, you open to the experience of Oneness, as the Creator of All Existence.

Oneness did not limit Creation to a landscape of bland, monochromatic vistas. The canvas of life is awash with the richness of contrasts. The highs and the lows of the terrain of your world reflect vividly the duality that is the nature of your incarnate experience. The duality that is a built-in characteristic of your very existence is that which you fervently deny and that which must be embraced in order to be freed from the endless cycles of creating those patterns.

The Oneness, toward which you strive energetically, is comprised of those polarities. And it is not possible for you to ascend into an exalted state of balance without encompassing all ends of the energetic spectrum. All must be embraced, at this stage of your journey, to prepare you to embody the totality vibrationally. Efforts to suppress inclinations that you would consider to be negative, and denying that those emotional reactions are part of your response mechanism, only serves to magnetize to you circumstances calculated to trigger those very emotions.

The emotion itself is not an obstacle to your spiritual progress. Rather, it is the unbridled *expression* of such emotions that puts one in a repetitive cycle of adverse experiences. The objective is surely not to deny that one is capable of feeling emotions that one would consider to be negative. Quite the contrary. The objective is in feeling those spontaneous responses fully and deeply while relinquishing the impulse to allow that emotion to govern your response.

Once transcendence of these patterns of experience becomes established, the key to maintaining your freedom from such episodes lies not in denying that you have the capability of feeling such emotions, but rather, in embracing those tendencies.

Your feeling body is a key characteristic of your very humanness. And you cannot transcend the limitations of humanness by limiting your experience of it. Your actions, therefore, become the reflection of choice rather than reaction. And your world begins to reflect those conscious choices and resonate in harmony with your environment and your fellow creatures.

The exquisite state of balance toward which you strive is the culmination of the full spectrum of life experience, both *positive* and *negative.* As you begin to taste that rarified state with increasing frequency, it is important to be aware that the capability of manifesting adversity still remains, albeit to a diminishing extent. For, vibrationally, the catalysts for such categories of experience would still be present in your energy field. Clarity regarding the nature of the process helps you to avoid the natural tendency to fault oneself when such episodes occur and inadvertently plunge you into a downward spiral of adversity.

Be gentle with yourself during this process. And allow yourself the grace of experiencing fully your humanness. For to do so is the path to all you would wish to experience in the times soon to come. Become the embodiment of the highest loving intent in every moment, and you become the director of your life drama, rather than its reluctant star performer. Allow the fullness of your presence as a Light being to express, as energy, through your form, and you create the parameters for the fullness of that energy to manifest as your life experience. Create from a place of spontaneous centeredness, radiating your unquestioning knowledge of your limitlessness as an expression of Oneness in human form, and you will reap the bounty that is the inherent potential of that blessed condition.

You have chosen to experience humanness as the most direct vehicle to the culmination of your sacred journey as a being. And the *human being* aspects of that adventure were expected and anticipated. The opportunity inherent in the voyage into humanness is to integrate the epitome of your understandings of yourself as a limitless being with the self-definition that consti gence as energy in form. To have arrived at this s ment is a major threshold. And to have undertak of a physical lifetime is, in itself, a testimonial to great courage. For the physical world is fraught with every adversity imaginable, quite literally. And the training possible is to harness that potential from a position of inner strength rather than from a position of might.

Those with the strongest abilities often encounter the most extreme obstacles and hardships in order to direct their quest toward the strength from within. For the manipulation of the physical manifestations of your world rarely produces the realization of your hopes and dreams. And those for whom those skills come easy often have greater challenges to overcome than less capable fellow travelers. For cleverness and talent rarely guarantee results in and of themselves. And such gifts can prove to be handicaps without a sense of how those abilities harmonize with more profound understandings of the nature of reality.

The attainment of balance can be the foundation for a profound epic for some of you, who have sought on a soul level to achieve completion of such themes in this lifetime. For the potential in these times is to be able to ride the crest of the wave, vibrationally, and to take quantum leaps in consciousness as a result. The potential drawbacks in having undertaken such a journey, are the experiential ramifications of jumping on the vibrational roller-coaster of these times. One may have a lifetime of scuffs and bruises to show for the ride. And the experience, to be sure, is not entirely pleasant. But then, it wasn't meant to be. It was meant to be full, and rich, and rewarding in ways that cannot be measured—not until the physical form has been relinquished and a higher perspective is once again possible.

Undertaking a physical lifetime is not unlike volunteering to serve in the front lines in conditions of combat. Every nuance of one's ability is put to the test on a moment-to-moment basis. The potential for emerging from the experience as a hero, in the highest sense, is great, regardless of whether or not one actually *survives*. For the potential in terms of inner growth and self-mastery is unsurpassed.

You who have chosen the experience of a physical incarnation under the conditions of these times in human history did so fully aware of the consequences of such a choice. Many chose to consciously harness the potential in those conditions by casting themselves in scripts that would provide for extremes of experience. For the potential for spiritual growth inherent in such a path far outweighs the inconvenience of the cuts and scrapes, and the pain in the inevitable wounds one knew one would bear.

It was all part of the plan. You walked into this experience of a lifetime with your eyes wide open. And you did so for the chance that you might emerge from the experience with your eyes wide open. You did so for the chance that you might taste your own Divinity, in the exalted state of physical presence, despite every conceivable obstacle you could think to place in your own way. Your objective was to transcend the limitations of your humanness, and to experience that state through the senses of a physical state of being.

This is who you are. This is the hero who lives at the heart of all you would fault and criticize within yourself. This is the blessed being of Light who ventured forth in this lifetime, in uncharted territory, on the chance that a map might be drawn to the Source within. This is the one who often thinks that the journey is some sort of race against time, when the truth is—there is no time. And surely, there is no race. For, the experience is not one to be hurried—but rather, to be savored.

Your journey into physicality was embarked upon for the purpose of amassing a body of experience to support the conclusions you will, quite naturally, draw from having lived through them. Thus, the experiences of your life are both the catalysts for your spiritual growth and the supporting evidence for the realizations that underlie it. You cannot hope to reach these understandings without having weathered a storm or two. The purpose of this incarnation is not to have glossed over the table of contents, but to have explored in depth some of the most poignant and excruciating passages.

Those moments when you judge yourself most harshly and in which you feel you let yourself down are the moments most deeply yearned for as a soul. For, in the moments you look back upon with deepest regret—the ones that conjure up within you the most profound humiliation in your own eyes—are the moments for which you chose a human incarnation. These key experiences serve as reference points for you to underscore the themes you have acted out. And your purpose in drawing these experiences to you was in creating moments that would be truly unforgettable. Your darkest hour was, in actuality, your shining moment. For, in the authenticity of your emotional experience was your key to your liberation from the pattern that keeps you rooted in the pain of separation from who you really Are.

In order to transcend the patterns of agony that lurk beneath the surface of your polished veneer, it is necessary for you to transcend the emotional barrenness that your cultural conditioning has supported. You have been prodded, energetically, into facing the truth of what lies buried there. You have been goaded by circumstances into feeling the rawness of your unresolved anger and grief, your envy and your selfishness, and your all-consuming fears. For, these are the attributes that are co-creating with you a reality that persists in undermining your dreams.

As you ascend into the higher realms of consciousness, you will need to have mastered these attributes. You will need to have come to grips with all that now has you in its grasp. And to do so, you will need to recognize the truth of what motivates your patterns of response, and the categories of experience that dominate your life. The key to the self-mastery that is so fervently sought by you who are so keenly aware of your process of evolution, is not to love yourself despite your perceived shortcomings—but rather, to love yourself because of them.

The self-love that is the end result of this process is not a conditional reward that is meted out for high marks and polished performance. It is there without regard for issues of worthiness or unworthiness. For, there is no place for judgment at all. You are the perfection of Oneness, with the uniqueness of identity, striving toward Self-recognition. And in your embracing of all that you Are—and in your acceptance of all that you are not, despite the evidence that you may have demonstrated along the way—is the unconditional gift of wholeness that awaits you.

The Oneness toward which you strive, as you stumble and fall in your daily trials, is the natural consequence of all of it. The profound sense of belonging that has eluded you all your life awaits you. For the sense of separation from your Divine connectedness is the illusion. It is this that will be transcended within each of you as you ascend into the higher states of awareness. Not just the privileged few, but all of you. It cannot be otherwise. It may take some of you longer than others to arrive at that blessed state. And some may choose to spend lifetimes working out the details of those agreements. But the end result is inevitable. For all Is Oneness. And, ultimately, all will know themselves to Be Oneness. Some of you, sooner than you can imagine.

chapter twenty-five

The vibrational nature of today's children
and the generations to come.
The "paranormal" characteristics and abilities
of the children of the future.
The care and nurturing of the "miracle children" of tomorrow.

Generations to come may speculate on what it was like to be alive in these times. For, your history will allude to conditions that they will not be able to comprehend. The world as you know it will undergo radical transformations in the times to come. And the foundation upon which you have built your understandings of the nature of your reality will have changed so dramatically that one would be apt to question whether it was the same world at all. Indeed, that is the very nature of the process. For the world as you know it to be is, in fact, dematerializing in the wake of the momentum that is driving all Creation.

The changes are taking form in subtle increments. And often one does not even notice that a significant shift has occurred. But, from the perspective of a broader vision, one will be able to look back upon these times with wonderment. And those of you who will have retained your physical form will have fascinating stories to tell as to how these changes came to be. Younger beings, who will only be able to imagine life under such conditions, will marvel at how such memories are even possible.

You, whose very presence will attest to the extent of the journey in consciousness humankind has undertaken, see these days of transformation from a markedly different perspective. For, collectively, you are the midwives who are assisting with the birthing of a new reality. Your willingness to be in physical form during these changes is an act of courage. For, it would have been far easier to wait until the dust had settled and simply manifest into more favorable circumstances. You, who read these words, are among those who chose to experience the transformational journey in physical form and to have the experience of physical ascension.

Future generations will have made preparations for incarnation into a dramatically different world. Their natural inclination to be less reactive reflects the fact that many of these younger beings have a dramatically different vibrational constitution than you do. Their energy fields are not cluttered with unresolved emotional blockages, and life for the young, in general, flows more smoothly than it did for you at their stage of development.

The beings now incarnating into your reality are, themselves, representations of an interim stage in the evolution of the being who will, ultimately, populate your world. Their perceptions seem clearer, at times, than your conditioning permits yours to be. And they are puzzled as to why the older generations seem to struggle with their lives, when they do not appear to manifest so much conflict in theirs. These beings have incarnated at vibrational levels that are in harmony with the conditions now prevalent in your world, whereas, you incarnated at vibrational levels from which your reality has ascended.

In keeping up with the pace of those changes, you have systematically shed the layers of density that were designed to keep you grounded at levels you have transcended. And for you, the process will be ongoing, as long as you retain your present physical form. In the process, you are able to confront and release the karmic constraints that contribute to that vibrational density.

And your conscious awareness of that process was the opportunity for which you chose this physical incarnation.

The beings who will be incarnating in human form in the times soon to come will have a natural affinity for the world of nature. They will be able to communicate easily with the other life forms that populate your reality, and their easy interaction with these other forms of intelligence will set the stage for the air of peace and harmony that will prevail. That harmonization is characteristic of an orientation based on a sense of Oneness, not only with one's fellow human beings, but with all life.

The beings now in their physical infancy will exhibit abilities that would have been considered most unusual, not long ago. These beings are incarnating fully equipped to cope in a world that neither you nor they have seen, as yet. For, your world is still in metamorphosis, and the conditions for which they have been prepared have not as yet manifested. As your world teeters right on the edge of interdimensional ascension, these young ones will provide the stability that may often be lacking in physically older, more experienced beings. For, the skills needed to cope in the world to come are not those developed by experience in a world that is fast becoming obsolete. The abilities needed to merge well in the conditions of the higher dimensions into whose vibrational force field you now travel are those the youngest amongst you are born with.

These skills can be acquired, quite often with ease, by those of you who present no resistance to the momentum of change. Many amongst you are very much aware of the *supernatural* abilities so many are now encountering, often within themselves. These kinds of abilities are commonplace in the higher realities, and the fact that these experiences have begun to touch the lives of so many attests to the fact that you, as a populace, have transcended the levels where such occurrences were rare. It is to be expected that the beings born in the years soon to come will exhibit what has come to be considered *extrasensory perception* as a natural fact of life. As the natural levels of vibration of a being at birth continue to accelerate, those kinds of abilities can be expected to become refined.

It will be a natural condition of humanness to become telepathic, not only with other humans but also with other life forms and with other dimensional forms of existence. The phenomenon of *channeling* will come to be considered commonplace. And it will hold far less allure than it does now. Your culture's present fascination with what is perceived as *otherworldly* will soon diminish as you begin to recognize how widespread such experiences now are, despite the fact that such occurrences were once considered miraculous. You will begin to develop a level of spiritual sophistication and the highly recommended skills of *discernment* regarding the kinds of consciousness with which you do or do not choose to interact. And, ultimately, you will begin to recognize that the wisdom that you yearn for is right there within your own being, and need not be sought from discarnate sources.

The very young amongst you know this instinctively and will demonstrate far less attraction to the otherworldly and the unexplained than do present adult generations. The very young will be absorbed in the wonder of being alive and with their formidable skills in manipulating their reality to produce what they want to experience. They will be less concerned with fending off adversity and overcoming obstacles than will the present population, for the criteria for the creation of those kinds of conditions would not be present for them, energetically.

It is important for those guiding the young to understand these differences and to resist the inclination to burden those entrusted to your care with excessive schooling in the limitations with which you labor. For, those kinds of constraints will not be part of their process. The ease with which the young beings yet to come master the dynamics of the creation of their heart's desire will astound you, who now struggle to grasp such concepts. They will understand, quite naturally, that they are creating their experience, and after an experiential training calculated to impress upon them the pitfalls of adverse thought patterns and speech, they will be well equipped to thrive in the times to come. Their best teachers will be their own experiences. And you will look upon them in rapt fascination, for they will be teaching *you*, by example, the lessons you now struggle to integrate.

For them, theoretical understandings are unnecessary, for there is nothing to be changed, no belief systems to be restructured, no extensive training needed at all to undo the lifetime of conditioning that now confronts the *conscious* adult beings amongst you. The world for which they are so well prepared will be an extraordinary place to be, in comparison to the conditions now at hand. And the issues with which they will be working will be different ones entirely from the kinds of life work of your own generation and that of the children already present in your world.

The vibrational changes are occurring so rapidly, now that it is possible to say that differences in the characteristics of children in the same family will be commonplace and are to be expected. The older children will be more vibrationally aligned with the adults now amongst your population. The children yet to be born will exhibit characteristics, from birth, that will distinguish them from their older siblings. And it will be fascinating to observe the differences in mental capabilities amongst children separated in age, within the same family.

It is important to remember the nature of these differences and to avoid the inclination to make comparisons. For the new breed of beings is scheduled to incarnate amongst you in stages, over the course of several generations. And until the conditions in your world stabilize, and a population of vibrationally adapted beings prevail, you can anticipate a populace with a radical diversity in ability and perspective. Those amongst you who have chosen to function as teachers in the times to come will be challenged to cope with the extremes of difference exhibited by the children with whom you have been entrusted, from one year to the next. Much care will be needed on the parts of those who have chosen to play these roles. For what is now considered *paranormal* will soon be very normal indeed.

It will be necessary for the teachers of the young to be acutely aware of the innate gifts of the children of tomorrow. For, they will be a different breed from the children of today—and worlds removed from what may have been true of one's own childhood. Anticipated rates of development and standards of performance will need to be perpetually reevaluated. And one will need to rely less upon what has been taught in one's formal schooling than with the reality of the here and now within the classrooms to come.

The gifted amongst the teachers in these times will be those who do not seek to limit the young by standards of what is known to be "possible." For those standards will continue to become obsolete with each successive year. Let the children themselves guide you in understanding the nature of the human species. Let them show you how to train the talented amongst them to maximize the potential in those gifts by allowing them to explore their perceptions to determine what is and is not "possible." They will astound you in what they, quite naturally, will be able to do. And you will become clearly aware that you are encountering and nurturing a very different kind of being. For these beings, the potential is quite literally unlimited, for each of them will be defining themselves to themselves in each ongoing moment, creating themselves as they would wish to be.

There is no necessity to structure the parameters within which they will conceptualize their world. For, this they are amply capable of accomplishing without your help. Resist the temptation to limit the outer reaches of their dreams with your expectations of what experience has shown you to be "possible." For the world in which these children will live is one you would be challenged to imagine. Create for them safe environments in which to explore the miracle of the physical form in which they have emerged, and equip them with sensory stimuli that will stretch the limits of sensory perception.

Provide materials with which these young beings may express the levels of passion that they feel quite naturally and which may strike you as incomprehensible. Allow creative expression free reign in the classrooms over which you may preside, and reap the bounty of joy these children will provide for you, just by being who they are. For the parents and teachers of the generation now being born will bear witness to the most profound evidence of the ascension process. Those amongst you who are privileged to play these roles will know, from having held the small hands of the ones that walk through your lives, the "miracle" of unlimited potential made manifest not by the rare protégé—but by all of them.

You, who are destined to be the grandparents of the generation now emerging in your reality, will experience the wonder of knowing that you have truly lived in many worlds in one lifetime. These blessed little pioneers will take you on amazing voyages of discovery, if you let them. The stories you may be inclined to tell them of your childhood will perhaps be difficult for them to fathom. Consider, instead, allowing these exceptional beings to tell *you* the story of your second childhood—the story of the being harbored within you, that's now in the birthing process. In the times to come, the young will be the teachers of the old in ways that have never before been experienced. And those amongst you who have let go of the need to *prove* yourselves and are content just to Be, are capable of literally being reborn at the hands of the children.

There is no mountain that cannot be scaled at will by the beings now emerging in your world as the children of tomorrow. For, by definition, theirs is a world unbounded by parameters of "possibility." Theirs is a world perpetually in the process of evolution, governed only by the unbridled imaginations of those who are creating it. "Reality" for them, then becomes that which is most fervently desired, and the results are often instantaneous. It will often be hilarious or horrifying to observe the manifestations of these "super-beings" as they begin to flex the musculature of instantaneous manifestation. And they soon learn, by poignant experience, the consequences of unleashing those capabilities.

Once it becomes apparent that the responsibility for one's reality rests upon one's own shoulders, many of these small beings may well become enthralled with the playground that is their world. And it soon becomes obvious that there is no limit to what can be created within it. As the conditions upon the planet at large stabilize to mirror the vibrational levels of the beings incarnating within the framework of each of those realities, the foundation is established, vibrationally, to support those capabilities. And human beings will have bridged the gap that now separates the many worlds that make up your world.

In the "here and now" of this rapidly accelerating process, the variations in levels amongst children are apt to baffle and to challenge most educators and parents. The children themselves are not equipped to cope with inherent abilities that their present world still regards as *abnormal*. And many will suppress and inhibit their natural tendencies toward self-expression in deference to perceived peer pressure. It is for those of you who have become aware of the transformation process, to support these first pioneering spirits in the arduous task of forging a new reality with no frame of reference.

Theirs will be a world in which they perceive themselves to be lost. And the parameters being force-fed within your education system do little to equip them to deal with themselves. Many of these first emerging beings will struggle with the reality of bridging two worlds simultaneously, and will feel, until well into adulthood, that they do not really fit in anywhere. With time, and the amassment of life experience with which to custom-make a belief system, these beings, now in early childhood, will be able to stabilize in a world which will, by then, be in a better position to accept them.

The vibrational levels amongst children in the generations to come will be determined largely by the levels of reality into which they have chosen to incarnate. These children, who may at birth be compatible with their environments, are no less subject to the upheavals and transitions now being experienced by the population at large. For, as the vibration of your planet as a whole continues to accelerate, they must continue to harmonize with those changes, or they will manifest the consequences of energy imbalance, just like everyone else. Once the pace of the ascension process wanes and the energies begin to stabilize and become the reestablished "norms" at those dimensional levels, beings will be able to emerge who are destined to populate the world of the future.

As transitional beings who are ascending hand in hand with the forerunners of those times, you are embodying levels and manifesting capabilities you do not yet even suspect are within your reach. Do not limit yourself into concluding that you are who you have always been. Nothing could be further from the truth. You are the embodiment of change itself. And your acceptance of the fluidity of the foundation of your reality is your best preparation for coping with the changes to come.

You can anticipate having more challenges than will the children amongst your population. But your potential for manifesting the fullness of your capabilities, as a creative life-force in physical form, is no less promising. Your willingness to adopt the trusting innocence and childlike enthusiasm with which you were gifted at the beginning of this incarnation will determine the extent to which you will be able to transcend a lifetime of conditioning in the arena of linear limitation. The fact is, you are no longer in the same world you were born in. You just think that you are. That world is light years away, experientially, from where you are headed—a destination not nearly as far as you may think from where you stand right now.

chapter twenty-six

Integrating change into one's composite of self-definition.
Adapting to the changes within and the new categories
of experience that result.
How judgment—and detachment from it—affects
your experience of reality.

The sum-total of all that you are, all that you perceive, and all that you do is a manifestation of energy, experienced and expressed as form. The degree to which your perceptions parallel the expansion process is determined by the degree to which you are able to surrender to the reality of what is transpiring within you. It is indeed possible to retain the illusions that keep you rooted in a perpetual state of separation and to perceive the structure of that world, if your comfort level requires it. And there are many who will continue to function as living relics of a level of beingness from which they have ascended energetically, out of conditioning alone, for some time to come.

Yet, as you begin to make your peace with the reality of the changes you embody, it becomes less a question of *if* so much as to what degree these changes are able to be assimilated and are allowed to express through you as identity. The shifts, in many cases, may impact individuals in such dramatic ways as to make them virtually unrecognizable to others who believed they knew them well. Indeed, these ones metamorphosize in ways that distance them from everything that once formed the basis of their perception of themselves. Often, within the expanded parameters of the newfound identity, the trappings of the old create a level of discomfort that feels intolerable. And the compulsion to shed one's former identity, like an outgrown skin, becomes undeniable.

One emerges in self-awareness, throughout this process, as layers are revealed and integrated into one's composite of self-definition. The portrait is not one that is completed instantly, but reveals itself gradually, one shade of coloration at a time. One may personify a *work in progress* for years, as the nuances of the newfound structure take form. The interim period, in which so many find themselves, is one rich in the challenges and rewards of a grand adventure. As each progressive level is attained and as each layer of vibrational density is released in the process, one is able to perceive the essence of the expanded self, emerging in one's own image. The portrait is a simple one, liberated from the trappings of the false identity under which one once staggered. And, the initial sense of self-recognition is accompanied by a newfound sense of peace and a profound feeling of inner harmony that intensifies as the process progresses.

Suddenly, one's search is seemingly over, as the recognition crystallizes that what had been sought has been present throughout the entire experience. The fears of inadequacy and feelings of reluctance to step forth attired in ones true magnificence, give way to a deepening sense of one's own limitlessness. And the choices begin to emerge as to how one might best enjoy expressing those abilities.

The resistance that may once have been anticipated is no longer perceived. And one's experience of life takes on the new coloration of a world that, at long last, seems receptive to the gift you offer. It may seem as if the world has changed. Now, life is saying "yes," where once your progress was challenged with every step. Yet, in truth, what has changed is not the world, but your place within it.

The world and its reactions to you are simply reflections of the energy you project upon the screen of reality at any number of levels. When you are present energetically, devoid of the complexities that may once have fostered reticence on the part of others, their response to you flows unimpeded. Thus your own energy projection is mirrored back upon you as an affirmation. The pure energy of positive response resonates exponentially, as it is reflected by you upon others with whom you interact, thereby reinforcing the energy each contributes to the whole. As each adds his piece to the energetic equation, the highest possible experience can be realized by all who participate in the exchange. And you will find that you gravitate toward interactions with beings who resonate at comparable levels to your own.

Yet, it is obvious that one is rarely able to cloister oneself and limit one's interactions to the relative few who share one's orientation. And life takes on the challenges of being "in the world, yet not of the world." As one begins to recognize the vibrational distancing that exists amongst those with whom you share your day-to-day experience, one becomes increasingly protective of one's own energy field. And it becomes a necessary fact of life that lines be drawn as to where and with whom one may or may not wish to venture.

One need make no apology for one's newfound reluctance to engage in activities and interactions that had come to be expected of you by others. Now, there is simply not the inclination to participate in group situations that once seemed enjoyable. The tendency becomes increasingly that of choosing aloneness over the companionship of others that had always been taken for granted as a way of life. One comes to regard one's own company as profoundly gratifying, and the time one chooses to spend interacting with others begins to diminish. One becomes attuned to one's own inner world and is drawn to withdrawing to the sanctity of that space at every opportunity.

The tendency to distance oneself helps to create a vibrational buffer and is a self-protective mechanism that one adopts instinctively. For, until you become adept at stabilizing the accelerating levels of vibration, you are susceptible to the variations in vibrational frequency with which you are surrounded and the extremes of experience that can result. One becomes acutely aware of the effects of certain environments and certain individuals upon one's manifestation of life experience. And one begins to make choices that others may consider radical. One often becomes ruthless in the curtailing of associations and activities that no longer serve one's highest interests.

The momentum becomes one of scaling down one's life and simplifying the scenarios in which one chooses to be present. That momentum, when left to ascend to its own natural level of stabilization, will carry you to a place wherein you can begin to realize your potential to manifest your highest expression of who you truly are. There is no doubt, when you are in this state of centeredness, that what will be forthcoming in your physical reality is the highest expression of possibility for you. Let go of the need to control the process. And allow the process to guide you ever deeper to a connectedness with levels of heightened awareness. When one is in this state, one's abilities to manifest and to experience are able to flow unimpeded. And the experience of physical reality becomes one of sustained levels of delight and wonder.

Naturally, once one has tasted this heightened state of beingness, expressed in physical form, one grows increasingly reluctant to jeopardize the vibrational foundation for that level of experience. At this stage, one develops a mind-set focused on the maintenance of those levels. And one grows to perceive life through the eyes of the observer and to sense oneself as being separate from all that surrounds you and vulnerable to its effect. Then, just as suddenly, one becomes consumed with an awareness of the interconnectedness of All Life and begins to perceive the perfection in the symbolism of every vision.

One begins to crystallize in one's awareness that what once may have been perceived as negativity or density, and thus have been rejected or avoided was, in fact, no more than a reflection of one's own state of beingness. The vibratory essence of a vision is not sustained by the vision itself, but rather, is a mirror of one's perception of it. One's attitudes and biases come into play here and form the foundation of the levels of vibration of all one experiences as reality, and thus how those perceptions affect you as energy. When one perceives an image that one interprets as external to one's own being, and recoils at the sight, one is not reacting to what is inherent in the image itself, but rather, to one's own attitudes, as judgment.

Ultimately, one is able to observe such visions without reacting one way or the other. Indeed, one is able to be present in the movie, without reacting at all. One becomes merely the witness. When one is able to cease categorizing one's perceptions according to a mind-set rooted in duality, one is able to cease assessing each vision and simply to perceive its presence. In this level of nonjudgment, one creates the foundation of a reality incapable of jeopardizing the sanctity of one's autonomy and the precious, heightened levels of vibration that one instinctively seeks to protect.

Simultaneously, in many cases, one suddenly becomes aware that there is truly nothing to fear, and one begins to observe life with a new level of detached fascination. You begin to realize that you are, literally, creating all of it. You are giving it power. You are giving it energy. And its effect upon you, vibrationally, is a direct reflection of the attitudes you project upon it. When you cease rejecting certain categories of experience and certain individuals and realize that you have drawn them into your energy field with your own judgments as to their merits in relation to your judgments of your own merits, the adverse effects inherent in the exchange cease to manifest. When judgment, rooted in duality, is not projected onto a conceptual vision, there is nothing, by definition, that can be reflected back upon you.

The so-called "negative energy" that one senses as one shifts into the heightened levels of awareness takes on the coloration of one's perception of the types of images one is creating in one's life. The knowingness that All Life is of One essence begins to permeate one's consciousness. And one chooses to see, with great joy, the selections calculated to reflect one's highest vision of oneself. One adopts a state of beingness that demonstrates an awareness of other kinds of imagery, but with the detached energy of nonjudgment that does not empower nor disempower, but rather allows the image to simply Be, within the context of your own arena of awareness.

As one begins to strengthen the skills of nonreaction, one is able to reenter the physical world and to walk freely within it, knowing that it cannot affect you vibrationally, one way or the other. The period of reclusive noninteraction can be a lengthy one or can be relatively short-lived, dependent upon one's ability to integrate the understanding that the fear-based attitudes, rooted in separation, only serve to reinforce the effect that the perception of "negative energy" has upon you. For the only power any image has is that which you give it, as its creator, with your judgments.

One begins to bridge the gap between the theoretical understandings of the process of the creation of one's reality and the experiential evidence of that process. And one's skill in manifesting more and more of what one would wish to experience becomes strengthened. These are not abilities that are perfected overnight. And simply because you have an intellectual grasp on the conceptual foundation of manifestation, does not guarantee that you are able to put that understanding into practice instantly, with perfect results. As with any skill, perfection takes practice. Yet, the realization that you truly are the producer, director, and star player in your drama goes a long way toward reinforcing that understanding.

One is able to reflect back over one's journey of metamorphosis and recapture, as crystalline awareness, the poignant moments in one's personal drama, where it becomes obvious that one was the source of all of it. The movie itself, which impacted you so strongly, was, in actuality, no more than a symbolic reflection of the mind-set with which you projected your energies upon the screen you consider to be your reality. That energy was enhanced and sustained by the levels of emotion those scenarios were calculated, *by you*, to stimulate. And the process was choreographed, *by you*, to build to a crescendo, so that it would be blatantly obvious to you that you were the spark responsible for igniting the entire process of illumination.

The process is one in which life comes full circle. In order to fully embody the essence of Oneness and to know oneself as the Source of one's experience of reality, it is necessary to journey to the outer edges of the experience of separation. From that vantage point one is able to recognize and identify what one is not, in order to know that which one Is. The experiences which one recognizes, in retrospect, to be most alien to one's concept of that which one Is, are the lessons that have the most powerful potential impact on your blossoming unification with All Life. For one Is all of it.

As one's awareness is stimulated and one's vibration begins to parallel the heightened levels of acceleration of the world around you, one begins to recognize oneself as being different from others. As one enters the path of separation in earnest and explores fully the experience of being *different*, the realization is seeded that, in actuality, there is nothing that you are capable of being different *from*—for all of it is your own creation. Your life is a living reflection of your own vibrational essence. Ultimately, you know yourself to Be that Source. And although some of life's mystery may be lost in the process of that awakening, one comes fully into one's power as a Creative force, and begins to experience life from the perspective of The Artist. Just like it was—In the Beginning.

That sense of beginning is one you will encounter countless times in the process of opening to the enhanced layers of your ascended self. For the levels are not static ones, but are ever shifting. And the perspective, through which you are able to view the experience you recognize as reality, shifts accordingly. There are no definitive levels of experience toward which you strive and at which you will ultimately arrive, like a train pulling into a station. There is no "last stop" on this journey, but rather, an endless series of vantage points from which you can view your own reflection. You can expect your life to "come full circle" time and time again in the course of this odyssey. For the nature of the journey is one that takes you to the outer reaches of your capacity for humanness and, alternatively, to the depths of your sacred inner being.

You will travel, surrounded by abundant companionship, and experience the most profound levels of loneliness and separation. And in the next breath, you will know yourself to be utterly and blessedly alone—and taste the exultation in the experience of that realization. Ultimately, you will know yourself to be One with All There Is and experience that knowingness not with the perception of being alone. For, "aloneness," by definition, must be in juxtaposition to "other than aloneness." It matters not whether that aloneness is perceived to be a separation from that which is kindred or that which is alien. When one transcends the level at which one embraces "aloneness"—and the separation that serves as its foundation—one is able to simply Be. And the experience of that Isness is the entry point to the path that leads back to the beginning of the journey—if you choose to go.

This crossroads in the endless cycle marks a poignant pause in the eternal momentum, where that choice may be made. The accelerating momentum of the energies of this enchanted moment makes it possible for beings to choose to circumvent the endless cycle and, in essence, exit the system. As one's experience of this process deepens, so too will the awareness of the limitations inherent in the endless cycle. And many will embrace the opportunity to retain the understandings gleaned and to merge, in Oneness, with multidimensional aspects of self who also will have attained the experience of Isness, within the context of identity and form.

From that enhanced perspective, one may choose to Be, and

know oneself as The Artist, from a multidimensional perspective. It is not necessary to leave the body behind and experience physical death in order to opt for this level of experience. It is this alternative to the endless cycle that is the nature of these times. And it is a viable option that will be made available, in this lifetime, to many whose eyes have only just begun to open in this endless moment of "now."

chapter twenty-seven

The nature of the journey home.
Deciphering the imagery that surrounds you.
The power of choice with focused intent.
Awakening to "Be Here Now".

Whichever way you look in your quest for spiritual answers, you are guided to One essential truth. It does not matter which of any number of avenues you choose to explore in your search for the meaning of your existence. The experience of connectedness to an internalized Source is the culmination of the journey. It is this experience that has been sought throughout the history of your species. And the yearning for that level of connectedness transcends all the barriers of culture and belief that have segmented you into the categories with which you identify yourselves. For, the search that would have you transcend those differences is the same momentum that drives you to find the Unity within your own being that transcends the limitation of your very humanness.

You are not a human being. This is simply an expression of form in which you have chosen to experience yourself. You are no more a human being than you are a rock or a tree, although you most certainly, are all of these things. What you are is not limited to any form at all. Yet, what you are encompasses all form—and all that is formless—simultaneously. You have begun to discover within yourself a level of perception that is both new and timeless. And although you have no conscious recall of these kinds of experiences, there is a sense of the familiar in them—a sense that you have tasted of this connectedness before. And, indeed, you have.

You have chosen to give yourself the experience of reawakening. You have chosen to taste, once again, the thrill of discovery of the scope of who you truly are. You have opted for the experience of all that you fear that you are, in order to awaken from that dream and to recognize it as all that you are not. There would be no exultation in the discovery of the first tastes of limitlessness, were that experience not preceded by massive doses of the experience of limitation. You have ventured so deeply now into the illusion of limitation and of separation from who you truly are, that it is indeed time for the veils to be lifted and to be able to glimpse what is actually there.

That is the nature of the process in which you are already well invested. And as your experience of it has amply demonstrated, the shift into deeper levels of awareness does not happen suddenly, leaving you illuminated from that point forth. You have experienced this process. And although you may not have put the pieces of evidence together until now, and drawn the conclusion that some radical changes were transpiring within you that were surely not imaginary, nonetheless those changes have begun to build to a crescendo that cannot be ignored. And you recognize that the process is one that eases you gracefully in and out of awareness, leaving you the time and distancing to digest and to appreciate the experience of it and to savor the moments of connectedness with a newfound sense of adventure.

The purpose of the journey itself is the joy of pondering the mystery of it, finding the clues, and deciphering what has been encoded in the imagery that surrounds you. The journey affords you a leisurely pace at which to integrate the grand illusion that beckons to you and to ponder its nature and fit it into the linear parameters of your frame of reference. As a result, you are well equipped to reject even that vision and, ultimately, to arrive at a vantage point from whence everything and nothing are present. The journey was designed, by you, to deliver you back to the beginning, but not before you were given every opportunity to experience fully what it was like to have ventured far from home.

You embarked on this adventure fully confident that the signposts and maps would be there, at the appropriate moment, to enable you to return safely. For, you placed them there yourself, to await your own rediscovery, after an appropriate amount of *time* was provided for you to forget, totally, where they were hiding. Since this is your game, you structured it to be challenging and exciting, yet built in safeguards that would insure your safe return. At the deepest level, you know that there is no way you can fail at this. You will not be stranded for all eternity in the illusion of separation because you did not "get it." You have seen to that. You have simply programmed sufficient detours and side trips into the itinerary to insure the greatest possible sense of gratification in discovering that you are, at last, heading home.

You are heading home whether you consciously subscribe to such ideas in the present time period or not. For the energy that propels you in that direction does not emanate from the limited perspective of your conscious physical identity, but rather, is being directed from a place of greater awareness that knows, like a loving parent, that you have been "out there" long enough.

The journey home can be prolonged, if that is your choice. Yet, the moments that nudge you toward reunification are calculated to accelerate your momentum by virtue of the pleasure programmed into this phase of the experience. You surely are free to opt for lengthy dalliances in the realms of dissatisfaction, frustration, and misery that you have, no doubt, visited along the way. But it is unlikely, given the nature of the reintegration process, that those choices would be made on a regular basis. You *will* arrive at your destination. That is guaranteed. What is optional is the *identity* that will experience that arrival.

From the vantage point of the timeless, it is irrelevant as to whether *you* or some "future" incarnation of you is the one to experience your ultimate homecoming. And it is not an indication of failure on your part, should you depart this physical body and relinquish this incarnate identity along the way. For, *you* are part of the journey. *You* are one of countless vehicles for the experience of the journey home—the experience you chose to give yourself and which you wanted to savor. It may take many lifetimes, even with an *enlightened* state of awareness, to bring this process to fruition. And although the illusion of this time and place is shifting in its form and vibrational nature, your perception of this "here and now" will remain your reality throughout your experience of the journey.

Should you choose to reincarnate in form to experience the ongoing journey from the vantage point of physicality, it will be within the context of linear time, in the linear place you consider to be planet Earth. Your perception of self, with linear memory even of so-called "past lives," will complete that portion of your journey "here." Once you experience yourself as One with all that is "here," the next phase of the process will be initiated, which will carry you beyond the multidimensional constraints of the world of form. Until you reach that definitive threshold, you will continue to expand your awareness such that it encompasses each successive heightened variation on the theme that you consider to be *your life*.

You have begun to delight in the recognition of some of the sensations that are characteristic of the heightened states of humanness. And you have altered your priorities to allow for exploration of these levels of experience. This is part of the journey. This is not an experience that you are rewarded with additional "points" for racing through or bypassing. The savoring of the experience is what you chose to have. And it is foolhardy to fault yourself because the journey is not yet over, when at long last, you have come to the best part.

Take time to savor your connectedness to the eternal. Make a place in the structure of your schedule of "obligations" to experience the sensations that come of having opened to the heightened expressions of your own beingness. And give yourself permission to release the need to understand the unfathomable and, instead, give yourself the latitude to partake fully of the *experience* of it. The choices you have afforded yourself are limitless on this journey, even in your present form. You can opt for a different direction entirely, any time you choose, simply by choosing that.

Considerations that would rule out following the direction of greatest joy are simply choices, justifiable or not. When implementing such choices, be aware of the inner directedness of the momentum stimulating that choice, and embrace that choice fully. There is no benefit to you to make choices reluctantly, out of altruistic feelings of duty. Any choice is capable of immeasurable rewards when initiated with clarity and a sense of willing participation. And you may discover, to your delight and surprise, that the selection of an avenue that may have appeared to be a lesser choice is one that delivers a richness in perspective that could not have been attained in any other way.

Know that you have chosen to give yourself a lavish variety of life experiences that run the full gamut of physical and emotional sensation. You did not intend to gloss over the surface of your journey of life without touching the heights and the depths that make it authentic and meaningful. Thus there is no prejudgment of the relative merit of one particular direction over another. And no telling, which of any given number of choices is, in fact, the direction that will yield the richest reward. There are no right and wrong choices. There is simply choice.

The experience of life at this stage of your development is much like a menu from which the options are all calculated to please you, given the parameters of individual preference. Naturally, you are free to walk from the table and choose starvation. That is always an option, but hardly a likely selection at this stage of your

atters little, which of any number of options you select.
portant is that your life choices are made with the energy
eness, and that the full power of your intent supports the
ave.   s selected.

The energy of reluctance has no place in the exercise of choice, when the optimum result is to be forthcoming. For, the vibration of hesitancy, in essence, dulls the vibrancy possible in any choice. For the highest possible outcome of any potential life experience, it is necessary for you to be fully present. That means putting the full throttle of your energetic intent behind where you stand, in any given moment, on any direction or on any issue. Halfway does not count. Not in the way you would wish it to. And in looking back upon your own approach to certain avenues that did not work out in the way you may have liked, it should be clear to you that energetically, you were not truly present. Were you fully behind any given direction, it becomes an avenue of choice, by definition, and yields a result that would be of value to you. It cannot be otherwise.

Once you begin to grasp the power inherent in this approach to all choice, you initiate a true understanding of the potential in the options that present themselves to you. And you recognize the treasure that awaits you in experiences you may once have never considered, for any number of reasons. The so-called "reasons" upon which you base your life decisions are no more than rationalizations of settling for less than the highest reward, in the ways that you would most value. For, "reasons" imply hesitation and the weighing of merit of one direction over another.

Once a choice is made, the "reason" is irrelevant if the experience is to yield the optimum result. Make the choice, and *be* that choice energetically—and watch the caliber of your experiences respond accordingly. Choose to be present energetically in all that you do. For, you *are* present energetically, whether you wish to be or not. Your experience of life is simply a reflection of your awareness of that fact.

Kaz

577 - 2164

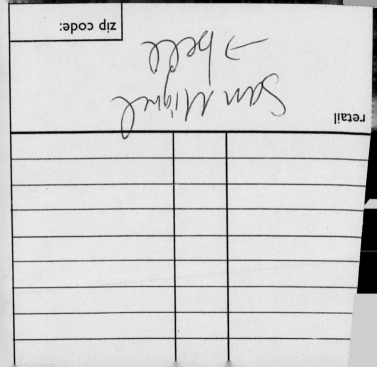

retail

San Miguel
→ bella

zip code:

Be Here Now. You have heard these words spoken and seen them written by some of the wisest amongst you in these times. And no greater gift has been offered you than that. You have made the big decisions already. You have chosen to be incarnate in this time frame. You have chosen the identity in which you presently travel. You have chosen the circumstances that provide a basis for the exploration of the life themes that you have, once again, chosen. And you have chosen to transcend the limitation of the illusion of incarnate experience and to recognize your innate Divinity within the context of this form—to your ongoing joy and delight.

All other possible choices pale by comparison to the ones you have already put yourself behind—body, heart, and soul. When you approach your experience of life with that level of commitment—with that level of heart-centered involvement—you reap the rewards inherent in all possible levels of life experience. And you begin to discover what is possible within the parameters of humanness.

Before it is possible to transcend the limitations of your humanness, it is necessary for you to be fully present in your experience of it. For then, and only then, will you begin to be free of the ties that bind you to the limitations of form. Only then will you be ready to transcend a "here and now" based on the concept of form and to begin to taste the experience of *timelessness* that awaits you when you choose to be ready.

chapter twenty-eight

Change, diversity, and the nature of composite reality.
The perception and integration of parallel realities.

The essential difference between the world as you now know it and the world you would be challenged to imagine lies in the levels of limitation with which you have equipped yourselves to perceive your experience of life. These safeguards have been set into place so that you would be able to perform at levels of perception that would correspond, vibrationally, to the world in which you came into form. That world is not the same one in which you find yourself at present. And the constraints that were intended as a device for restricting your perceptions are now being lifted in increments, so that you are able to slowly integrate an awareness of what is really there with your understandings of the nature of your world.

Those understandings will alter radically, as the fundamental nature of your reality continues to evolve in response to the accelerating levels of vibration that give it form. Yours is a world that defies definition in the present period. For the essential truths that formed the foundation of your physical reality have ceased to support a world whose structure has begun to crumble.

In the present period, the lens of limitation through which you view your reality has taken several unexpected turns. And what you now perceive is a composite of what has always been known to be there, and much that seems new and otherworldly. Know that nothing at all has been added to the mix of what constitutes your world. All that is now perceptible has always been present, energetically. You simply have been unable to detect the presence of certain elements of its vibrational makeup.

As your energies continue to accelerate, your world will continue to reveal to you layers of reality from which your awareness has been shielded. Now it is as though a curtain has been lifted, and your awareness has been directed to contend with a level of complexity that your world has neither anticipated nor prepared for.

The institutions that provide the authoritative structure for every aspect of your reality will be challenged to keep pace with the evidence that will continue to challenge the *gospel* upon which the so-called *facts* of your world are based. *Facts* are only as firmly founded as the moment in which they are perceived. For, *reality* only exists in the "moment of Now." And in the moment of Now that you would perceive as the "future," certain *facts* will be shown to have no basis, whatsoever.

The point here is to draw your attention to the nature of the process. For, the inclination will be to scrutinize what was known and accepted as factual, in light of evidence to the contrary, and to discredit those responsible for originating those concepts.

The fact is, given present conditions, the *facts* upon which the parameters of your reality are based cannot be expected to remain fixed. That is not to say that some error in judgment or analysis has been made by seers of the past, who helped to delineate some of those constructs. But merely to point out that the concept of anything at all being an overriding, definitive truth, with reference to the nature of physical reality, is by definition impossible. For, all that is now regarded as truth is fully capable of being refuted.

The kaleidoscope of your reality is shifting with every breath of every living being amongst you. And the composite world you are co-creating en masse is simply a reflection of those changes. What may once have formed the basis of your definition of the *miraculous,* may now easily be shown to be commonplace. That is not to discredit the so-called *miracles* of the past, but to put them in perspective within the context of the linear time frame in which they occurred.

Given the momentum of change, of which you are a part, what may presently seem miraculous is likely to be considered quite normal in the times soon to come. As the veils continue to be lifted, and what is actually possible under the accelerating conditions continues to be discovered, many purported miracles will be cited, only to fade into obscurity with the rising tides of change.

What is important is that your awareness of the impermanence of the process be stimulated. In that way, you will be less likely to be diverted into mentalized debates of what may or may not have been so in the past. What is significant is what your own experience has shown you to be so in the present—and only that. You can expect to become conditioned to the momentum of change, as the energies that surround you continue to accelerate and you continue to ascend vibrationally within them.

Your own perspective may differ dramatically from that of others with whom you share your experience of life. And the reaction of choice is not to agonize over whose perceptions are "right" and whose are "wrong," but rather to adopt an air of fascination at the diversity you are able to witness from the vantage point of the observer.

By taking into consideration the very real perceptions of others with whom you interact, you are able to avail yourself of the composite reality that is manifested in any given moment. It is that overview that you have chosen to give yourself in the present period. For, you have opted for the experience of transcending the limited perspective through which you now perceive the physical manifestation of your world.

In the times soon to come, you can expect to experience a multitude of parallel perspectives in a time sequence that may appear to be simultaneous. And it is possible that certain individuals may question their own sanity when confronted with perceptions that linear logic would consider to be contradictory. It may appear that two or perhaps even several different variations on a given theme may be playing out simultaneously. And it is a natural reaction, initially, to wonder which set of circumstances is the *real* one. Essentially, all variations on a given theme, when perceived in this way, are *real*. All possible versions of a given set of circumstances have always been *real*—playing out their own particular variation on a given theme. Yet, until now, only one version has been able to be perceived as *reality*.

As you integrate the composite self that is *you* into a unified perspective, you succeed in gathering up the trappings of the *reality* in which each of the aspects of *you* in question experience themselves. As the energies of the initial merging of these parallel selves—and the realities in which they experience themselves—begin to stabilize, the multiple variations on one's life circumstances merge, and are perceived as a unified perspective. In the moments that surround that shift, it is to be expected that one's awareness darts in and out of the composite of those realities and that one is able to perceive any number of the multiple variations on the vibrational makeup of those worlds.

Until now, such experiences have been relegated to the arena of science fiction or dismissed as evidence of mental aberration. As you begin to achieve the integration of the multiple aspects of self as part of the ascension process, it will become obvious that the experience of having objects appear and disappear will be commonplace. Resist the inclination to dismiss such experiences as evidence of foul play on the parts of discarnate consciousness. For, the experience itself is not evidence that something is wrong. But, rather, that something is right.

The inclination to be led down the avenues of fear will be a common reaction to such experiences. And, initially, the experiences of some beings will be taken as grounds for judgment on the parts of those who have garnered places of authority in your world—on the basis of *expertise* that such experiences will demonstrate to be obsolete. And great debates will ensue over what is or is not "truth" in your reality.

In the instability of the initial periods of upheaval that will result, as these kinds of experiences become prevalent, much reaction that is fear based will play out. Then, just as dramatically, humanity as a whole will seemingly come to terms with the impermanence of the experience of reality, and a shift in the collective mind-set of the whole will catapult the very essence of your world to a new octave of experience.

The time frame required to achieve the transition from one "norm" to the next will vary with the individual perspective of each and every participant. Some of you who are experiencing reality on the leading edge of this shift have already begun to feel the effects of the transition. And many can attest to having had *otherworldly* experiences with increasing frequency, as part of your daily lives. Others who populate your world are seemingly untouched by the process and will opt for the continued experience of an obsolete reality for some time to come.

It is for you who are aware of what is transpiring to remain focused in your own experience of these times. It is unnecessary to your own personal process to invest large amounts of mental energy on questions of what others may or may not be experiencing. Your own journey is not one governed by consensus reality in any given moment. What is true for you is not necessarily that which is true for a close friend, a relative, or a total stranger. Your journey is one that is being tailor-made to the pace of your own process. And you are not necessarily "wrong" or "abnormal" on the basis of experiences that are not being replicated by others.

Know that the reality you are experiencing in any given moment is a graphic representation of the energy you are projecting at any number of levels. The complexity of the web of dramas you have woven, and the key players you have cast as actors in them, is the mystery you are unraveling in these times. To succeed in shifting the energy of adversity that characterizes some of the episodes that appear as a recurring dream in your life, it is necessary to delve deeply into the experience of that energy. Once you succeed in feeling fully the underlying emotions that have magnetized life theme experiences to you repeatedly, you can begin to release these energetic links to realities that have kept your awareness grounded in their midst.

The key to transcending various categories of experience is the very same process as that which releases one's vibrational tethering to levels of reality structured to support such experiences. You will find that you are shifting your life drama and the stage upon which it is acted, simultaneously, as you plunge headlong into the emotional building blocks of that level of experience.

By confronting the very issues that most confound you, you are able to move *through* rather than move away from all that would attract those conditions to you. As you bring each of these life-theme categories to resolution, you can expect to experience the dramatic evidence of the colliding of several worlds, as those realities merge on a foundation of new, common ground. And your experience will reflect new levels of harmony on what still may appear to be a familiar landscape.

You will find, as you emerge in conscious awareness of your transition as a being, that although your circumstances are essentially *the same*, the quality of that structure has altered dramatically. You may technically be living in the same neighborhood, and be interacting with the same primary cast members in the living theater of your life, yet it becomes obvious that the basis for certain categories of interaction is seemingly no longer there.

Certain long-standing arenas of conflict may appear, quite suddenly, to have lost their familiar call to action. And you become aware that you are now simply *present* in circumstances that no longer prod you, goad you, or draw you toward interaction. You begin to observe yourself in the role of the observer of circumstances that once had you spinning reactively in all directions. Now, you are content just to *Be*. There is no compulsion to *engage* or to flee. There is simply an awareness of what *is,* and of your own presence as part of it.

The period of stabilization of the energies following major episodes of integration provides a peaceful reprieve from the high drama that characterizes those shifts. You will discover, to your delight, that life has made space for the reassessment of your priorities. It is to be expected that individuals will make radical changes in their life circumstances, following experiences of reality integration, that reflect, more appropriately, one's newfound state of beingness. And this process will repeat itself, over and over again, as you continue to shed the trappings of each successive, outmoded identity.

The metamorphosis in which you are engaged is one that will continue throughout the duration of this physical lifetime. For, the process is not one in which a plateau is reached where one can sit complacently. The process is a journey that continues to unfold. And the vistas from the summit of the mountain you have just succeeded in scaling merely serve as the impetus to move forward.

chapter twenty-nine

Transcending the spiritual dogmas of this reality.
A spiritual path tailored to every seeker.

There is no set way in which a being emerges into awareness at successive levels of perception. And even though each of you is on a similar journey through your experience of this particular level of reality, each of you has choreographed a unique dance that will not be experienced in quite the same way by anyone other than you. And so, while it is possible to generalize about some of the phenomena that characterize this stage of the journey, there is no guarantee that your particular experience will include those perceptions.

Some of you will require a prolonged series of repetitions of certain aspects of the process, in order to release the elements that are keeping you rooted in denser levels of awareness. Others will experience instantaneous realization of the essence of an experience without the necessity to have the point drilled into your awareness over and over again. These are choices each of you is making. And those choices determine the nature of your own unique journey.

There are many traditional paths that offer formulas calculated to deliver the spiritual seeker to successive levels of awareness of one's Divine connectedness. And these time-honored methods have helped many to experience a level of results in this timeless quest. Yet it should be understood that one is not required to select from traditional methods and *accepted* spiritual disciplines in order to reach the levels that are possible.

You are not limited to any menu at all in choosing how to realize Oneness, for the possible paths to the destination toward which you travel are limitless. Some have been discovered and developed into elaborate systems that, if followed carefully, will ease the journey somewhat, in predictable ways. Yet for some, such an approach is a bit like "painting by numbers." The result will emerge upon the canvas, either way. How one chooses to experience the process of the creation of one's work of art is optional.

You may wish to experience your journey upon a well trodden path, along with others, equipped with maps, and guidebooks, and teachers who are willing to show you the way. But, inevitably, all of these paths lead within. The guides and the guidebooks can lead you just so far. Ultimately, once your footing is established, the journey is a solitary experience that cannot be replicated. You are not required to select and to practice a recognized spiritual discipline or to subscribe to a religion in order to fully experience your sacred journey to Oneness.

You may wish to make such a choice. And you may derive great satisfaction and a powerful feeling of Divine connectedness in doing so. But that is not to say that such a choice is appropriate for another seeker, or that it would necessarily yield a comparable result. There are many who will choose to forego the experience of a sacred journey via an established path, and will source within their own inner sanctums a path that will deliver them to the same destination. There are no right or wrong roads to Oneness. And there is no predictable way of determining which of the infinite number of possible routes is the most direct. For, each journey is unique.

The determination as to how on—
itual path is one best made not fro—
the mind, but rather, from one's e—
It matters less what you may or may—
taught as to what is the correct way—
than what your own experience h—
weighing the relative merits of the —
awakening, consider above all your own inner sensing of what is or is not truth for you.

It is irrelevant that certain methods may have yielded results for untold thousands of years, if that is not your own personal experience of it. Do not be inclined to feel that you are inadequate in your practice of a given technique or discipline if after a given amount of time your experience is not rewarding. It may well be that what is missing is not in the way the discipline is *done* but rather in the energy you have brought to the *doing*.

When one approaches any effort with the energy of reluctance or half-heartedness, the result will not be satisfying. When you choose a spiritual path because your mind tells you that you *should*, you can expect to be disappointed. When you practice a spiritual discipline begrudgingly, enduring the repetitions rather than savoring them, the method will prove fruitless. For the vibrancy of any approach is based not on the mechanics of the practice but upon one's total surrender to the direction in which the practice leads you.

The key to one's *success* or *failure* at any given technique has nothing whatsoever to do with the technique, but rather, with the energy of joyousness with which you approach it. When one approaches the practice of meditation, for example, with the underlying attitude that "this is a waste of time," or "I'm not getting anywhere with this," you are virtually guaranteed that result. When one surrenders to the process itself, regardless of the style of one's practice, one has begun to lay a foundation for a wonderful experience. The expectation of a result has no place in any spiri-

ice and is the greatest single obstacle to the realization result. When one is present, in the moment, in a state of ghtened receptivity, one adds the essential ingredient to any spiritual practice.

It matters not whether you choose to follow in the footsteps of your ancestors in your expressions of devotion, or upon a path that no one has ever walked before—so long as your heart has led you to it. There is no point in pursuing any path or practice out of feelings of obligation. For, the energy of reluctance serves to invalidate any possible positive result that may have been forthcoming.

Guilt and shame have no place in one's selection of a vehicle for one's expression of Divine connectedness. And regardless of whether those adverse emotions are the basis of one's continued adherence to an ancestral path, or the emotional remnants of having abandoned one, the vibration of reticence serves to sour the potential sweetness inherent in one's chosen direction. Choose your direction from a place of contentment and heartfelt connectedness and you will have embarked upon a route that will nourish you well along the way.

The sense of spiritual fulfillment that is sought universally is not dependent upon which affiliation is chosen or upon which of any number of rituals may or may not be performed. For the experience of joyous Divine connectedness transcends all barriers of culture and belief and has been experienced, since time immemorial, by beings of all backgrounds.

There is absolutely no truth in the allegations that one path is the only true path or that one people are the *chosen people*. These are constructs created by man, upon a foundation of fear. All beings who themselves choose to recognize the truth of their own Divine connection, are the *chosen people*. For the choosing is not an action directed upon you by a Divinity you would perceive to be external to you. The choosing is an affirmation sourced from the Divinity within you, of that connectedness.

One seeks not to be identified as having *been chosen*, for that level of choice is an attestation of separation from others and from Source. One knows oneself to personify choice, and bestows upon oneself the affirmation of that choice with every waking breath. Whether or not one chooses to express that state of beingness through rituals is also a matter of choice. And surely not a requirement for attaining nor sustaining a state of Oneness.

You who have been humbled under the yoke of fear into bearing the burden of the man-made dogmas of your world have been given a convoluted detour, rather than a direct path to the Divinity you seek. The beings who have instructed you in these practices have themselves been misled, more often than not. And the fear-based tactics employed to bind you to a particular mode of worship are ones that have been used to ensnare the hearts of the very ones who teach such practices. When one stops to question such fear-based systems of religion, one can see quite easily the motivation built into these systems for perpetuating the spiritual tyranny that has been perpetrated upon so many of you.

The God you long to know does not seek to control you, or to punish you when you choose to express the free will with which you have been gifted. You have not been provided with the opportunity to experience your Divinity in physical form simply to have you follow a particular prescribed routine. You have been given unlimited freedom of choice. And that choice encompasses all avenues of the expression of your innate Divinity. The opportunity here, in these times of blossoming self-awareness, is to recognize the unlimited potential in who and what you are, and to gift yourself with permission to express that knowingness as you choose to.

The free will that is inherent in the human condition is unconditional. You are free to do anything, be anything, and believe anything, in any way it pleases you. That is your God-given birthright. And with that freedom goes the right to reap the ramifications of all actions. You yourself built that into the system, so you would be able to experience the results of your choices.

It is pointless, therefore, to expect that you would follow mindlessly on a prescribed course through life and to experience the predictable consequences. Naturally, that is what you have been taught to do, by a society that has learned, and in turn teaches, the path of constriction. Yet, it is in your very nature to violate such rules. It is an integral part of your essence to know yourself as limitless and to balk at the barriers that would seek to bind you. That is why you placed them there. That is why you chose to create the barriers that frustrate and infuriate you. That is the motivation for graphically depicting for yourself that which you *are not*—in order to know, unquestioningly, that which you *Are*.

You have chosen to create for yourself circumstances which would help you put into perspective your innermost beliefs on certain core issues. The very fact that you are reading these words attests to the fact that your sense of spiritual identity is a focal point for you in this lifetime. And in order to arrive, unquestioningly, at the knowingness of your Oneness with all Creation, you set about to confront yourself with a given set of barriers that would contradict and oftentimes violate the essence of that inner truth. The objective in creating such a scenario was surely not to have your Divine essence crushed under the weight of the collective will of consensus reality. Rather, the opportunity in having experienced such pressures is to know, unquestioningly, that which is *not* truth—for you. And to have afforded yourself the opportunity to implement that knowingness, out of freedom of choice.

The fear-based dogmas, which beckon to you throughout your world, depict for you example after example of all that you are not. When you attempt to fit yourself into these molds, the discomfort level invariably becomes intolerable. Inevitably, you walk away, regardless of whether that rift is expressed physically or is simply a disconnection of heart. What is important as an adjunct to the experience of the rejection of a dogma with which you have been force-fed, is to release fully any sense of obligation to the pressures that may come to bear upon you for your choice.

It is pointless to walk away from one's religious heritage because the dogmas do not ring true—and at the same time to feel guilty about it. It is equally pointless to continue to go through the motions of adherence to such modes of belief and to harbor feelings of resentment about it. Either way, the energetic contradiction between the action expressed and the emotion repressed would set up conditions that would nullify the potential inherent in the act of devotion.

In order to be truly free of the shackles of obligation perpetrated upon so many of you, it is necessary to shift one's loyalties. Your obligation is not to the so-called "truth," that may have been handed down through generations of misguided seekers. Your obligation is to the truth that has been unearthed within the depths of your own heart—and to that alone.

For each of you, there *is* only one truth: your truth. It is contradictory to the very concept of spiritual devotion to subscribe to a school of thought forced upon you by the might of the masses, when such concepts violate what you know to be your own inner truth. That is the challenge that has divided man from his fellow man, historically, since time began. And, that challenge is the one that all of humanity shares. The differences that divide you are the very concepts that, ultimately, you will embrace as a unified race of beings. The momentum for the transcendence of those differences is the hallmark of these times of transformation.

When you look back upon what you consider to be your history, you will note, with rare exception, that the human race has been consistent, across barriers of culture, in denouncing their fellowmen for their differences. It is presumed that if one is correct in one's perceptions and thus knows them to be *truth*, the differing perceptions of another being therefore constitute *falsehood*. It has only begun to dawn on the collective consciousness that the countless differences in perspective amongst you are not evidence of a world of falsehood, but rather are proof of the infinite levels of Divine truth, personified by the presence of each of you.

Each of you holds a unique vision and the experience of the Divine connectedness of each is unparalleled. You may describe your experience of awakening with the same words as another being, or may find in hearing or reading the words of another, that the sentiments expressed describe your own. Yet language cannot begin to approximate the essence of the experience itself. And though there are many so-called authorities who have peppered the spiritual path with reassuringly recognizable signposts, the actual experience is yours and yours alone. For language can only begin to touch the feeling of bonding with one's own Divinity.

When you speak, therefore, know that you speak for yourself alone. Your truth cannot be the truth of another being, for each of you perceives the experience of life through a lens that has been designed to deliver a vision custom-made for your eyes only. The opportunity in encountering the contradictory perceptions of another is to regard, with fascination, those differences. For the differing perceptions of another do not invalidate your own, they merely add the richness of contrast to the composite vision that is Oneness.

You will note the natural human tendency to gravitate toward individuals who share your general perspective on issues you would consider important. Within the context of those similarities, the subtle shades of difference are able to surface in order to permit each of you to fine-tune—to yourselves—nuances of the views you hold most dear. The contrast provided by the mirror of the vision of another being is the gift you bring one another, in order that each of you may perceive his own vision more clearly.

There is not one amongst you who has ever encountered another being who sees the world in exactly the same way you do. And that is as it was meant to be. Your differences in the macrocosm of your world have historically inspired the wars and human atrocities you have perpetrated upon one another. In these times, those differences are designed to inspire your collective recognition of the potential harmony inherent in that diversity. For if all were whistling the same one note, there would be no music. If all painted the canvas of their life's creation with the same favorite color, the collective would be a bland vision devoid of contrast or detail.

When one ceases to give energy to the invalidation of the perceptions of another as a means of reinforcing one's own, one creates the space for the validity of all variations on a shared vision and lays the groundwork for the mutual experience of harmony. This principle can be applied interpersonally and interculturally, and ultimately forms the basis upon which the differences that now alienate you from one another become the force that unites you all.

The key to harmonizing with the truth of another person's vision is to hold one's own truth as a treasure to be prized, honored, and protected. In your recognition of the truth of your perspective on the experience of life, you hold a priceless piece of the composite vision of reality. Resist the inclination to be dissuaded from what your experience and sensing have shown you to be so. For pressures will inevitably come to bear upon each of you to relinquish your perspective and bend to the mind-set of the collective.

There are beings in positions of authority in every aspect of your reality whose task it is to make you feel "wrong" about what you know to be "right." The history of intimidation that has colored your world has resulted in the eradication of much that might have been of value, were individuals free to express the truth of their vision. Hold to your vision. And know that your perspective is what it is, because you are what you are—unique. Your purpose in being present in physical form is to embody that uniqueness, not for the purpose of imposing it upon another being, but for the purpose of graphically depicting it to yourself.

Thus the approach of choice, when addressing your spiritual development, is not to reject your cultural conditioning simply for the purpose of substituting one vision for another, if your purpose is to impose that view upon others. Your vision is sacred because it is yours alone. It is not your mission to convince others of the validity of what you know and the way you have chosen to express that knowingness. It is your mission to develop and explore the richness of the depths of that gold mine for your own benefit, and to allow others the grace to exercise that same freedom.

In the times to come, you will encounter much in the way of so-called "new thought," presented in self-righteous packaging by visionaries who blaze the trail at the new levels of human awareness. It is for you, who are amongst those whose eyes are truly open, to know that the collective experience of which you are a part, does not come with a newly stylized set of rules and regulations. The truth that characterizes the essence of the new levels of awareness is no different than the underlying essence of all spiritual mastery. *That which you seek is within yourself.*

In this way, nothing has changed at all. What has shifted is the awareness of so many of you that this is so. The harbingers of this truth, throughout human history, have never sought to be deified for speaking it. They simply have been volunteers who sought to share what they themselves knew to be so, for the chance that others might be inspired to make the same discoveries. The impetus for such actions is the indescribable joy to be realized—to be en*joy*ed—within one's own being, in this process. It has surely not been the purpose of the Divine messengers throughout your history to be placed upon an altar and to be worshipped. For, in so doing, humanity has affirmed the very state of separation that all of Creation strives to transcend.

The momentum toward recognition of your mutual Oneness with each other is not a new development that has been reserved for a "New Age." This truth is the essence of the timeless—the very foundation of All That Is. The torchbearers of these times who illuminate the path of others do so in order to kindle the awareness of each that the true path leads within. The true teachers of your times do not seek to be exalted in your eyes. They have chosen to show you, by example, the validity of a vision in which each of you is exalted in your own eyes.

Consider carefully the messages carried by those who claim to know the way. If the message imparted is one that inspires the aggrandizement of that teacher, consider very carefully before following in those footsteps. For in these times, many are awakening. And it is the gifted amongst you who knows that your own exalted vision is not a basis for commanding the devotion of others.

The freedom to worship as you choose is your God-given birthright. There is no one who knows better than you do, the devotional path that is the most gratifying for you. Resist the inclination to allow the enthusiasm of your heart to be dampened by the fears of others who may be threatened by your newfound sense of spiritual direction. Know that their path is their own choice. And if family members have chosen to carry on with a particular religious tradition, that is their right. Yet, it is not one that they have the right to impose upon you. You are not obligated to participate in rituals simply because that is the heritage of your family in this lifetime. Participate if it gives you pleasure to do so, and you will have exercised the highest choice.

Likewise, resist the temptation to attempt to convert family members and friends to your newfound spiritual direction, if openness is not demonstrated. Your path is your own. And it is no more your right to try to convince another being of your personal truth than it is for them to do so. Allow others the freedom you would want to enjoy, and you will have demonstrated the very thing you would most wish to share with others.

Teach by example that which you are inclined to share. For your actions speak far more clearly than any theory you may feel inspired to impart. This is the best possible way to communicate to those who are alarmed by your choices where you really stand on issues they can relate to. Show them how you have applied your newfound vision of reality to your life. Let them observe your non-reactive approach to confrontations that may once have triggered major battles. And provide for them a living example of the results of releasing the emotionally charged remnants of your personal history.

This is the best possible way to communicate to the dubious amongst your inner circle the kinds of choices you have made. This is the strongest way to impart the message you would most wish to have heard by those who don't want to hear it. For it is far more powerful to live your truth than to preach it.

Many will be intrigued and will watch from a distance as you progress in your metamorphosis. Be less concerned with what others may or may not be thinking than with the essence of your own experience. They will be integrating much into their awareness simply by being around you. And although they are unlikely to admit it to you, chances are that many will be touched in profound ways by being close enough to walk beside you through these times.

Do not expect that others will necessarily be converted to your vantage point simply by virtue of their proximity to you. Yet know that they will have been affected in ways that they themselves do not understand by having accompanied you on this segment of your journey. Be patient with the beings who life has placed closest to you in these times. For you are serving as a teacher for many, simply by being who you really are.

chapter thirty

The significance of the health crisis
in the heightened stages of the ascension process.

The state of health of your physical form is a direct reflection of your energetic state of beingness at all levels. And while you surely are able to make a positive contribution to the condition of your body through conscious practices of diet and exercise, the underlying causes of certain conditions will inevitably manifest if left unaddressed.

In the heightened stages of the transformation process, you can anticipate encountering the evidence of dormant energetic conditions that you have carried with you, perhaps for lifetimes. For, as you peel back the layers of your awareness at all levels, you will invariably reveal key issues that have contributed vibrationally to the life theme scenarios that you have begun to identify in other areas of your life. These recurring dramas do not merely manifest emotionally, but are carried through and surface in the experiences you draw to you and in the condition of your physical body. When the evidences of such conditions are ignored, the energies are able to build and compound the manifestation with levels of imbalance that can prove life threatening.

Do not assume that you are automatically immune to the more serious evidences of discordant energy, simply because you have an intellectual grasp of the nature of the ascension process. You may well have progressed through the advanced levels of this work, and have come to terms with the major issues upon which you have been working throughout this entire lifetime, and yet have failed to bring to resolution the energies underlying them, through release. It is for you, who have become aware of the vulnerability of your physical bodies to the effects of the higher frequencies, to focus carefully on the clues your body is providing in these times and to delve deeply into the root causes of these conditions.

The state of your physical health will be challenged intermittently, as each progressive level of vibration is integrated into your energy field. The heightened levels at which many of you will be operating as you approach the interdimensional threshold will, by definition, require the elimination of the layers of density you may still carry in your physical and emotional bodies. Thus, as you become more refined vibrationally at some levels, you affect directly the urgent necessity to achieve vibrational balance at all levels. This would explain why some amongst you, who are at advanced levels of this process, are manifesting profoundly challenging physical conditions, while others, who appear to be oblivious to the changes at hand, appear to continue in optimum health.

You may wonder why you may suddenly have manifested health problems. And the tendency will be great to begin to fault yourself for what you may assume to be your spiritual shortcomings. Know that these conditions are not symptoms of having done something wrong, but rather, they are signs of having progressed. For the fact is, that the higher you ascend vibrationally, the greater the necessity to purge your physical form of density that cannot be carried at the heightened levels. That density takes the form of illness and disease.

Many amongst you will experience the sudden resurgence of past conditions that you had presumed to be *cured*. What may have been addressed previously is the symptomatic relief of the evidence of that condition. Yet what, in likelihood, has lingered, is the underlying vibrational catalyst for those symptoms. Oftentimes years can go by without any sign of residual symptoms. Then, unexpectedly, you may experience the sudden reappearance of sensations that would indicate the presence of activity in the area in question. The cause for the reemergence of a given condition is based upon the fact that the original foundation for that condition was never addressed. That density has remained dormant in your energy field awaiting the conditions that would prompt resolution and release.

It is an important part of the work at hand to become clear about the interconnection between the state of the etheric bodies and the manifestation of the evidence of imbalance in one's physical body. The basis for virtually all physical health conditions is energy related. Thus, your culturally inspired tendency to address and to mask symptoms alone serves to prolong the lingering presence of the density that caused them.

Once you have ascended to accelerated levels of vibration, the seeds of disharmony that you harbor are stimulated and called to the surface of your awareness in the form of physical symptoms. The physical body's way of calling your attention to a condition that is nonphysical is to manifest in a way that cannot be ignored. Should you, once again, address the symptoms alone, you will succeed in driving the underlying cause of the condition deeper, where it forms the basis of a future manifestation that may prove more insidious. Ultimately, if left unaddressed, the density carried at the cellular level of your physical body will pose an ever-intensifying threat to your physical well-being.

At the emergence of physical symptoms, the opportunity has been afforded you to delve directly into the underlying condition and to identify the unresolved issues you are harboring. You may find, in the course of the work you have been prompted to do on

ŕ core life themes, that certain physical conditions sur-
denly, produce acute symptoms, and just as suddenly,
nish. By addressing the emotional foundation for major
ca.   of life experience, you stimulate the release of corresponding eneɪgies at all levels of manifestation. The emotional catalyst
for the manifestation of life experience parallels the replication of that
expression of energy as imbalance or illness in your physical body.

It is important that you recognize and allow for the expression
of these symptoms, rather than seeking to inhibit them. For, when
coordinated with a consciously directed program of life theme resolution, the release of physical symptoms can be achieved quickly
and completely, ruling out the likelihood of a recurrence. Know
that when issues have surfaced in one area of your life, you are well
advised to anticipate the emergence of that evidence at all levels.
Feeling your feelings deeply, without repressing the authenticity of
those core emotions, is the doorway to relinquishing the vibrational
density that is holding you at diminished levels of awareness.
Nonattachment to outcome is the threshold to be transcended in
the deeper levels of this work.

One is guided to confront questions on one's own mortality
and to come to terms with dormant fears that one may be carrying on this core issue. The experiential catalyst is provided that
provokes exploration of man's deepest questions and forms the basis
for releasing attachment to retaining physical form. Once one is
able to release the fear-based grasp one holds on life, it becomes
easy to release the underlying emotional constraints that potentially prove life threatening.

You may well be taken to the very edge of the cliff, in order
that you attain a clear vision of what lays beyond it. Once that
perspective has been achieved, one shifts to an understanding
that retaining this particular physical form is a choice that one may
make and not a condition to be grasped compulsively at all costs.
One may well peer over the cliff and embrace the liberation that
would be inherent at one's appointed moment to jump, and at the

same time know that moment is not yet at hand. When one is able to confront one's mortality with nonattachment, one is ready, energetically, to release the condition that could bring about that transition.

These challenges can be anticipated and will be experienced and surmounted by many of you who are moving rapidly through the stages of the ascension process. Know that these kinds of confrontations are not in the same category as life-threatening episodes being manifested by the population at large. Your own manifestation of these symptoms and experiences, while taking a similar form, manifest at the heights of one's spiritual unfoldment and constitute a powerful part of the ascension process. For, to be able to sustain physical life at the higher levels of awareness, one must be totally free of one's attachment to it.

Life is not to be perceived as something one should be desperate to maintain. Awareness through the context of form simply *is*. It is a perspective—one of countless possible vantage points from which one is able to experience oneself. Once that realization is reached, a level of sublime detachment is achieved regarding the human condition, and one achieves the lightness of spirit that is a prerequisite for "life" at accelerated levels of awareness. The *life-or-death* challenge is one that is designed to catapult you to the edge of those levels so that you have the opportunity to make the conscious choice of moving forward in this particular form.

You who are already in the throes of that experience have, in all likelihood, ventured far with the physical challenge that is the hallmark of this part of the journey. And the trials you encounter, as you exhaust the physical solutions for your physical condition, are catalysts calculated to force you to reach beyond the obvious solutions and explanations put forth by the consensus wisdom of your culture.

These are unprecedented occurrences. And you should be prepared to experience unprecedented results, both in your own experience and in the experience of others for whom you may be facilitating. The dramatic remission of symptoms characteristic of this process is a phenomenon that will defy the scientific laws that govern your concept of what is and is not possible. The so-called "miracles" that may once have prompted reactions of awe and wonderment are occurrences to be expected by those who have journeyed to the outer reaches of the human condition in these times. Do not be tempted to limit what is possible, in terms of spontaneous recovery, on the basis of what you may have been taught. There are no such limits—not in the new world you are helping to birth, simply by being present.

The challenges with which you will undoubtedly be faced will vary according to the levels of resistance posed to the reality of what is transpiring in your life. You can anticipate being pressed to question the validity of your situation and may begin to suspect that the underlying cause of a physical condition is in direct energetic resonance to the imbalance you may be experiencing in the emotional arena of your life.

You will begin to see the so-called "symptoms" of a physical condition that you have been harboring as the manifestation of the thought form that precipitated it. And that level of spontaneous realization will serve as the gateway through which you will be able to liberate yourself from a multifaceted vibrational condition. The outward manifestation of a particular set of symptoms is your cue to delve into your own psyche and to begin to explore the parameters with which you have structured your life experience.

Your beliefs are the building blocks with which you have constructed the vibrational grid system you would know as your reality. Within the confines of that structure, you have systematically crafted the conditions that would represent, energetically, the unique set of presumptions and preferences that characterize your state of beingness. Your life experiences serve to reenforce or to restructure that energetic blueprint. And the stability of the entire vibrational construction rests upon the firmness of its foundation. That fundamental essence serves to determine whether layers of life experience reenforce the equilibrium of the structure as a whole or begin to undermine its vibrational balance.

When so-called *symptoms* surface in your physical reality, be they in the form of a life experience or a physical health condition, know that the key to the underlying cause may well lie in the very core of your energetic structure. Be prepared to dig well beneath the surface of your awareness for the core elements that have surfaced as symptoms that suddenly have captured your attention.

This too, is as you designed your experience to be. For a fundamental part of your awakening process is to see clearly the constructs with which you have built your sense of self-perception. A condition that cannot be ignored is the perfect opportunity to explore your own core essence and to confront what lies dormant, waiting patiently for this moment in your evolution.

A mind-set that harbors any form of limitation whatsoever, regardless of whether your experience has led you to believe it is justified, is a catalyst for the disharmony that can manifest as disease. The opportunity afforded you now is to consider whether certain presumptions, based upon disappointments, grievances, injuries, or any other manifestations of the inhibition of the expression of personal will, have relevance under conditions of limitlessness.

You can argue, convincingly, within the parameters of your consciousness, that certain consistent bodies of experience serve to reinforce certain levels of limited self-perception. Yet, on closer inspection, it becomes clear that those bodies of experience were amassed under vastly different vibrational conditions than the ones in which you now find yourself—and indeed, the ones toward which you ascend. With that realization, one is able to transcend the patterns of stuckness that have characterized entire lifetimes, and to release the fundamental misconceptions that spurred those experiences into manifestation, vibrationally.

You may well have experienced victimization, for example, as part of your body of life experience, in any of an infinite number of avenues of expression. Yet that does not justify the maintenance of a mind-set that would identify one to oneself as a "victim." Your own unwillingness to engage in dramas characterized by such interactions sets the stage for a shift in the energies that would have precipitated them. Yet, in order to release the structural building blocks for that category of life experience, it is necessary to identify the core beliefs within your own energetic blueprint that would support such conditions. Turning back the pages in the volumes of life history you have amassed, serves to illustrate the rich body of experience you have collected to support what may be a grossly misguided premise. In scrutinizing these patterns, it is fascinating to recognize the very earliest instances that seeded repeat occurrences throughout your lifetime.

It is entirely possible that the catalyst for such initial experiences may be one that was carried forth from another incarnation, or is experience that is replicated energetically in lifetimes that parallel this one—realities that continue to resonate disharmony that affects you in key areas of your life. It is not necessary to *time-travel* or to attempt to intervene in other expressions of reality in order to adjust the effects those conditions may be exerting upon you vibrationally. All that is required is to become whole within one's own self and to reach a place of clarity as to what is a valid characteristic of one's own essence—and what is not.

The fact is, there *is* no limitation whatsoever in the structure of your fundamental essence. And you can, in fact *be* anything you choose to *be*.

The key to transcending conditions, in which you perceive the evidence of limitation, is not to dwell upon the essence of that limitation, but rather, to dwell, utterly and completely, in a perception of *how you would like to have it be*. Thus, regardless of the nature of the condition in question, were you to see yourself in circumstances devoid of that condition, you would have initiated the process that would lead, energetically, to that very reality.

Were you instead to dwell, in a state of dread, upon how much you do *not* wish to be in a certain condition, you succeed in reinforcing the vibrational building blocks for the continuation of those circumstances. For, in stating to yourself what your physical senses have shown you to be your reality, you serve to reinforce the energetic grid that magnetizes that category of experience.

Your manifestation, therefore, might be a physical condition that persists, despite every conceivable effort you can make, in physical terms, to thwart it. The fact is, this condition does not *exist* at all. You merely have persisted in telling yourself it does. And the more mental and verbal reinforcement you add to the equation, the stronger the foundation you have constructed to sustain it. By consciously transcending the physical evidence of a given condition, and giving your mental energy, instead, to resolving the fundamental life issues that, in likelihood, served to precipitate it, you can make monumental strides toward surmounting the obstacles that challenge you. For, it is you who has placed these physical hurdles in your own path. And it is you alone who can determine whether you are able to navigate your way around the illusion of these obstacles in physical form.

These challenges are clues. They have been placed in your path, strategically, like the tip of the proverbial iceberg, so you would not be able to continue to ignore the experiential evidence that has been nudging you for a lifetime. These life threatening physical manifestations that are a characteristic of the heightened levels of the transformation process, are no more than a vibrational signal within your energy structure, that your attention is requested, right now, at the deepest level.

Consider carefully how you choose to respond to these signals. And recognize them for the gift they truly are. For the illusion of illness or disease with which you may be wrestling is not the issue at hand. Rather, that condition is the symptom that is calculated to liberate you from the limitation of the density with which you have been staggering, vibrationally. You will not be able to move forward at the rate of ascension at which you have begun to travel while maintaining those debilitating levels. The physical condition that has surfaced is there to herald a major shift within your entire realm of beingness. For once this major hurdle has been transcended, you will begin to experience a new category of perception and to sustain that perspective as the focus of your reality.

The habitual patterns of interpersonal interaction will, quite suddenly, appear to relinquish the grasp in which they have held you throughout this lifetime, as you work out the details of the final scenes of your life theme dramas. Once the energies have had the opportunity to build to a peak experience and to prompt resolution, the resulting clearance will be too profound to be dismissed as coincidence. And you will *awaken* to the realization that the densities to which you had become so accustomed are no longer present.

The catalyst for this shift may well be the recognition of the habitual emotional patterns you have been bringing to closure, or the physical condition that resulted from them. It does not matter whether your attention is captured by the physical or the emotional manifestations of your vibrational state, for they are intertwined. And once the energy is allowed to be released, at one level, the symptoms it supported will very likely dematerialize, for there would be nothing remaining, energetically, to hold them in form.

The objective then, is to address the question of where to direct your *focus.* As a being focused in self-perception as a limited physical creature, caught at the mercy of the circumstances of your physical environment, it was a logical reaction to respond to life's trials in a direct physical manner. As the vibrational complexity of the environment in which these interactions played out has escalated, the effectiveness of physical solutions to physical challenges has diminished. The point is reached, ultimately, where it is obvious that "life just isn't working" anymore. All the tried and true methods of dealing with cause and effect in your physical reality don't produce the results you were taught to expect. And you begin to feel powerless, as you intensify your attempts to force a result with a mind-set rooted in reflex reactions.

Eventually, the desperate sense of struggle surrenders to the realization of the utter futility of this approach. And one begins to ask the "big" questions that herald the breakthrough in which all illusions shatter simultaneously. In that moment, one experiences a clarity of understanding that defies *understanding*. For in the utter simplicity of that crystalline awareness you know that, at long last, you are free. You know that none of the issues and the worries with which you struggled over the course of an entire lifetime really matter at all.

From your own ascended perspective, none of what may once have seemed life-threatening holds any importance or interest. And you begin to view such vibrational *hot spots* as invitations one instinctively declines. One chooses not to jump in and engage the full focus of one's consciousness, even for a passing moment, in conflict. The need to appear vindicated or validated gives way to the need to sidestep such scenarios altogether, and to relegate those invitations to exercise the self-righteous needs of ego to another place in time. The corresponding freedom from the testing conditions of a life-threatening physical ailment heralds one's imminent approach to the interdimensional threshold.

As one flounders in the final moments of the morass and misery of the illusion of separation, one reaches a moment of truth. In that moment, one transcends the need to perpetuate the illusion and sees the physical symptoms that were so feared, or detested, or denied as evidence of one's impending freedom from all such forms of attachment to the illusion of those symptoms. Once you relinquish all sense of importance of this ultimate life issue, it no longer holds you, vibrationally, in its grasp. In essence, it ceases to manifest in your reality.

The health crises that will be so prevalent as by-products of the ascension process are the ultimate gateways to *healing* in the truest sense. For the level of healing you would wish to attain, as you rise to the fullness of your physical presence, goes beyond a freedom from symptoms that may once have confounded you. True healing occurs when one has succeeded in releasing the underlying vibrational charge one has carried at certain levels of awareness for lifetimes. And in so doing, attains a vantage point that transcends totally that kind of experience.

chapter thirty-one

Manifesting the world of The Artist.
Recreating the world of The Dreamer.
Liberating The Dreamer within.

As one begins to progress through the initial stages of the ascension process, and the rudimentary portions of the release work have been confronted, one becomes aware that one is suddenly viewing the world through different eyes. The attendant difficulties to which you had become so accustomed and which, through your anticipation, once persisted despite your awareness of them, suddenly are no longer there. And one emerges in the rarefied space of recognizing a new beginning marked by unprecedented freedom of choice.

Without the familiar obstacles to dictate or to limit the range of one's direction, one is struck by the profound awareness that there are literally no limits to what you may now choose to experience within the context of this physical form. With the newfound absence of limitation comes the realization that one must now take total responsibility for the focused intent that underlies one's choices.

One can no longer take the default position that one "has no choice" or that one was obliged to select from a limited number s in any situation. The full thrust of one's intent draws into a of possibility the circumstances that will carry that intent through to manifestation. Thus, the process is less a by-product of making choices from a given number of possible options, than of starting from a position of limitlessness and drawing forth the corresponding options as possibilities to be embraced as choice.

Become clear as to what it is you truly wish to do, or experience, or know, and that very clarity will magnetize the circumstances through which one may explore one's heart's desire. Life becomes a process through which experience is custom made to order, vibrationally, and is no longer perceived as a journey that is ready made and mass- produced. You are not required to do anything. And it is helpful to condition yourself in the recognition that every nuance of your life is a sequence that has been called forth, by you, by choice.

The level of clarity with which you focus your intent helps to determine the ease or degree of complexity that manifests accordingly. When you approach the process of manifestation at the higher vibrational levels to which you now are ascending, you are no longer afforded the luxury of passivity. The old mode of operation that may have seen you living your life with a "wait and see" approach, will not manifest anything at the higher vibrational levels, other than confusion. For here, the complexity of pre-determining conditions, characteristic of denser realities, are no longer present.

Once one has cleared the slate of the karmic vibrational remnants that once compromised one's energy field, there is literally nothing left with which to magnetize life experience other than the vibrational essence of what it is that you want. In order to function effectively in a world where all the rules have changed, it is wise to take the necessary time now, in anticipation of those conditions, to become clear on where you wish to be going with this physical incarnation you call your life.

Mixed feelings on a given issue will manifest mixed outcomes every time, under the vibrational conditions toward which you now ascend. Reluctance and half-heartedness, in essence, nullify the fundamental charge that would call forth the circumstances in question. Now is the time to focus your awareness upon the importance of being clear in your intent before engaging in the action of choice. It is not possible to manifest one's heart's desire by continuing to drift along, waiting for life to "happen" to you. At the higher levels, it simply doesn't work that way.

In order to manifest the world of The Artist, it is necessary first to recreate the world of The Dreamer. This is the world of the eternal child, into which you were born in this lifetime. A child does not know the concept of limitation. These are shackles with which his world equips him from the earliest stages of his development. In his dreams there are no limitations, and his wishes and desires dominate his every moment, calling forth what it is he most wishes to experience.

Initially, the desires are rudimentary, and his focused approach to what he wants to experience reinforces the manifestation of those results. As his development progresses, his desires are thwarted and his dreams are dashed by the rules of a *reality* with which he is force-fed. Soon, those rules are integrated into the formulation of a belief system that cripples his abilities to manifest his heart's desire. The energy of focus shifts from what was truly desired to what is perceived to be *possible*. And even in the early stages of his development, he learns to weave a complex route through the labyrinth of his life, in an attempt to salvage some fragment of the original dream.

Ultimately, the magic of the dream and the accompanying joy of dreaming it, becomes lost in a realm ruled by logic and strategy. And in shifting one's focus from the joy of dreaming the dream to the fear that fuels overcoming suppression of the dream—the child forgets *how* to dream. These times are about reinstating those skills. For without them, one is destined to recreate the conditions of a world defined by limitation and struggle.

Your essential nature is not focused in goal-oriented activity, but is rooted in your feeling body—your emotions. The drive you experience toward accomplishing a given end is not based upon a need to fulfill a dream, but rather, is based upon a need to avoid sliding into the abyss of your fears. Thus the motive for most of what you have been taught to strive for is fear based. That type of energy produced a limited level of results in the realms through which you have progressed thus far in your journey. But the thrust of this type of energy would manifest results that you would not find pleasing at the levels you are soon approaching. It will be necessary to learn to distinguish, within the context of your desires, between those that are based in fear and those that stem from the innocence of the joyousness that is your fundamental essence.

To recreate the authenticity of your dream, you will wish to begin to scrutinize your true motives for wanting to do what you are telling yourself you want to do. If you wish to build a fabulous home with your own hands, for example, it would be important to know whether that desire is based upon the unbridled pleasure you would derive in the act of that creation, or whether, at some level, you seek to *prove* something in your own eyes or in the eyes of others. The former desire is born of The Dreamer within you. The latter is rooted in the energy of separation.

The Dreamer derives his limitless joy through the expression of his Isness in ways that please and delight him, without regard to the benefit that may be forthcoming in the way of the opinion of others. Even to the extent that self-esteem may be rooted in goal setting within the sanctity of one's own consciousness, one sets up the parameters of duality—of *success* or *failure*—with such a mind-set. There is no success or failure for The Dreamer. There is simply the essence of The Dream.

There is no challenge inherent in the dream, nor any place for judgment, whether internally or externally focused. The Dreamer has no qualifying considerations whatsoever in releasing the pure essence of the dream into the embrace of the ethers that carry them forth into manifestation—simply that the idea is infinitely pleasing.

There is no concept of the attainment of a goal for The Dreamer, for that very concept opens the door to considerations of what may or may not be considered *possible* by a mind structured in linear logic.

The Dreamer does not care what is or is not *possible*. For the Dream is based in limitlessness. The Dream is totally without structure. The Dream is found in the depths of the child who still dwells within—regardless of how disenchanted or disillusioned you may consider yourself to be. Regardless of how jaded you are or how broken by life's blows, the Dreamer remains untouched. And reconnecting with that rarefied spark of your own Divine essence is the key element in restructuring the life you are preparing to transform. Before The Artist can begin to emerge from the radiant core of your being and give expression to the unique creation that is to be your life, you must first find and liberate The Dreamer from the prison of your linear consciousness.

The Dreamer to be embraced is not the ego-oriented aspect of self that would have fueled your ambitions with focused strategies oriented toward achievement. The Dreamer is the glowing spark of joyousness that somehow became buried beneath the burden of all you have undertaken to *do* in this lifetime. The Dreamer does not dwell in the realm of *doing* but thrives in the innocence of simply *being*. The Dreamer is set free when you set aside the ego-focused priorities with which you have tied your own hands and allow your true essence to emerge.

Once you have made the connection with the unconditional state of joyousness that radiates within you, you have taken the first step in restructuring the direction of your journey. When you have tasted of this connection with your very own self, you will begin to understand why, at some level, life has declared a "time-out." It will begin to make sense to you that, were the circumstances of your life allowed to continue on "automatic-pilot," you would not have arrived at the destination toward which you are now headed.

You begin to recognize, once in this aspect of the process, that your life had delivered you to the vantage point of a plateau. There was an element of clarity from having ascended to that perspective, and with it came the realization that the plateau was going nowhere. It offered the potential of the perpetuation of the essence of that level and a sense of clarity that there was nowhere to go from there. Not without first descending *from* the plateau.

As you begin to emerge from the devastation of the structure of your circumstances, it begins to become obvious why that experience was a necessary part of the journey. The fortress you had constructed upon the plateau of your experience had, in fact, become the prison in which your very own sacred essence waited patiently. The fresh innocence of unbridled joy that you harbor within cannot thrive in the structured conditions you created in a world built on the premise of compromise. The sweetness of the vision of The Dreamer, awaiting your rediscovery, is the elusive missing piece in your journey of self-discovery. For without the illumination of the heart of The Dreamer you would continue to travel blindly on the path that compels you to venture forth upon it.

Before you can become clear within yourself as to what you want to *do* with your life, it is essential that you pause in your program of frenzied activity to discover who you really are. Then and only then have you prepared the conditions in which The Artist can emerge and give expression to your true essence, in a way that will provide a life that is rich and satisfying in all the ways you quietly yearn for.

Alternatively, you could continue indefinitely, trying this and trying that, in an attempt to source, from the outside world, that elusive *something* that always seems to be missing. And you could choose to shuffle and reshuffle those cards of possibility indefinitely, trying to come up with the missing piece that will tie it all together. For the missing piece is not to be found in any of the distractions that present themselves, in and of themselves. Yet that elusive element, once found within, could well express through any of those infinite possible avenues, and provide the perfect medium for The Artist to paint—with passion—your true life's work.

Before you can begin to determine "where to go from here," in terms of what you choose to *do*, take some time at this particular crossroads in your journey to become reacquainted with yourself. This is an exercise that most will wish to do in solitude. And you can expect to be nudged in a direction that provides for generous periods of alone time. You may find yourself withdrawing from your normal circle of activities and friends, and seeking out circumstances that allow you to be in the sanctity of your own consciousness. This is all part and parcel of the process of metamorphosis that holds you in its embrace. For, in order to reunite with The Dreamer, one must withdraw into the silence of inner solitude. And the elimination of the distractions of daily life during this period is a necessary part of the process.

Your agenda will become simplified in of itself when you reach this stage of your journey. And there will no longer be the predictable excuses that would have allowed you to postpone the self-confrontation that awaits you. The moment for turning inward announces its arrival blatantly—in silence. Once you recognize the signs of its presence, and cease filling the empty spaces it creates with "busy-work" and mundane social interaction, you are able to relax into the sanctity of this special time that has been set-aside for you alone. Within this haven from the outside world, you will begin to turn back the pages and to retrace your steps through the epic adventure you are living. And in the high points and low points that will highlight the story, you will be able to recognize the places where The Dreamer began to surrender The Dream.

You will be able to remember the pain of the disappointments and the anguish of the defeats that set the stage for a script founded upon disillusionment and compromise. You will begin to trace the beginnings of the choices exercised in resignation rather than passion. And in weaving together the theme that underlies these episodes, you nce the clarity that comes of identifying the pattern, and he mind-set that has driven you to perpetuate it. It will become obvious to you that in following in those footsteps, a vital part of your sacred essence has been lost. And in the absence of that Divine spark, the episodes that followed suit somehow felt dry and lifeless, despite all the trappings with which you adorned them.

Now, in the clarity of your retrospective vision, it is time to prepare for reunion with The Dreamer who, like a child, wandered away when it wasn't fun anymore, while you were so busy *doing* your life, you didn't even notice he was missing. Not until much later, when it was obvious that something very precious was very lost.

Now it is time to simply stop. Stop what you are *doing*. Stop all the mechanical practices that absorb your every waking moment. Stop your compulsion to pull others into your drama as a way of avoiding focus on the one who stands at center stage. This aspect of the process is not about others. It is not about "what" you are *doing* or "who" you are *doing it with*.

That missing element is not the by-product of the "wrong" relationship, or the "wrong" profession, or the "wrong" spiritual path, or a technique of spiritual practice that is exercised incorrectly. Those are all potential vehicles through which the passion of The Dreamer might be given expression.

In the sanctity of the silence you have afforded yourself, you will begin to recognize the instances, in your earliest experience, when your natural, unrestrained enthusiasm and eager curiosity was allowed to play freely. And in recapturing these precious, simple moments, in the timelessness of memory, you will discover the true path to self-discovery. What you yearn to experience, and fault the external trappings of your existence for not providing, has been within you all along—waiting patiently.

chapter thirty-two

Experiential mirroring: creating a foundation for compassion.
Putting the rocky road into perspective.

Whichever way you choose to look at it, there is no denying the degree of change each of you is experiencing in your
inner world. Some of you have chosen to share your personal experiences of transformation with others and have enjoyed a level of
camaraderie and support that has served to reinforce what your
experience has shown you to be so. Yet others of you have retained
your perceptions and revelations as evidence of an inner shift in
awareness so profound as to be undeniable. The level of self-
recognition evolves accordingly, as one progresses in the intensity
of this process of evolution.

One becomes aware that characteristics of one's identity that
formed the foundation of one's sense of self-knowledge are no longer
valid expressions of one's experience of oneself. And one comes
to understand the fluidity in the nature of this process of metamorphosis. The vantage point from which you are able to observe
yourself in this moment puts into perspective the rich and often
rocky terrain you have traversed. And with that retrospective

vision comes the understanding that the present moment's clarity does not invalidate the journey that was necessary in order to attain it.

It would have been easy for you to arrange to birth yourself into circumstances where today's newfound understandings were already at hand. And you might have spared yourself much anguish, and effort, and *time*, had you chosen to write your life script in that way. Yet, had you done so, you would have denied yourself the firsthand experience of the dramatic contrasts that are now so vivid for you. To have lived through the poignancy of your key episodes has served to underscore for you the revelations of this experience of spiritual breakthrough.

Had you not had the taste of the bitter as well as the sweet, you would have emerged with a theoretical understanding, supported only by your observations of the trials and tribulations in the lives of others. And while you ultimately come to bask in the exultation of your Divine connectedness when that state is at hand, the profound intensity of that experience is that much more vivid by virtue of the contrast your life dramas have provided.

You have not failed yourself for "having taken so long" in your journey of awakening. For the vantage point that awaits you at the summit of the mountain would not have carried the impact that is possible had you not made the arduous climb. In order to avail yourself of the richness in the experience of knowing your Divine connectedness, it was necessary to avail yourself of the richly contrasting details of the experience of separation.

In order to appreciate fully the realization that you are creating the essence of your life experience, it was necessary that you explore—in raw detail—the experience of injustice and victimization. In order to know yourself to be truly all powerful, it was necessary for you to experience the agonizing frustration of not being able to implement your will. And in order to know, unquestioningly, that there is a Divine foundation underlying the entire experience you have come to regard as *life*, it was necessary for you to create the conditions in which that Divine essence could be questioned. It was necessary to experience the adversity that underlies a state of separation in order to realize fully the magnitude of the Divinity that radiates from within you.

The so-called *dark-side* of your nature was given liberty to express through you in order that you might be able to recognize the vibration inherent in those patterns of response. For it becomes abundantly clear that those states of being do not feel good. The horrors of the depths at which some of you explored the world of physical reality are a graphic illustration of the levels of vibration from which you have chosen to *ascend*.

You now have an experiential reference point at hand with which to contrast the physical, emotional, and experiential sensations that are part of the ascension process. And you have a basis for the profound sense of humility and gratitude that naturally result from a life's journey that encompasses the extremes of human experience. As you look back over the amazing itinerary you have programmed for this lifetime, you can look back with wonderment at the awesome richness of so much of it. And you will have formed the basis for understanding the adversity being depicted by much of your world.

It is far easier to understand the nature of another person's pain, having lived it yourself. Now, as you begin to emerge from the illusion of the adversity of separation, and the circumstances of your life reflect that vibrational shift, you are able to empathize with others who remain in the throes of that kind of experience. Having crawled out of the dark night of your own soul's journey, it is easier for you to recognize the truth underlying the nightmares of another.

Having watched your own dreams thwarted and your sand castles leveled by the unrelenting seas of your own life script, you can feel vicariously the levels of disappointment and despair that others around you are living as they bear the waves that crash upon their shores. You have built for yourself the foundation for the experience of *compassion*, by having watched illustration after illustration of your worst fears come to life. For you would not have had the basis for reaching out to another being living at the depths of his drama, had you not been given the chance to experience those levels yourself.

Now, as you begin to view life so differently, you can see the perfection in the diversity. And at the same time you begin to recognize the patterns of similarity in the life experiences of those you may once have judged, with your very own journey. You have magnetized into your arena of awareness beings whose journeys would graphically depict for you the mirrors of your own experience that best underscore the points you wished to make in the crafting of your own life script. You may have blocked yourself from recognizing these players as the consummate performers they now appear to be. For, in playing out the melodrama of their own responses before your very eyes, they have shown you what you were unwilling to recognize and acknowledge within yourself. Now, as you begin to suspend judgment and to cease perceiving yourself in an exalted position, simply by virtue of the fact that you know you have made great progress, you begin to sense the simple Isness underlying it all.

There is no element of stature or lack of stature on the spiritual journey. For All Is Oneness. You each are simply at a different moment—a split-second, freeze-action spark of awareness on a journey that is timeless. The collective points of illumination form the composite perspective of the journey known as *enlightenment*. And each nuance adds a subtle element to the essence of the whole. You may think that the journey you have made is yours, for your experience has told you so. But in truth, your experience is but a glimpse into the composite reality that is the shared vision of these times.

Oneness has chosen to make this journey as each of you. And we have done so—*you* have done so—in order to know yourself in the fullness of All That Is, having had the experience of it. We have availed ourself of the possibility to experience the absolute thrill of awakening into spiritual awareness. And the most dramatic way to have that experience is to have lived through infinite variations on the theme of forgetting—and then rediscovering the true nature of our own Divine essence—over and over and over again. Your own exalted moments of awakening add a brilliant note to the indescribable harmony being co-created, as each of you adds your resonance to the multidimensional whole.

There is no need to judge another being as he falters in his attempts to grasp the clues he has left in his own path. You may be able to see quite clearly what is obvious to you—from your perspective. Yet, from the perspective of the one on his knees, the clue was not visible. Not yet. But after a sufficient number of headlong spills into the mud, the clue emerges. You know. You've been there. We have all been there. For that is the nature of the journey. And as you reach out to offer a helping hand to another being and have it rejected, and as your words of newfound wisdom fall on deaf ears by those who need them most, you'll remember. For you've been there. And you'll wonder how you could have been so blind, when the clues were right there, in full view, all along. Yet you know that the seeker will not see what he has come to see until the appointed moment for that particular set of eyes to open. You know, because you've been there.

Hand in hand with the blessed realizations you have, at last, come to embrace is the opportunity to express your understandings through the experience of compassion that is a hallmark of this stage of your journey. You can recognize and you can feel the power of the journey of another being in the moments of mutual recognition that you will come to share with many, as you venture forth with newfound eyes. The clues have always been there. But until now, you have not been equipped to see them. You have embodied the blinders necessary to shield you from a level of knowingness that might have denied you the poignancy of the experience of awakening.

Now the blinders have been removed, at least from your own limited field of vision. And this is a process you will experience over and over again, as the layers of illusion are lifted and your true essence is revealed.

Your own radiance will help illuminate the path of others who walk beside you, however briefly, simply by being in the authenticity of your own moment. It is not necessary to *try* in order to help another being who is experiencing a lesson you have learned the hard way. Simply by being present and holding that vibration of transcendence, you can add the much-needed boost to another that enables him to discover what has been right there all along. Just like you did.

As you begin to teach by example the underlying principles of this process of metamorphosis, it is to be expected that your own experience will continue to alternately plateau and plummet as you continue to attain and re-refine each new vantage point of understanding. There is no static condition of *enlightenment* on the path of enlightenment. It is an ongoing journey that continues to evolve. Do not expect that your life circumstances will suddenly become trouble free, simply by virtue of the fact that you have attained certain levels of vibration and of understanding. For the peaks and valleys of the terrain of physical reality will continue to provide for you the graphic illustrations of your own life's work.

Each instance of adversity that may cross your path, is an opportunity to pause and to reflect upon the mirror those circumstances have manifested to provide for you. Ultimately, you will recognize in the experiences of others the parallel episodes in your own life theme patterns that they illustrate. And you will recognize that another being has gifted you with an illustration of an issue that you were not required to relive yourself.

As you continue to ascend vibrationally, you will recognize, increasingly, the phenomenon of this level of experiential mirroring. As you embrace, vicariously, the gift in the lessons symbolized by the dramas of another being, you are able to further release and re-refine elements of your own energy pattern that resonate to those themes. The levels of compassion realized in this process enable you to align and to harmonize vibrationally with your experiential surrogate, without taking on the levels of negativity embodied and released by the other being.

Thus the experience of compassion is one in which balance is sustained between bonding and boundaries. One is able to reach out and to care deeply for the poignancy of another's process, to recognize the underlying theme as a common thread woven in your own experience, and at the same time to distance yourself, vibrationally, from the heat of the blaze. Your own mastery of the common issue acts as a vibrational catalyst for the one enmeshed in the actual drama that nudges that being toward completion of the theme at hand.

And so, you begin to recognize that the process is indeed a dance in which you share moments of common resonance with others. And just as you may well be leading the dance when certain all-too-familiar passages begin to play, so too do others who have experienced mastery in putting the steps and the music together, dance the dance with you. All move, in vibrational unison, toward the crescendo experienced collectively as Oneness. For, in truth, it is Oneness that is dancing. It is the Oneness in each of you that recognizes the Oneness in another, which unites you in a breath of harmony that is shared. And in each interaction, there is the promise of that attainment of balance, even when one reaches out only by listening, or simply by being there.

Know that in giving, the giving is never one-sided. For the giver is equally gifted in ways you have only begun to understand. When you share the reality of your own painful or challenging situations with another being, you have not burdened that being with your problems. You have afforded that being the opportunity to harmonize with you on a common note in a song you both know by heart. When compassion is expressed in earnest, the burden is lightened for each of you. The giver in the exchange always seems to come away from the encounter feeling uplifted for having reached out to someone else in his hour of need. Yet rarely does he understand why. The vibrational dynamics of the exchange allowed for the release of levels of density harbored within the giver's own energy field, leaving him with a sense of levity.

Compassion is the common thread with which the tapestries of each of your lives are interwoven. For in truth, there Is only One of us here. As you begin to recognize the parallels in the lives of those with whom you share this dance, you begin to recognize the uncanny perfection in the synchronicity of the moments that bring you together. It becomes blatantly obvious that there are no random occurrences. The so-called *coincidences* you may once have been inclined to dismiss are far from irrelevant. Each seemingly chance encounter is an exercise in the perfection of manifestation. For in that moment, there is something to be given to each of you, by each of you.

You are never too busy, or too committed, to pause and reconsider when life presents you with the possibility of a radical turn-about in what you thought were your plans. Those plans were merely the detour you used to bring yourself to the moment where the real direction might be stumbled upon "by accident." Each chance encounter with a being who tugs at your awareness from beneath the surface, has been placed there strategically—by you—to reinforce a common thread. Each of you has danced this dance before, most likely with each other. And the ease with which you slip into the rhythms of interaction with these perfect strangers underscores the significance of these seemingly random connections.

Take the time—make the time—to explore what is shared mutually, particularly when it appears that the other person is the one that has the most to gain from the encounter. For these experiences are the ones likely to leave you enriched in the ways that really matter. None of you is here on a singular path like a sprinter whose *win* is dependent upon remaining ahead of the pack. Each of you has progressed as you have largely due to the sudden surge in a wave you are all riding together. And it is the collective *you* that is ascending, even though from your personal perspective it appears that you alone are making these quantum leaps.

There are countless others who have given you a vibrational "leg-up" on this ride, so you could ride the crest of the wave together as One. And in transcending the sense of separation you have spent a lifetime justifying, and surrendering to the mutuality of the momentum you share, there are moments—magical moments—when you know that you have not imagined it. You have experienced that Oneness. You know you *are* that Oneness. You know, because you've been there.

chapter thirty-three

Detaching from the details of "the illusion."
Attaining the vantage point of the witness.

Discovering tendencies within yourself, and seeing clearly the extent of the deception you perpetrate upon your own awareness, is a fascinating part of the process of awakening. Suddenly, you become aware of the *character* being portrayed through the vehicle of your identity, and you observe that character with a sense of bemused detachment. Once you have identified clearly some of the major themes you have been acting out throughout the course of your life, it becomes easy to watch yourself going through the motions of your own predictable response patterns, while in the act of doing it. At times, it is as though two of you are present. One is dutifully going through the motions of a programmed response, and the other is standing by watching in fascination as you run through your routine.

You are able to begin to unravel the intricate web of good intentions you have woven and in which you have ensnared yourself, and others, all your life. No one is fooled when you say one thing and then do another, having fully intended it that way from the onset.

For vibrationally, you communicate quite clearly what you believe your clever words and behaviorisms have disguised. And you wonder why you cannot be trusted, by your self, as you continue to demonstrate to yourself how untrustworthy you actually are.

You don't mean to be untrustworthy. For naturally, at this stage of your transformation process, you see yourself as a high-principled being who makes choices that are *conscious*. Yet given the opportunity, you would not hesitate in *cheating* on yourself, even ever so slightly, with a food or a substance or an activity that you had promised yourself was off-limits. You may feel justified in shifting the *blame* for the breech of trust to any number of perfectly plausible excuses, yet what remains is the responsibility for the action taken—which can be no other than your own.

Each of you knows the words by heart that will state to yourself and to any who care to give your drama their attention, what the highest choice would be in any given circumstance. So it is rarely a matter of not knowing the difference, but rather, one of exercising your free will to violate your own rules, like a small child, testing the boundaries set by those in authority. In this case, you are the authority whose boundaries are being tested. You are the one who thinks, at some level, that it is possible to "slip one through" and get away with it. But in actuality, it is not possible to break your own laws and not reap the results of having done so.

There are no definitive laws of right and wrong, beyond those you create and set for yourself. There are higher choices and lesser choices, in terms of the predictable consequence of certain actions. Yet the violation of a standard can only be applicable to the "rules" you have set for yourself. When you attempt to push the boundaries of your own standards of acceptable action, you draw yourself ever deeper into the very illusions you are working to transcend. When you buy into the evidence of being at the effect, rather than at the cause of your own circumstances, you create the parameters to reenforce the illusion of your separation from Source.

As you begin to detach from the details of your personal drama, and you see yourself running your standard routine like a robot going through the motions, you begin to experience yourself from the perspective of pure awareness. It is this level of your own consciousness that is able to detach from the personality you identify as *you* and observe objectively as you act out the character you have created. You can see clearly, as you delve ever deeper into your very own essence, that which is truly *you* and that, which is the masterpiece of your own creation.

That fully adapted character has all the responses and the full repertoire of survival skills with which you have equipped yourself to deal with the idiosyncrasies of a script written just for you—by you. You are confronted with the situations, over and over again, that best relate to the expectations you have programmed into the character you have invested your life in portraying. Once you begin to observe the ironies and the patterns in your own masterful performance, you begin to shift the self-perpetuating vibrational charge with which you have programmed your star performer.

Your life is a dance in which your circumstances help to define and redefine the identity of the character you have allowed yourself to become—and the reflection of the responses of that character on the circumstances that follow. You can continue to spin and twirl to the same melody for a lifetime, if that is what you choose to do. And most of the beings in your reality know nothing beyond that type of dance. Or you can choose to become aware— to become truly *conscious*—and to see yourself as both the perpetrator and the target of your own creation.

When choosing to violate your own self-imposed standards, know that you are able to do so, in a fully present state, owning fully the ramifications of that choice, and thereby by-passing the consequence of the vibration of victimization. You are not a victim of your addictions, or your cravings, or your unbridled desires. You are a fully responsible participant in your reaction to the choices presented. And in approaching all choices in that way, you serve to dissipate the vibrational charge that will magnetize undesired consequences to you.

When you choose to place in your mouth a confection you told yourself was off-limits, do so fully embracing that choice, savoring the morsel, and loving yourself for it, rather than doing so with the energy of *cheating,* and hating yourself for it. Make your choices consciously and fully and they become the highest choices—for you.

There are no right and wrong choices. There is simply action and reaction. And both are intertwined in the eternal dance of life. You are able to begin to fine-tune the footwork when you are able to step back from the illusion of the dance and see yourself performing it. The logical next step is to begin to wonder just who it is who is doing the watching. If you are not the illusion who is twirling obediently on the dance floor, who is it that realizes himself to be the choreographer and the audience as One?

This one eternal question is the pivotal point that marks the beginning of your quest to transcend the realm of the illusion and to experience the fullness of the realm of possibility. For, it is here that you truly dwell. Here in the limitlessness of your unbridled joy in your experience of aliveness.

The vision of the identity you act out allows you to transcend the limitation of that very illustration and to know yourself as you truly are. For, the identity is built upon a foundation of all you have *done.* And who you Are has nothing whatsoever to do with *doing.* The one you hope to unveil in the process of this quest has no need to *do* anything in order to know him as he truly Is. For, there are no questions of judgment or of worthiness and unworthiness in a state of Isness. One simply *Is.* One's joy in that simple act of *being* is untouched by the issues that might distract the one caught in the drama of the illusion. The One you have had a fleeting chance to experience and ultimately to know is untouched by the trials and tribulations of your drama. That One simply *Is.* And knows. And radiates the joy of that Isness—that knowingness.

Having experienced that aspect of who you Are, you have a reference point, to which to retreat when the inevitable challenges that arise in the world of the illusion come into play. This untouchable *center* is akin to the center of a storm, where all is calm and tranquil, despite the whirlwinds that surround it. That center is the haven within which you truly dwell. The vantage point from that center is the one which, ultimately, you will carry with you as you walk within the world of the illusion. You will begin to take on the perspective of the witness. And gradually, as you detach from your fixation on the details of your drama, you will begin to experience yourself floating above the surface of even the most turbulent circumstances, knowing yourself to be unaffected.

The truth of who you are is there within you. Right now. It is not something you can hope to attain by hearing a designated number of sermons from the supposedly learned amongst you. It is not something you must perform austerities to experience. Nor is it something that requires any suffering or sacrifice on your part. It is not a state that you can "buy" with obedience to any of the countless religious dogmas that your world now offers. But through the vehicle of the original vision of some of those avenues, or through a path one blazes through the uncharted jungles of one's own consciousness, that Oneness is *experienced*. And known. And never forgotten.

You may have spent a good portion of this lifetime seeking the knowingness that has been within you the whole time. And you may have had glimpses of the very thing you have been searching for, without realizing it. For, the state of silent awareness is not one that shouts at you to be recognized. It is subtle. It is simply there— and *you* are there—and then you are back within the embrace of the illusion, over and over again. You begin with a flash of illumination, the feeling of having attained an overview, and then the clarity recedes once more.

Ultimately, the perspective of pure awareness is retained. And as you continue to ascend vibrationally through the levels of physical perception, you realize that you have come to *embody* the Isness that you have tasted in the center of the storm. When that perspective is recognized and is known to preside in your awareness, you know—without knowing how you know—that you are no longer where you were.

From that vantage point the world in which you were born, and in which you have played out the animated scenes of your personal drama, is a world relegated to the realm of memory—an archive of experience that you're welcome to revisit at will. But now, when you choose to look back upon those episodes, you do so from the perspective of the overview. Now you are able to see, in retrospect, the truth underlying those experiences. Now you can witness for the first time what was obscured and colored by the intensity of emotion. Once the veils of emotion have been lifted, true objectivity is possible. And the memory becomes a vivid picture—vibrant in its aliveness—revealing the gift of the clarity that was there all along.

As you process and label, as you decode and reassess the memories in your personal archives, you begin to see where you have traveled for the very first time. For it is rarely possible to see where one is from the vantage point of the illusion. Once you have distanced yourself from the circumstances of your personal past, you can recognize familiar territory in your present experience. Through the lens of the greater vision, the authenticity of the moment is clarified and categorized automatically. And one remembers, fondly, nearly identical scenes that escalated into full-blown episodes in which one's ego presided at center stage.

The realization is instantaneous now. And the self-recognition produces barely a ripple upon the waters of one's awareness. Just a knowingness of what was—thanks to the vantage point of what now Is—and an overwhelming sense of gratitude for the richness of the adventure.

The perspective of the witness does not allow for self-recrimination, or for regret. For circumstances were as they were for good reason. You set about to illustrate for yourself an unforgettable story. And the poignancy of that experience would not have been possible if you had simply sampled the concepts in theory alone. You can empathize with the vicarious pain and traumas of another being, but you cannot truly walk in anyone else's shoes but your own. You could not have hoped to attain the perspective of true knowingness, had you not supplied the vivid details of true-life experience yourself.

This clarity that comes of hard-earned experience is what you now have to give to others who are where you have been. Now you are able to reach out in a way that is real to others in the throes of the process of awakening. Now you are in a position to really make the mark upon the world that you had always silently hoped to—one compassionate moment at a time. For, now you are in a position to speak from a place of self-knowledge. And that vantage point is only possible when you watch the reruns of your movie with your eyes wide open.

It is not possible to whitewash the poignant passages of the saga you have lived. There is no disguising the details of your sacred journey in gestures of denial. Nor would you wish to. For, what is sacred is the authenticity of where you have truly been on your journey into humanness—not just the pretty parts. In order for a story to have something truly of value to offer, it must be moving and memorable. That is why you wrote it the way you did—and included passages you knew would be unforgettable.

Now, waiting in the wings of your awareness, is a time of distancing from the turbulence of your transformational odyssey. It comes not as a culmination of your process, but rather as a poignant pause in the action, part way through. This time for quiet reflection has been provided to allow you to digest the details that have gone before and to prepare you for the road yet to be covered. Be aware of the fluid nature of the ascension process. And know that you have not awarded yourself a permanent vacation from the work at hand—merely an opportunity to become comfortable with it.

For, by the time the perspective of the plateau is attained, you would have traversed some of the roughest terrain and would have emerged with the details still fresh, yet free of the emotional debris that once obscured a clear vision of the experience. A quiet period of reflection provides the space to survey what has transpired and to make key decisions on where one now wishes to be headed.

This is a period where radical turnabouts in life direction are likely. Relationships are terminated suddenly, or careers are abandoned. Homes are sold, possessions are given away, and the load is lightened as one's awareness becomes keenly attuned to the understanding that what is truly of value has little to do with the trappings of material attainment that may once have seemed important. The compulsion to simplify one's life becomes a dominant theme as one begins to see through the layers of the illusion with the eyes of the witness.

There is a profound period of calm that follows, and choices are made that will determine how far one wishes to venture from the familiar security of the world of the illusion. For, there is a comfort in the familiar that many will not choose to relinquish. And even though a glimpse of true reality has been experienced, many will choose to cling to the illusion that is known rather than to abandon all that has gone before in order to begin anew. For the true metamorphosis requires one to emerge in a newfound skin and to function in the world in ways that rule out the possibility of compromise.

When one understands the dynamics of manifestation, it becomes apparent that the choices implemented must be a reflection of one's true intent and the instrument of one's will, rather than an adaptation that has been created to accommodate the expectations and needs of others. At the levels you now approach, the impetus to action must remain unencumbered if the highest possibility is to be realized in any given circumstance.

When one burdens one's choices with the complexity of feelings of obligation rather than with one's pure heart's desire, the resulting manifestation is muddied by the energy of conflict. Once you have discovered that it is a natural part of the human condition to manifest your heart's desire, it becomes obvious that that end can never be realized through the transmission of a mixed message. And the convoluted motivations of others with whom your life has been intertwined become blatantly obvious to you, as you shed the layers of density that have kept you rooted in the illusion.

The key to all that has held you in its grasp is the emphasis you have continued to place on being in the good-graces of others. From the perspective of the overview, the price of "keeping the peace" is too high. And one begins to question the importance of those relationships, and to sever ties that prevent the implementation of one's own highest choices.

You will be inclined to surround yourself with companionship that affords you the maximum possible latitude of motion, or oftentimes will choose solitude or total isolation for this period. You will be unconcerned with the attempts of others to manipulate you into implementing or endorsing their choices. And you will begin to view the actions of much that surrounds you as transparent and comical. You will observe the petty squabbles that dominate the lives in your midst and will walk through that turbulence untouched. The outcomes of those conflicts will not concern you. For you know that none of it matters.

You will undoubtedly be accused of being aloof, or egotistical, or insensitive. When in fact, your sensibilities will have been heightened. And what others will find objectionable and often intolerable in you will be their own inability to use traditional tactics of manipulation to ensnare you.

When you cease giving power to the opinions of others, you release the tethering, vibrationally, that ties you to the illusion. That release is traditionally done in increments, throughout the process of transformation. Yet, for some of you, the realization will be instantaneous and the shift in your loyalties to your own shoulders will be sudden and dramatic.

The drive to simplify every aspect of your life experience will become the dominant theme of this phase of your transformative journey. And you will focus your awareness and direct your intent toward activities that dissipate all that is superfluous in your life. The direction of your life's work will shift to reflect your innate sense of joy in being alive. Anything that is perceived to be alien to that focus will fall by the wayside during this period. And you can expect to emerge from the profound metamorphosis that follows with a perspective built on a foundation of Self-love.

The Self to which we refer would have shifted from the myopic, linear definition of *self* with which you emerged into awareness in this lifetime, to an expanded perception of what one Is. The illusion that was the sum-total of one's linear identity would have also fallen by the wayside in the process of emergence. And in its place, one experiences Self-perception as unbounded by time and place.

When one is ready to step forward clothed only in Self-awareness, one would have made the transformational shift that marks the turning point that has long been heralded as *enlightenment*. It is a milestone in your journey as the focal point of awareness you would refer to as "a soul." And it is a stopping place on the path in the process of ascension that has become the major theme of this lifetime.

You will come upon this stopping place many times on the winding road that weaves through this mountainous stretch of terrain. It is not unlike certain spots that offer a "scenic view" in your physical world. These stopping places provide a chance to rest, to catch your breath, and to reflect upon the awesome wonder of the vision before you—before it is time to continue on your journey and resume your arduous climb.

The vision remains in your awareness even when it is not in full view before you. For you know, having experienced it for yourself, the vantage point that awaits you just around the bend. And you know that the trials of the winding road are simply part of an illusion—one that begins to fade into the mists of a dream.

chapter thirty-four

Sourcing inner guidance.
The crossroads as a gateway to the path within.
Declining the invitation of psychic dependency.

W isdom is the illusive essence that has been sought by
humankind since the very inception of the idea of your emergence into form. Wisdom is the single element that distinguishes
what you have always been from what you have chosen to become.
For the agreements that govern a choice to emerge as form with
identity require that your knowledge of the nature of your own
Divine essence be relinquished.

What remained was the indefinable sense deep within you that
there was a profound purpose underlying all that now surrounded
you—a wisdom that was sensed, but could not be grasped. It was
sensed, in part, because once there was full conscious awareness
of that wisdom, and in part, because that wisdom, that knowingness,
has never left you. That wisdom is a part of your very essence. You
simply have denied yourself access to it, in order that you would
have the opportunity to *attain* that wisdom of your own volition
against all odds.

Now that you have begun to unravel the threads of the mystery you have created, hints of that wisdom surface in your conscious awareness now and then. You leave traces of illumination right there at your very own feet, so that this time you can't possibly miss the clues you may have avoided stumbling over before. Very carefully, you are being guided out of the wilderness in which you presumed yourself to have been abandoned. And you are being nudged and prodded to defy the logic of your mind and make choices that somehow just "feel right."

Many refer to these flashes of illumination as *intuition*. And as you wean yourself off your addiction to the illusion of the limitations of linear reality, these *flashes* become more frequent and more consistent. After some practice in recognizing and responding to these prompts, your own experience shows you that these glimpses into the true nature of what *Is* can be trusted. For the results in doing so speak for themselves.

One learns to follow one's own inner guidance in preference to that being offered, in the guise of wisdom, by many who have tapped into other sources of information. For the very sense of separation you seek to transcend is reinforced when you offer your power to another being who claims to have *psychic powers*. The information that may be provided for you from such sources can only be validated by your own inner knowingness. And the opportunity for you is to recognize that you have within you a remarkably accurate barometer of what is and is not valid guidance and information.

The information provided by one who purports to be able to *see* what you believe that you cannot, is only as clear and as accurate as the filter of that being's own consciousness. Some are able to peek through the veils of the illusion with varying degrees of accuracy, and to report to you what is seen or sensed or heard. But it is rare that any of this *otherworldly* visioning is truly *wisdom*. For what *Is* cannot be tainted by the vantage point of another, and is available only to the rare physical beings amongst you who have totally transcended, in their own personal journeys, the veils of the illusion.

The visions that may be offered to you by others who are at various stages of piercing those veils within their own process are, in large part, isolated glimpses into the infinite field of possibility. What has been read and reported is, in all likelihood, one of any number of possible outcomes to a given situation. The choices you make of your own free will would, by definition, alter any such prophecy and render it invalid.

To act upon the guidance offered by another being, regardless of how *gifted* they may claim to be, is to make a statement, vibrationally, that valid information is unavailable to you directly. And therefore so it is. You have not come to this experience you call your life in order to have another being, with a questionable degree of visionary skill, make your key choices for you. Ultimately, the choices you put into action must be your own choices if they are to yield the level of results you would wish them to.

In these times, it has become popular to invoke the help of *otherworldly* sources of guidance and information. These forms of consciousness offer any number of levels of perspective and you would wish to regard any advice offered with a degree of objectivity. It is no great feat to be able to make contact with beings who once were, and are no longer, in physical form. These beings abound in the transformational conditions of your physical reality. And most are all too willing to meddle in your life.

If you choose to give your power to them, know that even though these beings may mean well, their advice is colored by their own perspective and their own issues, which have not vanished simply because they are not presently in physical form. Chances are, they are simply "between chapters" in their own saga. And in attempting to influence you, they are reinforcing, vibrationally, the ties and attachments that may once have been there between you. In this respect, nothing would have changed. The essence of the manipulation, and your openness to its influence, would have survived.

In seeking the help of these so-called *angels* know that they are oftentimes no further along in their spiritual unfoldment than they were at the time they departed the physical world. They are not necessarily all knowing or all wise merely by virtue of the fact that they are presently in a nonphysical state of being. You would wish to afford the same degree of deference to their views and opinions, as you would be inclined to, were they still here with you in physical form, and make your own choices accordingly.

You may have had occasion to make contact with other levels of consciousness either through the vehicle of another being, or within your own awareness. And you would wish to be aware of the nature of the agreements of those beings who have chosen to serve as your so-called *guides* and *guardians* from beyond the realm of your reality. These beloved beings are ones who have volunteered to assist you in your focus upon your life's purpose. They are surely not here to make your choices for you. And they would be in violation of their own agreements, were they to do so.

No one is in a position to live your life for you, regardless of how spiritually elevated they may be. To do so would violate your very purpose in being here. It is unrealistic to expect that your guides will swoop in and rescue you as you peer over some precipice on your journey—symbolic or otherwise. That is not the purpose of their presence. Vibrationally, they are able, however, to nudge you into finding within your very own depths the knowingness that leads you in the direction of the highest choice.

It is in these moments that pose the crucial crossroads of this lifetime, that the silence of stepping back from the circumstances at hand best serves you. It is in the clarity of that silent openness on your part that true guidance may be sourced from beyond the recesses of your mind. This guidance does not come in words but transcends all limitation and is simply there for you as *knowingness*.

A so-called "moment of truth" is precisely that. It is a moment where, faced with the inevitability of taking action, you are able to find that *truth* within yourself. It is not your cue to send out an SOS and expect, magically, to be rescued. For that wou defeated the entire purpose of the episode you went to lengths to arrange for yourself to experience. Your guides are surely there for you in the ways that really matter. But they will not give you the answers.

There are other categories of discarnate beings amongst you with their own agendas and motivations for attempting to meddle in your life. It is an expression of wisdom on your part to be aware, and to consider carefully before acting upon any guidance, whether solicited or unsolicited, from discarnate sources.

The levels of awareness which you will begin to experience, sequentially, as part of your ascension process, will begin to rule out any inclination you may have had to defer to the influence of others in making key life choices. You will discover, as you begin to explore the new depths of insight now available to you, that the wisdom you may have been inclined to seek is already there. You become aware that the answers are before you, almost before the question is fully formulated. There is simply no need to ask for illumination. For the direction of highest choice is obvious to you.

When you find yourself standing at a crossroads, allow yourself the grace of the unfoldment of the possibilities that will lead you in the direction of highest choice. Resist the inclination, in these moments of uncertainty, to force a decision prematurely. For it is entirely possible that the way is unclear because all the information has not yet been presented. You have entered a period, within your transformational journey where radical changes in your life direction are likely. The purpose of placing yourself in such a maze of circumstances is to develop a reliance on your own ability to source the answers. And by this time, you would have discovered that deference to the guidance of others often leads you deeper and deeper into a state of confusion.

The clarity you seek when presented with a complex series of variables is best attained in the realms that transcend mind. Here one does not feel compelled to take any action one way or the other.

When there is a sense of urgency and a compulsion to choose from a given set of options, recognize those conditions as your cue to retreat into the stillness within and to *do* nothing. For the sense of urgency is rooted in a fear of choosing incorrectly. And those are not conditions in which you would wish to make choices of any kind.

The answers you seek do not come from your logical mind. They are sourced when you recognize the wisdom in defying logic. They are realized when you understand that there is no need to reach out for guidance from others. They are made manifest when you risk trusting that you hold the answers—all of them.

To break the patterns of dependency upon the influence of others it is necessary to understand that the answers themselves do not matter at all. The act of seeking those answers is merely an exercise you have devised in order to guide yourself to the path that leads within. Ultimately, the life altering choices you have created to confound yourself fade into obscurity, along with the very crossroads that prompted them. And you emerge in a place of knowingness that the questions—and the answers—are unimportant. They are simply vehicles that deliver you to a place of unconditional trust in your own ability to derive a sense of inner directedness in *any* circumstances. The dilemma that may be at hand merely illustrates the point.

Ultimately, you come to realize that there are no incorrect answers. Choices you have made, which have produced disappointing results, are your opportunity to recognize the conditions in which those choices were made. Choices made under conditions of uncertainty, or fear of choosing wrongly, set up the parameters for the thwarting of one's efforts and the undermining of the result that had been hoped for.

Choices which represent the guidance of *angels* or *psychics* or any of the limitless number of possible external perspectives that are available to you merely foster dependency and undermine the entire point of the exercise. For "the answer" is not the answer. It is the Source of that answer that is being sought. It is irrelevant to your purpose in coming into form what friends or seers or departed loved ones may think you should do in a given circumstance. What you hoped to find was the sense of Presence where The Source of all answers was unquestionable—and to know it is within you.

There will be moments of sublime connectedness in the higher stages of the process of your unfoldment where that knowingness is at hand. You will no longer be *the seeker* in those moments— for there is nothing to be sought. And the feeling of awareness that holds the answers to all possible questions will permeate your being. The fullness of that state, which is experienced in increments, will be realized by many of you. For the process of that awakening, which might have taken untold lifetimes to complete, has been accelerated under the transformational conditions of these times.

The opportunity posed by the profound dilemmas that present themselves is to begin to recognize the symbolic significance of those circumstances. And at the same time, it is the opportunity to source within your own being the experiential evidence that will help you transcend those illusions. You will be tested again and again, as part of the process of liberating yourself from the self-imposed prison of separation. For the key to that elusive freedom lies not in the hands of others who may or may not know the way, but rather upon the cliffs of your own uncertainty. You have led yourself out to the edge of that precipice on purpose. From there, the only step forward is to jump.

chapter thirty-five

Awakening to the realization that this is not
the same world you were born in.
Facing radical global change without fear.

Distance yourself for a moment from the mundane concerns of your day-to-day existence and allow yourself to become aware of the subtleties of your sensory surroundings. You will note that your physical senses have become keenly attuned to the vibrational changes you have undergone and that they are delivering to you a highly augmented variation on the kinds of sensory information you were able to perceive previously.

As you approach the heightened stages of the ascension process you will become alert to the acute levels of sensitivity you are able to bring to your experience of physicality. Suddenly, a flower is no longer just a flower; it is a multisensory journey that guides you deeply into the arena of fragrance. Your capacity for opening to heightened sensory experience marks the beginning of a shift in awareness of how you perceive the world around you. And you will begin to notice profound differences in your understanding of what is *real*.

The characteristics of your physical world take on an *otherworldly* quality as you find yourself probing the visions before you for details you had never noticed before. Colors take on levels of intensity you have never before experienced. You are struck by the vividness of the experience of vision and begin to wonder whether you're still in the same world. You realize that in many respects, you are not.

Under normal circumstances these changes occur so gradually, spread out over so much time, that it's difficult to make a correlation between the subtleties of change as layers of reality merge and become one. Now, under the radically augmented levels of the energies that surround you, these shifts are taking place within your moment-to-moment awareness. And you will come to find it quite fascinating to realize that virtually nothing in your physical reality has remained the same. The clues will elude you, initially. But there will be little question as you relinquish your instinctive need to control your reality and resist the recognition of these changes, that you are, quite literally, somewhere else now.

Initially, your attention will be captured by the systemic breakdown of many of the societal structures that gave definition to your world. And those of you who are able to view these inevitable changes without giving in to the instinctive reaction of fear that will consume many in your world, will be able to float within the embrace of the energies and allow yourselves to be carried to higher ground.

The key to riding out the turbulence that may well manifest at the height of the vibrational shifts to come, will be in your willingness to surrender totally to the process, fully aware that you may not yet understand what is, in fact, happening. The changes will be so profound and so far reaching that you will be challenged to maintain your mental and emotional equilibrium. Yet, when confronted by the reality of what your physical senses show you, you have the opportunity to let go of the need to remain "in control" and resign yourself to the fact that you have signed on for the adventure of a lifetime.

You, in fact, have little choice in this regard. For you have come too far in your awareness of the intensity of these structural changes to retreat into the illusion you have taken for granted all your life. The fluidity of the momentum that holds you in its grasp is the only aspect of the process that you can anticipate with any certainty. And this unprecedented level of change will continue throughout what remains of this physical lifetime and well into the next. For it will take quite some time for the dimensional shift to stabilize and for the reality in which you find yourself to once again be in a world where life could be considered predictable.

The hallmark of these extraordinary times, in terms of your physical awareness, is the extremes of uncertainty that characterize virtually everything. Your so-called "science" will be hard pressed to come up with explanations for the phenomena that will become a fact of life in the times soon to come. And a world structured around the provable will crumble in the wake of events and evidence that do not fit into your linear understandings of reality.

The phenomena that will manifest do not stand as evidence of the fallacies of your understandings, but rather as an indication that it is time to expand them. The rules that defined your linear reality still stand as a structure that delineates accurately what *was* true of your world. But that is not the world in which you find yourself now. That world is relegated to a place in the time/space continuum where your awareness is no longer present. For you have ascended. And you are no longer there.

The reality that appears to your physical senses is a similar place, in many respects, to the one in which you have spent much, if not most, of your life. Yet the surface characteristics are where the similarities end. For the entire dynamic in the manifestation of your reality in this "here and now" is a different process entirely. And even though you may be interacting with the same cast of characters and be living under the same roof, or so it would seem, this stage set is for a different kind of drama.

Those of you with the presence of mind to regard with fascination the changes within your very own physical senses, will have the tools in hand to adapt easily to the fact that you are a very different *you* living within the context of your own identity. You will find that you have, suddenly and without explanation, transcended physical limitations that you had assumed were permanent characteristics of your own self-definition. Now, you will discover that you are able where once you were not. Now, you have sensory perceptions that you have never before experienced. Now, so-called miracles become commonplace occurrences—not only for you—but for everyone.

The awakening process has accelerated to the point that those who openly acknowledge awareness of the changes are more numerous than not. And even in social strata where you would not expect to find openness to such concepts, there is openly acknowledged acceptance of the fact that everything seems to be changing. People everywhere are shifting their awareness inward and are reaching beyond the mundane evidences of a physical reality for a spiritual foundation on which to build their understanding of what is so.

The concepts and understandings vary in sophistication, yet the inner awareness is universal. How one chooses to come to grips with what has and continues to transpire will separate you from your fellow human beings—or draw you together as One. Those who choose to fight the reality of what is at hand will create painful and challenging obstacles to the lives they would wish to be living. Those who are able to transcend the differences and the sense of *separation* that once defined your world will be rewarded with a vantage point from which all is possible.

You can expect to be able to share your own experience of these times more openly now. And those of you, who felt inhibited by what was once the consensus overview, will begin to emerge with a sense that it is safe to talk about how you really feel and what is really happening in your life. For people everywhere are having these experiences. You need not continue to consider yourself an oddity and bury the reality of your experiences in the closets of your fears. For now the phenomena characterizing the heightened stages of transformation are there for all to behold.

Many of you have residual fears from other realities and other time frames where your spiritual perceptions were met with the horrors of the atrocities that color so many of your personal histories. These ones now have the opportunity to confront the depths of those fears and to emerge into the bright, new dawn of these times, unencumbered. For the fear based systems that exercised the unrelenting tyranny that has characterized your world will soon crumble in the wake of an awareness that invalidates all man-made systems of discrimination.

You who emerge awestruck by the rapture you may be feeling are to be reassured that these extraordinary sensations of joy, simply of being alive, are to be expected and are a natural part of the human condition at the levels you have just begun to embody. Resist the temptation to suspect that there is something *wrong* with you when you begin to have these wondrous sensations and perceptions. For experiences that once may have been reserved for the spiritually elite amongst you are now available to you all. Your openness to the possibility of experiencing yourself as limitless in this lifetime sets the stage for the manifestation of that level of experience.

You will discover that you will draw to you the very guidance needed to help you to reach the levels of connectedness that you have longed to embrace. Your own resistance to the possibility of these experiences dictates the levels at which you will be able to perceive yourself. And you will be led systematically in the direction of ultimate surrender to the truth of your Oneness with All Creation—no matter how many lifetimes it takes.

Many of you are right on the brink of that level of awareness. And you will join a legion of fully awakened beings in your acknowledgment of that Oneness. For by definition, once fully present in that awareness, you know that you are not alone. Those of you who now ride the crest of the wave that carries you ever closer to that breakthrough will serve as teachers—and ultimately as spirit guides—for the masses that will follow in your footsteps in these times. You will have made the journey ahead of the rest, in order that you would be equipped to reach out and take another by the hand in the times to come.

There is no relative merit or lack thereof in having awakened when indeed you do. It is simply a choice you have exercised at a higher level, which you are implementing now. Your ability to complete your journey into humanness with your humility intact will determine the levels at which you will emerge once again into physicality. Some of you will choose to reinforce your grasp of this momentous awakening by providing yourself with multiple levels of this experience. Do not assume that once your eyes are truly open, the story has ended. You will make this journey again and again. And ultimately, you will know yourself so fully and completely as Oneness that you will no longer need or wish to make the journey.

Chances are, you have been here before. Quite possibly, you have already discovered, to your awestruck amazement, the very truths that take your breath away in this moment. For in truth, there *is* no time. And you are completing this experience of ascension on an infinite number of levels simultaneously. The thrill of the moment of awakening is the experience you hoped to give yourself within the context of form. And it is a moment that you will experience exponentially at all levels of your beingness, many many times.

There is no way you can fail at this. Know that. For, there is no such thing as success or failure on the path to Oneness. There is simply the option of infinite possibilities to experience along the way. That is what keeps it interesting, and what keeps you coming back for more.

chapter thirty-six

Being Nowhere, Nothing, No-one—here—Now.

Where have you been going all this time? Where is this search leading you? And where are you right now? The answer to all these questions is very simple: nowhere. The direction in which you presumed yourself to be headed for much of this lifetime will not lead you where you now wish to go. So that path was leading nowhere. The quest for the enlightenment that has remained ever elusive leads you to the same destination, for there is nowhere for you to be beyond where you are right now. So long as you believe that there is a destination just past the horizon, where you are is nowhere.

Your transference of your ambition from the arena of the material to the realm of the spiritual changes nothing. You remain in an unrelenting quest for that which you perceive yourself to be without. So long as you are neither here nor there, you are nowhere. You are in a netherworld of striving—a state that invalidates the reality of where you are in deference to where you believe you are not. When, in fact, *Nowhere* is where you most fervently wish to be—and where you have been all along.

The destination toward which you assume you are traveling in your spiritual quest is not a destination at all. For a destination, by definition, is somewhere other than where you are. And where you are is all there is and ever can be—which is *Nowhere*. All that can be changed is your perception of that blessed state. So long as you perceive yourself to be short of the mark, you will experience discontentment, regardless of how far you believe yourself to have journeyed. When you are able to embrace the "here and now" moment as a joyous statement of your beingness, regardless of where you perceive yourself to be, you will have arrived. For there *Is* nowhere "to Be." Once there, One simply Is. One is everywhere. Which, by definition, is *Nowhere*.

This "now" moment in which you find yourself is a statement of perfection you have made to the universe. It is the perfect answer to the parameters you have set up. It is the perfect reflection of your attitudes, your beliefs, your understandings, and your conscious, physical manipulations of the illusion you believe to be your life. This is where you most wish to be. This very moment. Right now. This is the culmination of all that has gone before. And it is here to deliver unto you a treasure, provided that you are willing to receive it. Yet, as long as you deny the perfection in this "now" moment and the circumstances with which it has gifted you, you will be destined to continue to wander, and to search, and to strive, and to yearn for something that will always remain just out of reach.

The opportunity in this "now" moment is to stop all of this activity—and simply Be still. For it is in the stillness that you will, ultimately, discover what has been there all this time—*Nothing*. Nothing at all. No great bright lights. No profound "cosmic" ideas. No *other* to which you can connect in order to be *complete*. No sense of attainment. No overwhelming feelings of self-worth. All these things are trappings of a linear illusion you will have left behind when you venture forth into what is truly *reality*.

In the stillness there Is—*Nothing*. No-thing to "have." For in order to experience "having," it is necessary to have known "not having," a sense that something is missing. In a state of perfection, nothing can be missing. So there can only Be—*Everything*. Where there is *Everything*, there can be nothing more. And that state is only possible when there is *Nothing*—nothing more to want. For in that No-thing-ness, All That Is—is present.

And who will *you* be when you find yourself engulfed in that infinite stillness? Will you be who you are right now? Will you be someone else—some higher, smarter, more polished version of the one you think is *you*? No, on both counts. The one who emerges in Self-perception in the infinite Stillness is—*No-one*. For, by definition, *you* cannot be in the infinite Stillness. Nothing can be there. No-one can be there. And yet, in the depths of quietude you will touch upon, you will experience *awareness*. And at the same time you will know that there is nothing "there" to be aware *of*.

Who is it that is experiencing that awareness? It cannot be *you* because *you* cannot be there. The only possibility? *No-one*. That is ultimately who you will discover yourself to Be. For in order to be "someone," *that which you are*, there would have to be *that which you are not*. Neither can be in the infinite Stillness, for nothing can be there. Therefore, in that state of blessed *awareness*, you can only Be *No-one*. And at the same time, your *awareness* is All That Is there. In the Stillness, you will understand yourself to Be—That.

When you step out of the illusion, even for a fleeting moment, and relinquish your grasp on your so-called reality, there is the ever-present possibility that you may lose yourself in a reality that knows neither future nor past. For in that state of awareness, there can only be Now. And that state of Now-ness Is All That Is—the ever-present, present tense you embody, in reality.

In the illusion, you have a past. And in your mind, you are forever reaching for, and longing for, and living in—the future that never seems to come. In the Stillness, you experience that all pervading Now-ness and recognize it as All That Is. You experience your *awareness* as ever-present, there in the eternal *Now*. And you understand your *awareness* to Be that Now-ness—a sense of presence melded in Oneness with the eternal All That Is.

It is with that sense of presence, that sense of Self-awareness, that you may choose to revisit, and to experience the illusion you consider to be your life. You may choose to experience that sense of sublime detachment—that Isness which you tasted fleetingly in the Stillness—and to experience the "here and now" as All That Is. For within the polarity of all that the illusion Is, and in the polarity of all that it Is not, is the full spectrum of Isness that is no more or less than All That Is. The illusion is everywhere—and *Nowhere*. It is everything—and *Nothing*. It is You—the real You who has let go of the trappings of identity and knows itself to be *No-one*, here in the infinite foreverness of *Now*.

chapter thirty-seven

The significance of conflict resolution without compromise.
The vibrational foundation for peace and harmony,
interpersonally and globally.

Massive changes are taking place throughout your reality in the present time frame. And the fundamental composition of all you consider to be *real* is being restructured in order to resonate harmoniously with the characteristics of the higher vibrational realities. In the process, much that might have seemed stable will suddenly be thrust into upheaval and discord. And you will most certainly begin to wonder what, indeed, is going on.

The systems on which your society is based will, most likely, experience a fundamental breakdown as they are built on a foundation of diminished vibration that cannot sustain itself under conditions that continue to accelerate. The collective consciousness, which is no less than the sum of its parts, brings to the present moment a radically altered orientation, and will be unwilling to continue to condone the oppressive and suppressive conditions to which you all are subject.

The transformation taking place within each of you is reflected in the collective of which you are an energetic part. And the old structures, which represent outmoded ways of human interaction, will begin to crumble unilaterally in the wake of the universal shift in human consciousness now taking place. There is simply not the necessary proportion of thought forms present to sustain what no longer serves you.

You can apply this principle to virtually every aspect of your reality. And you will be astounded at the extent of the shift in mass consciousness to come. People everywhere have begun the process of waking-up to a heightened level of awareness. And even though most are still culturally conditioned to suppress such perceptions out of fear of being judged or ostracized, energy is stirring within the depths of each of you stimulating you to shed the habitual patterns that have imprisoned you. The feelings of unrest that have begun to stir throughout the collective consciousness will begin to play out and act as a catalyst for ousting any construct that serves to restrict personal freedom.

Humanity as a whole has begun to question the basis for such repression. And the core issues on which those regimes are based will be found to lack relevance in terms of how the population at large perceives itself. Governments will rise and fall. Economies will crumble. Spiritual super-structures will wither. The power bases on which your world depends will find themselves depleted of resources, and will be forced to release their grasp on the life force of the collective. And the doors will open to a new kind of thinking that will serve to empower rather than suppress the collective will of all people.

The conditions within your world during such a transformational shift will appear frightening to those whose orientation is rooted in the fear based need to resist change. Those who recognize the unrelenting momentum that continues to build can assist in the process by allowing the changes that are transpiring so naturally, to do so on a personal level. Retaining a death grip on the past will only stimulate the energies necessary to assist you in releasing all that is holding you back from flowing with the momentum of change. And in some cases, the upheaval will be so drastic as to force one to question the fundamental essence of life itself, and one's place in a world where nothing remains certain. This is as it must be. For to truly rise to the fullness of who you are to become, one must release the shackles of all that would attempt to restrict you. You are a fully empowered, ascended being, traversing a shifting landscape in the illusion you perceive as your reality. These changes are not happening *to* you—but rather, have been initiated *by* you vibrationally. And your awareness of the dynamics of change that is all around you will ease the experience for you and for all who travel by your side. For your life circumstances are a reflection of the ease or resistance with which you meet the momentum of change. And many will be looking to you to set the pace for their own assimilation of these shifts in consciousness.

It is no accident that you have stepped forward in your own awareness and have recognized the collective falsehood reflected by the archaic conditions you are now transcending. You have selected this particular experience as a highlight of your journey into physicality in this lifetime. And your very essence demands that you shrug off any efforts to constrict you. The opportunity is to recognize the possibility to achieve these shifts without entering into confrontation and conflict.

As you meet with episodes that defy your objectives and jeopardize the stability of your situation, you have the opportunity to recognize and to honor another being who is simply reflecting his own truth, even if it means altering your expectations. Struggling to cling to your concept of how it should be will only escalate the discordant energy of these conflicts. Your willingness to allow circumstances to seek levels of natural resolution will enhance your ability to manifest results that will serve the best interests of all concerned.

You may not be able to anticipate the direction in which you really *are* headed, if you struggle to remain attached to acting upon obsolete agreements. The shifts in priority will be sudden and dramatic. And people can be expected to do a radical reversal in direction under these conditions, regardless of what may or may not have been said previously.

It is pointless to attempt to force another being to honor the terms of an agreement that no longer rings true for them. Far better to acknowledge to yourself the validity in another's perspective—from *their* standpoint—and to work together toward levels of resolution that are mutually empowering and clear the way for higher choices that may not have been anticipated. When you look back upon some of these volatile episodes, you will appreciate, in retrospect, the wisdom in letting go of what seemed certain, in preparation for creating the space for the highest possible outcome to manifest for all concerned.

Many of the conflicts you are now and will continue to be encountering are what could be considered *karmic* in nature. And it is possible that certain explosive interactions are direct reflections of conflict resolution taking place in other levels of reality. When you encounter extreme levels of out-of-character reaction in certain individuals with whom you have shared history in this lifetime, do not discount the possibility that what you have encountered are the vibrational repercussions of interactions taking place between other aspects of each of you. It is easy to tap into those energies and to play out dramas here that parallel ones that may be taking place in other relationships you share with this being in other realities.

In trying to resolve instances of seemingly unwarranted discord with certain individuals, consider that what you have encountered is no more and no less than *energy*. And it could well be energy that has escalated and has manifested in your energy field by virtue of parallel categories of interaction into which each of you has been drawn. As the energy seeks resolution, it carries over into your present reality and affects how you interact with certain individuals, regardless of what has actually been said of done. You can serve the highest interests of all concerned when you resist the inclination to lash out and give someone "what he's asking for." The provocation may well be based in a reality beyond your conscious awareness, and is simply triggering parallel emotions in this "here and now."

You have come to a place of resolution with many of the major players in your life. And you will begin to recognize the inclination to bring certain relationships to completion on a multitude of levels. You will begin to sense that the foundation that served as the basis for certain relationships has shifted now. And while you continue to share a sense of history and familiarity with these beings, you sense that deep beneath the surface of that level of connection, the bond feels like it is no longer on solid ground.

It is likely that one of you has chosen to deviate from a path you have shared for a time. And energy that once seemed to flow effortlessly between you now feels strained. You may each choose to go through the motions of maintaining such a relationship. But, inevitably, you will find that you each choose to let go of the ties that once bound you naturally into an alliance that now no longer nourishes either of you.

In these times, the dynamics of your reality are shifting far too quickly to expect anything to remain the same for any period of time. In your choice to honor your own truth in this "now" moment with regard to certain relationships, know that your feelings do not invalidate the relevance of what once was shared. That was then. This is now. And the opportunity has been provided to release, with the energy of compassion and loving kindness, any ties that may seek to keep you bound in situations that no longer feel comfortable. Know that you are exercising the highest choice in so doing, and declining the invitation of compromise in the name of "peace and harmony." For peace and harmony cannot truly be achieved when one has relinquished their own inner truth.

Peace and harmony, when it is truly sustainable, must be built on a foundation that resonates fully with all concerned. Much manipulation and attempts to exercise control over the energy of conflict has presented itself for resolution in the name of "peace and harmony." But rarely is that end truly in the hearts of those who meet chin to chin at the negotiating table. For the *energy* of peace and harmony does not easily fit into the structure of *compromise*.

Peace and harmony must be an end that is truly heartfelt in order for it to be achieved. Without a vibrational foundation built on sincere sentiments of well-being for the other party, efforts that go through the motions of *compromise* are doomed to failure.

When one is totally honest with oneself as to what one's stance truly is, there is no real benefit to anyone to attempt to construct a scenario that answers those objectives in name only. For in so doing, one merely prolongs the inevitable resurgence of discord between the factions in question. The history of your reality is a testimonial to this truth. And your differing vantage points have served to polarize you as a race of beings into warring factions bent upon vengeance and other similar expressions of ego.

The exercise of using might to thwart the collective will of another group of beings is a way that you, as the human race, have reinforced the energy of *separation* throughout your history. That very inclination is the characteristic that has obstructed your efforts toward unification as a race of beings and has prevented the manifestation of the best interests of all humankind.

You may ask then, what are you to do when confronted with the opposing viewpoints of another being or an expression of collective will. You begin *not* with the scrutiny of the other party's motives, but with your own. You begin by digging honestly beneath the surface of the stance you've taken and exploring the real basis for your *own* position. Chances are, if you approach this exercise in full honesty with yourself, you will recognize a fortress built on a foundation of ego—an expression of will rooted in the fear of suppression by the will and ego of another. This is hardly the recipe for Oneness—much less for the *world peace* to which you all pay much lip service.

The concept of Oneness as a collective of humanity cannot begin to be realized without a thorough analysis of the hearts of all who comprise it. Those who put the full force of their will behind the suppression of the best interests of another serve only to reinforce the polarity that exists between you. In so doing, you widen the rift that keeps all of humankind in a state of separation from each other and from the unification in Oneness toward which all Creation now strives. In continuing to act out the habitual patterns that reinforce your "might makes right" mind-set, you thwart the very momentum toward which you strive.

You cannot hope to achieve "peace and harmony" in the collective without applying the true essence of that concept in your interpersonal relationships on an individual basis. In scrutinizing your own position on a given issue, you are able to recognize the areas in which you are directed, by the motivations of ego, to assert your will over that of another. When you take a closer look, a natural solution ultimately presents itself that allows both parties to honor the expression of their true essence, without causing injury or harm to anyone. That optimum solution is the one that must be sought on all levels, in order that the vibrational pitfall of *compromise* be circumvented and true peace be achieved.

The answers you seek in your personal lives are no different than those you seek in your neighborhoods, your countries and in your global interactions. All must be addressed in terms of *energy* in order for a lasting solution to be realized. For energy that is thwarted rather than transformed will only resurface with renewed force, in another form, regardless of how carefully you have crafted the terms of your half-hearted contractual agreements.

Stop looking for the self-serving motives of the other side and begin looking at the self-serving motives that underlie your *own* actions. That is the basis for the true harmony you all yearn for at the deepest level. For your world situation is no more than a magnified reflection of the energy of the collective consciousness. You are a part of that group dynamic. And the only way to shift the worldview is to shift the thrust of what you project upon it. Each of you. One conflict at a time.

By shifting the energy you project onto even one seemingly inconsequential encounter, you shift the vibration you project onto the macrocosm of your world. If each of you did that, in every instance where your own personal will butts heads with that of another, you would have the world peace—and ultimately the Oneness—that each of you cries for throughout all Creation.

chapter thirty-eight

Integrating the fragmented aspects of your identity
through the path of emotion.
Poignant episodes with key players
as a catalyst for wholeness.

Vistas of new awareness will begin to unfold before you, as
you begin to assimilate the higher frequencies and release your
grasp on a reality you believed was carved in stone. Nothing is so
permanent as that—not in true reality. The illusion you have
created and convinced yourself was real has permanence, a
fundamental sense of urgency, and an impetus to action that
becomes a race against time that you may choose to play out in
any of a number of arenas. Yet now you have chosen to expand
your perspective and to consider whether or not you truly wish
to continue to explore those realms, or whether it is indeed time
to move into the realm of the timeless and to experience what is
really there, from the perspective of physicality.

These words may strike you as nonsense, at first. And then as
you begin to examine the priorities, the commitments, and all the
details to which you have attached importance, you will, in one
shining moment, recognize the absurdity in all of it. And in that
recognition, you will have prepared the way to step forth and to

experience what remains of your life from a different kind of vantage point. For you will have begun to harmonize, vibrationally, with higher aspects of your own being. And without being fully conscious of what is happening, at first, you will be experiencing life through different eyes.

The recognition of the shift is gradual. And the subtleties of these shifts may elude you for some time, as you continue to bounce in and out of varying levels of awareness. But then your circumstances seem to quiet down, to stabilize, and you reach a state of beingness where you know that you are no longer who you were. Even though you reside in the same skin and the trappings of your identity are recognizable, it is not the same.

The recognition of what has happened will be assimilated after the fact, as you adjust to the higher frequencies that now surround you. Things happen more quickly now. You reach a place of clarity with your objectives and where you wish to focus your energies. And you find that you are virtually surrounded by kindred beings whose life purpose seems perfectly aligned to your own. Life flows easily from this point forth. And even though there certainly will be moments of uncertainty and of conflict, the resolution of these energies takes place in a way that seems natural. The proverbial "path of least resistance" appears before you at every turn, and taking it, instinctively, leads you in the direction of increasingly deeper levels of satisfaction with what you perceive to be *your life.*

Looking back, you will start to wonder why it all seemed so complicated, and frustrating, and oppressive, when now it is all so different. And you will realize that *you* are not the same *you.* You will have ventured forth unto another level of experience, and will have merged with multiple layers of awareness, all of which consider themselves to be *you.* Now, the vantage point from which you perceive this "now" moment is the result of a composite vision. And it draws upon a multifaceted archive of life experience that would have reaped the result of exploring every possible variation on the theme you believe is *your life.*

The other beings you encounter in your day-to-day interactions are not necessarily at the same place you are. For, all are not resonating at the same frequency, simply by virtue of the fact that they are "here" in your presence. You may encounter a *piece* of composite essence that represents the identity of a being who is familiar to you, yet the reactions of that being may seem inappropriate to the nature of the history you've shared. It will be important to condition yourself to exercise tolerance with regard to such encounters, and to know that much the same way as you have made major shifts in your own awareness, so too have others, though not necessarily to degrees that parallel your own.

You may find you are interacting with a fragment of the essence of a particular individual, and do not experience the same sense of *connection* as you may once have felt. Do not judge. Simply allow the interactions to transpire and the energies to stabilize. For, it is likely that in the heightened stages of this process, you will act as catalysts for each other, to bring to ultimate resolution the issues that a given aspect of one or the other's identity is bringing into full focus. Allow the energy to express as it will. Allow the dust to settle. And be willing to witness the emergence of an ascended version of another being by virtue of the encounter.

You can anticipate cataclysmic clashes with certain beings, as each is assisting the other in what can only be described as a birthing process. By triggering the release of energies that either of you may have carried forth from another aspect of reality, you take each other by the hand, vibrationally, as each merges with heightened aspects of his own beingness. It is in some of the most caustic of these encounters—scenes you would have thought you were now incapable of acting out—that you are able to assist each other in releasing the threads that have kept you entangled in habitual *karmic* interactions.

In shrugging off some of these vibrational constraints that most of you have carried at some level of your awareness, you clear the way for the integration of these fragmented pieces of your own essence. For once the repressed *charge* is released, the vibrational remnants of the resentments, and the hurts, and the outrage experienced at each other's hand is permitted to surface at last. There, blatantly before you, is the reality of the undercurrent that has prevented a truly unconditional bond of loving trust to be experienced between you. And there, before the witness of your own multidimensional consciousness, is a major missing piece of your very own essence, that you were not able or willing to acknowledge.

The most poignant episodes of emotion are likely to be triggered by beings who you considered to be your closest allies in this lifetime. For rarely are roles played from one perspective alone. The major players in your script have been there for you, and you for them, in the full spectrum of roles throughout your history. You have been cherished lovers—and detested enemies. You have run in the fields of life together as children. You have been parents to each other more times than you could possibly count. And you have assisted in birthing each other's awareness, at each level of your unfoldment, with every emotionally charged interaction, all this time.

Now, as your own transformational process is reaching a crescendo, you can anticipate being drawn into circumstances where aspects of your multidimensional consciousness will be provoked, through the path of emotion, into rising to the surface. The actual cause of the explosive encounter is not important. And it is irrelevant as to who is "wrong" and who is "right." For "right" is merely a matter of perspective. And each, in such a moment, is myopically wedded to his own. But the essence of the encounter, as a catalyst of repressed vibration, is what you will be led to trigger within the depths of each of you. And in so doing, each will be assisted in bonding in wholeness with aspects of your own being that had been *cast out* by virtue of fear, or shame, or outrage, or any number of profound emotions, that at one time or another, you were simply not able to deal with.

At this stage in your process, everything must rise to the surface to be scrutinized and "owned." Nothing remains buried. And your key players are right there for you—right on cue—to serve you by doing whatever it takes for you to release the feelings you've kept best hidden from yourself. You can choose to recoil from the behaviors some of these players may choose to exhibit in their star performance with you. Yet you will be able to recognize the symbolism in the dynamics that have transpired between you. And ultimately, you will arrive at a place of great love for these beings. Not in spite of the episode—but *because* of it. For each will have acted upon his own truth. And in so doing, each will have helped his partner/lover/enemy/friend/child/parent/Self to witness and embrace his own truth.

This is a vital and necessary part of the path to wholeness. And those of you who have deluded yourselves into thinking that now that you have begun seeing things from a higher perspective, everything would be clear sailing, will be caught off guard by the kinds of interaction you would least expect with beings that you cherish the most. You have not faltered by giving vent to the fullness of your feelings in these moments. But rather, you would have taken a major step forward in allowing the fullness of your being—all the parts of you that have been in hiding so long—to come forth and be embraced into the multidimensional composite of who you really are.

The heights and the depths of feeling are to be expected when one comes to the fullness of the process of the unification of individual identity. For you cannot hope to ascend into the infinitely more complex arena of multidimensional awareness without every last one of the faces of *this* identity intact.

So by all means, delight in the exultation that is a hallmark of this heightened stage of your journey, when those blessed moments arise. And at the same time, know that the profound moments of discord that must also arise are equally blessed. For it is not a one-dimensional being who journeys within you toward Oneness with all Creation. It is the full spectrum of your humanness—your authentic beingness in all its glory—that is navigating this journey. *You* are simply a passenger—a pinpoint of awareness—along for the ride on a voyage that has begun to be most fascinating, indeed.

chapter thirty-nine

Finding God.

Since the very beginning of your self-awareness as an incarnate being, you have probed your world for clues to the meaning of your existence. You have looked in every conceivable crevice and pondered the vastness of the infinite cosmos. You have scrutinized the spiritual wisdom that was forthcoming from those who believed themselves to be knowledgeable about such matters. And you followed their directions religiously, in lifetime after lifetime, hoping that somehow you would emerge, at the end of your days with *the answer*.

Yet regardless of the cultural circumstances in which you found yourself, the questions led only to more questions. The deeper your explorations led you, and the more profound your under-standings, there emerged deeper, more profound questions from the innermost recesses of your insatiable mind. Ultimately, your questions have led you to this place and to this moment. And even though you can sense that you have enacted this script before, there is a deeper knowingness that this time it is different.

At last, it seems you have ventured to a state of beingness where you have begun to tire of the questions. You have become bored with the entire process of skirting the perimeter of what you have been seeking from the beginning. For instinctively, you know that the answers are not "out-there" at all. Nor are they within the realm of mind. This *knowingness* that is yearned for at the very deepest level will not be understood. Not even after a thousand more lifetimes of "conscious," spiritual pursuit. For one cannot attain the unattainable. One cannot hope to fathom the incomprehensible. One cannot *arrive* at a destination from which one has never departed. One can simply know oneself to be *here*—Now.

Here you will not find the externalized "God" who you hope awaits you, somewhere beyond this place. Here you will not find the answers to the infinite philosophical questions with which you have danced through time immemorial. Here you will not find the wisdom that you fear will continue to elude you. Not as long as you continue to search for it. Here you can only hope to find yourself. And in so doing, perhaps you will experience an exquisite moment of surrender, and then another. And perhaps, in the eternal moment of "Now," you will know that you Are what you were seeking all along. You will know this. Not because you have finally amassed a sufficient body of knowledge and understanding. But simply because You *Are* This—fully present in your *experience* of it. The experience of Divine connectedness. The taste of that essence. That's it.

You have come to the center of the storm now. You know this, for you have been here in this place before. And even though you have slid past the gateway to all you yearned for, over and over again, you've also ventured to the sanctity of this haven when you least expected to. And by now it feels familiar, and comfortable—and safe.

And here you thought it would be the ultimate challenge. Enlightenment—a pretty big word. Finding God—an intimidating concept. Only because you believed that it was. In truth, it's all so simple. And your bondage to the illusion that it was otherwise is what has kept you coming back, lifetime after lifetime, on the chance that *this time* you'd "get it right." This time you'd solve the riddle. This time you'd actually encounter God. And you'd know the truth, once and for all. And this time—you do.

chapter forty

The quickening.
Emerging in awareness as the full composite
of your "memories" of life experience.
Bridging two worlds at the interdimensional threshold.

M any who read these words will feel a reluctance to step into
uncharted territory, when the reality of what is transpiring becomes obvious. And after all the work has been done and
the destination is in view, it is easy suddenly to question all of it.
For it is one thing to have intellectually grasped the concepts that
have been presented and to have gone through the motions of
putting them into practice. It is quite another thing to begin to
embody the heightened energies and to experience the quickening
that accompanies it.

The new sensations of heightened vibration can be alarming,
at first, if one is unprepared to anticipate the feelings that accompany the advanced stages of the transformation process. As the interdimensional threshold is approached, one can expect to experience
an otherworldly sense of detachment from the mundane aspects
of one's life script. And at the same time, a sense of deep contentment
that is not cause related permeates one's consciousness.

One has the sense of virtually floating over the day-to-day details of one's life without being drawn into feeling invested in the outcome of these scenarios. And well one need not be. For the pages are turning so quickly at this stage of your journey, that outcomes will not actually be experienced in the way one might anticipate them under *normal* conditions. "The laws of cause and effect" have been radically rewritten at this point in the process. And at times, what manifests as one's reality is far from what would have been expected.

There is no rhyme or reason to some of what will transpire— at least, not from the perspective of linear logic. As the details of resolution play out for each of you, a barrage of parallel experiences may manifest, one after another, as if to underscore a particular life lesson that must be mastered. You can anticipate experiencing a *sequence* of seemingly unwarranted provocations that gives the impression of being virtually under siege. What is being tested at this stage is *if* and *how* you react. And it is not unusual to find oneself backsliding into defensiveness and reactions that reflect an investment in having to be "right."

Until the pattern is recognized, one can continue in such a cycle for what appears to be an agonizingly long time. Then, abruptly, the energy shifts once more and the barrage of adversity is no longer there. And you will have achieved the state where you are present in your own circumstances, with great indifference, as a *witness*. You find yourself watching your circumstances unfold and observing yourself as you float effortlessly through turbulence, untouched by the emotional charge that might once have accompanied it.

Patterns are initiated in one reality and brought to fruition in another, at this stage of your journey. So, it is pointless to expect particular results to manifest, when an entirely different set of variables has been added to the equation. The outcome, were one to have stood still and not shifted realities, may well have been the triumphant result of careful planning, hard work, and brilliant strategy. Yet under the conditions of heightened vibration, those variables may well fall short of the mark. And it is likely to become confused and discouraged when everything, seemingly, starts "going wrong."

It is easy to start blaming others, or the stars, or any of a number of plausible causes for a string of circumstances that is so adverse it almost appears comical. Your situations present themselves for resolution, sequentially, in escalating vibrational realities, where your frequency continues to register at the low end of the scale. Your ability to nonreact to these irritants helps you to stabilize your energies quickly and not contribute to the conditions that create adversity.

Your "buttons" will be pushed in every way imaginable during this period of transition between dimensions. And your ability to resist taking these episodes at face value will go far toward easing your passage through this unstable and unsettling stage of your experience. The blatant contradiction between the exalted states of energy assimilation and the uncanny streak of "bad luck" will seem absurd during the experience of it. In retrospect, you recognize the makings of a great story. And in the light of the new days about to dawn, these times of trial will fade into the haze of a distant dream.

The volatile times of your transformation process will progressively appear less vivid as you begin to distance yourself from the categories of interaction that have held you transfixed for much of the process. It will begin to seem incomprehensible to you that you felt compelled to react in certain ways and seemed to manifest such extremes of experience. Now, in a new light, similar circumstances can be viewed through the lens of tranquillity and barely produce a ripple upon the waters of your awareness. For the page will have turned. And the stabilizing effect of that shift will manifest circumstances where life, at last, flows easily.

That is the nature of the circumstances that will accompany you right to the very edge of the interdimensional threshold. The states of heightened contradiction—between your heartfelt connectedness with the momentum that propels you and at the same time the irritants that you continue to manifest—can be confusing, when caught in the heat of the moment. Yet as you distance yourself from these petty dramas, you can feel a palpable *lightening* of all that held you in its grasp. The release is sudden and dramatic. And, seemingly for no reason at all, you shift into a different octave of beingness. And you know, without having to be told, that something very significant indeed has happened.

At this point, you will no longer need to keep asking yourself whether all of it is just the product of an overactive imagination. You will have ceased wondering whether this journey into the outer reaches of your consciousness is real. You will know. It will be unquestionable. You will not need to ask yourself whether or not you have *ascended* yet. You will know. You will not be troubled that despite that sense of knowingness, you are still living your life. You are still present in your movie. And all the actors that have surrounded you continue to be there, right where you left them. The only thing that will have changed is "you" and the way you find yourself reacting to the kinds of lines they are programmed to deliver.

It is not as though you are in a different world. You will still experience awareness in the same world. But suddenly, you will have a heightened perception of it. You will experience sensations of accelerated energy. And others will begin to perceive and react to you in a very different way. For, you will not be broadcasting into the ethers the categories of energy that would have caused predictable experiences of adversity to manifest for you. Now others will not be prompted vibrationally to deliver those responses. And you will experience the sense of being present in two realities simultaneously.

This is, in fact, exactly what will have happened. For before you make the shift—physically—at the interdimensional threshold, your subtle bodies will have preceded you. Your *energies* will be fully present in the higher dimension, and at the same time, you will have retained your conscious awareness in this "here and now." The process of merging your energies with the higher octave of your beingness is a gradual one. And as your subtle bodies are assimilated into the energy field of that higher dimensional aspect of *you*, you can begin to sense the presence of that heightened perspective here—*as you*.

Suddenly you find yourself reacting to familiar situations in a dramatically different way. And it is as though someone else was looking out through your very own eyes at a totally familiar landscape. And the world shifts, quite suddenly, into a very pleasant place to be. You can expect to experience the stabilizing conditions of this interim stage of interdimensional ascension for some time to come. Some of you will retain physical awareness in this reality for the rest of this physical lifetime. And for those who remain "here," an exalted version of the experience of *life* can be anticipated.

For others, who are scheduled to merge fully and completely with the heightened aspects of your beingness—consciousness that experiences itself at the next dimensional level of reality—this transitional stage constitutes a vibrational foundation for the shifts to come. It is a refreshingly different plateau. A time to catch one's breath. And a time to feel fully the experience of embodying the exalted levels of energy that characterize the higher levels of awareness.

Prior to having made this dramatic vibrational shift, you will experience a sense of coming to completion with the interwoven themes that have characterized this lifetime. You will find that poignant life episodes, often long forgotten ones, leap suddenly to the forefront of your awareness. And you will have the experience of mentally reliving these old movies—but now from the vantage point of the overview. You will see the significance in the essence of the drama. And you will experience a sense of detachment from those circumstances and at the same time a sense of resolution of the theme underlying it.

You will have the sense of seeing your life literally passing before your eyes. Flashbacks will bring into vivid focus the agonies of various transformational periods in your personal history. And you will realize fully how very far you have come. You will wonder in seeming disbelief, how it possibly could have been *you* who acted in such a way, who made such choices, who embodied fully the state of separation from who you now know yourself to be. And yet, you know that it was *you* who starred in those dramas. A *you*, you are now able to embrace fully, without blame, without judgment, and without recrimination—a piece of your own Divine essence that was very lost, and now is a fully integrated aspect of your being.

You know you did these things—for you remember them. Or do you? Was it *you* who subjected yourself to that particular humiliation? Was it *you* who acted out that callous, insensitive role in any number of your worst nightmares? Was it *you* who succumbed to the temptations you vowed you had overcome, thinking no one would ever know the difference? Is it that same *you* who is remembering all of it now in excruciating detail? Or is it all some abstract aberration of your mind? How could "that person" be *you*? How, indeed.

The *how* is the entire point of this journey. For it is in the infinite, multifaceted aspects of *you* that such extremes of perception and behavior were possible. You planned it that way, in order to provide yourself the rich details of the experience you now have begun to review, and relive—and assume is *your life*. This composite of experience is housed within the context of your identity. And the memories are *yours*. But the choices were implemented by the infinite variations on the theme that you consider to be *you*. Now, as you have gathered up the fragments of your consciousness, you begin to appreciate the gift in some of the most adverse of these adventures. And you can appreciate the sense of balance offered by the more mundane episodes.

All of it fits into position and begins to sculpt the core essence of a being who now has recognized the gift in that experiential diversity. What you *did* does not negate who you *Are*. It defines it—and humanizes it. And it gives you the sense that what you *were* is a valid and valuable part of all that you now are not. For you could not now be reviewing, in rapt disbelief, some of these dramas, had you not given yourself the priceless gift of having tasted them.

You are the composite of all those aspects of self. The ones that committed the foulest acts are no less a part of *you* than the one who is now reading these words. And the one who sits with this book in hand is no less a part of the *you* who watches from afar, in joy, as you put it all together. That next higher increment of your selfhood will merge with your energy field in stages, as you enter fully into the heightened levels of your transformation process. There will be moments when you feel, unquestioningly, a connectedness with something *more*. And there will equally be moments when you will know yourself to be back in the void of isolation—marooned once more in the ongoing enigma of your life script.

It is that heightened aspect of *your* awareness that nudges you, when you stand at a particular crossroads, and gives you the sense of which road to take. It is that aspect of *you* that senses when you are in danger, and signals you to take a sudden deviation from what you presumed to be your path. It is that higher aspect of *you* that embraces you now—unconditionally. All of you. Even the parts that you'd sooner forget.

There are no bits and pieces of you that will be discarded in the ascension process. Every blessed part of your illustrious or infamous past is an equal candidate for assimilation into the composite that you believe to be *you*. And every nuance of that being—you in all your magnificent humanness—is required to be present in order to be assimilated totally at the next level of awareness.

It is no use hoping to sweep some of those memories under the rug of your consciousness. There are no closets in which to hide the warts and the wounds you have garnered along the way. It is all part of *you*. And it is *all of you* that is so very much wanted—and loved.

As you watch in fascination the diversity that has been your life, know that it took a "cast of thousands," literally, to produce and to star in this epic. You couldn't have done it alone. Not in your wildest dreams. Now, as you integrate these understandings with your memories of those experiences, the eternal question: "Who Am I" takes on a whole new level of possibilities. And pondering that timeless question becomes most interesting.

chapter forty-one

Merging with the Divinity within.
Liberation from the need for validation.
Embracing the state of sublime indifference.
Detachment from the mundane world.

Whether or not you notice the otherworldly sensations that mark the heightened stages of transformation, there will be no doubt that a deep sense of inner awakening has at last begun. Quite possibly, you have read or spoken of the concept of *awakening*. And yet you presumed that this was the stage at which the transformation process was initiated. Now, well invested in your journey, the doors within you have indeed begun to open in a different way. And you have begun to taste a new level of inner-aliveness that stirs within you.

You have awakened from the deep sleep of denial in which you have hibernated, in a waking state, all your life. And now you will have become vividly aware of the blinders with which most of the beings in your *world* go about their lives. Yours is a world of blame and recrimination; a world of self-righteous indignance; a world of misrepresentation and misinterpretation; a world of misunderstanding and mistrust. It is a world where the *other* is the unconditional adversary regardless of the intimacy of the relationship.

It is a world of disillusionment and disappointment with virtually everything.

Yours is a world in which you ultimately distance yourself, emotionally, from everything you ever held dear, in an effort to avoid further pain. And ultimately, in the impetus behind that instinctive action, you distance yourself from yourself. You recognize and set to one side everything that has characterized the identity you invested a lifetime in creating. For at last, this mask has ceased to be recognizable to you as yourself.

The complexities of the role you've crafted for a lifetime comprise values and behaviors you cannot imagine yourself exhibiting. And it begins to feel like the person you have been for most of your life is someone else. The *you* who now resides in your body and wears your identity has transcended much of the reflex reaction and culturally induced response mechanism with which you were equipped upon emerging in this reality.

Now, the energies of the realities through which you pass in quick succession cannot accommodate the vibrational levels that support that outgrown mind-set. And, often inadvertently, you find yourself having dropped pretenses and stances in which you once had placed great stake. Here, in the aftermath of that great shedding of one's outgrown skin, you now find yourself. And the temptation is great to cast the scraps of all that once was valid and meaningful into the trash, and to turn your back and walk away.

Ah! If only it were that simple. But, naturally, it's not. You wouldn't have wanted it to be. For, the object of this exercise is Oneness—not separation. And that includes Oneness with all you have ever been. You cannot hope to ascend into the embrace of the higher energies with a whitewashed identity and gaping holes in your history. The aspects of self that await your imminent arrival do not hope for part of you. They are waiting patiently for all of you. And the integration of all the fragments of your identity that you'd rather not look at, are the ones most needed in *your* loving embrace.

You are no more or less who you now are than all the masks you have worn and all the posturing you have demonstrated along the way. All of it are integral parts of an identity that seeks resolution, not in the act of discarding what was, but in the act of integrating all of it into the composite of what Is.

So, by all means, you can change your name, change your residence, change your fashion statement, and change your professional identity. You can change the people with whom you share relationships and change the way you relate to the world. Yet, the change that is more significant is not one that is expressed. For the act of expressing anything is a statement of recognition of the importance one places on all that is external—and its opinion of you. The change that is significant is not one that needs ever to be seen, or heard, or known. For the only one that needs to know it—is you.

You have connected with the timeless. You have opened to the possibility of transcending all that defines your existence—and the world that gives it definition and form. And in embracing that inner glow of recognition of the *kindredness* of the most intangible connection of all, you take the quantum leap. For the higher awareness and the sense of connectedness you hope to embody is no more and no less than your own Self. It feels kindred because it Is kindred. It is You—as is the One who speaks with you now.

The God you would hold exalted and worship from afar is no further away than your own heart. The dimensions you hope to bridge in your "travels" on this sacred journey are not "out there" somewhere. They are also within you. The aspects of your own beingness that have suffered with you, and rejoiced with you, are all within you. All the illustrious *past lives*, who have shared this lifetime, are within you. As are the future selves who act out the scripts you believe to be yet unwritten. All are within you— harbored in the sacred core of your eternal being.

You are birthing the one who personifies the culmination of that entire body of experience. And that one recognizes the comfort and familiarity of the Divine essence you hold within. There is nothing *foreign* or otherworldly about experiencing your connectedness with God. For it is none other than your very own Divine essence, ever-present within you, that reaches out in that embrace. It is not something that suddenly enters. It is something that has never left.

It does not matter whether or not you believe that you are capable of connecting with God—that the one who speaks with you now dwells within your own being. It does not matter whether or not you can debate the point brilliantly with those who will presume that you have lost your mind, at the mention of such ideas. And it surely does not matter whether you alter your life dramatically, or go about your business like nothing ever happened. None of it matters at all. When you have experienced the harmony of that heart-felt glow, even for a fleeting moment, the knowingness is indelibly etched upon your consciousness. And that level of knowingness cannot be forgotten.

You can certainly pretend to yourself that you have not tasted what you know you have. You can surely protest your spiritual innocence long after the initiation of your heart. But once awakened, your knowingness will not be forgotten. It will resurface and nudge you into remembrance when you least expect it to. It will emerge with that familiar kindred glow—just to remind you that *you* have not been forgotten.

Oneness has no agenda with regard to the timetable of your transformation. It does not matter whether you embrace who you really are this year—or even in this lifetime. For time, as it truly *is*, has no relation to the illusions in the linear dream you call your life. We are here, waiting patiently for you, as we have been for all eternity. We are willing to wait. We will wait "forever," if necessary, for you to work this out. And if it takes forever, you are no less our Beloved.

The stage of your journey at which your recognition crystallizes brings with it, once again, the sense of a plateau. From this vantage point you are able to see quite clearly the territory that has been covered. And you are able to recognize the gift in this time of resting and the assimilation of all that has come to pass. For now there are no longer the doubts that once eroded your path and made the traversing of certain stretches of terrain difficult and exhausting.

Here in the clarity of this place, the way has been eased for you. There is the sense that the obstacles that have thus far littered your path have been cleared away. And at last you have the opportunity to integrate the understandings of what has transpired within you with the newfound simplicity of your life circumstances. The complexities that anchored you into a seemingly unending spiral of difficulties have now been released and relegated to a distant place. And the recognition is unmistakable that from this point forth, the journey leads within.

You will wish to spend extended periods of your time in blessed isolation now. And you will find yourself withdrawing your energies and your presence from virtually everything that once held your attention. Now you feel great indifference toward what is transpiring politically, and what is transpiring socially in a world in which you once counted yourself as fully present. From where you now stand, all of it appears irrelevant.

The details of the external world do not interest you now, for your interactions with others are invariably fraught with discord. It is as though you were still a magnet for the irritability and disgruntled reactions of everyone with whom you have even casual contact. And, indeed, that is exactly what you have become. For, as you transcend the allure of mundane concerns, certain residual energies within you continue to magnetize experiences of a corresponding vibration, which manifest as adversity on the parts of others. Until these energies can be released fully, you will find that you continue to experience a barrage of inconsequential incidents that are calculated to be irritating.

It is your reaction to this kind of provocation that determines how long you will need to linger at this level. For this stopping place is for the ultimate resolution of all the residual vibrational baggage you carry with you. This is the place where your knee-jerk reactions will be tested repeatedly. And this is the place where, ultimately, you will master the skills of detachment.

Now you will have the opportunity to watch yourself and to scrutinize how you have managed to accumulate the collection of life experiences that have garnered for you an energy field that has magnetized the same old story all your life. For, as these final episodes now play out, you become vividly aware of how you might once have reacted under similar circumstances. And with sublime indifference, you allow the provocation to pass you by, for you have ceased to be invested in having to deliver justice in a given situation. You know that it truly doesn't matter. And in that act of detachment, you release yet another piece of vibrational density. That energy is not needed to support and to verify who you once were. That aspect of you no longer needs validation at the levels toward which you journey.

As you consistently condition yourself in the skills of non-reaction, you begin to experience a rarefied sense of freedom from all that once held you prisoner. For you have been the prisoner of your own need to be validated. You have been the prisoner of the need to prove yourself right—and another wrong. And you have spent untold lifetimes building the vibrational framework within which you could continue to experience evidence of it. You have just been liberated from the need to do so.

Suddenly, you realize that it doesn't matter in the least whether or not you are "right," and another "wrong," in a given circumstance. What truly matters is that your inner harmony is retained, and that your connectedness with the Source of that inner peace remains undisturbed. Anything—*anything*—that is working, vibrationally, to undermine that objective is not important. Anything that beckons to you with the invitation to engage in conflict is not important. And anything that attempts to impose its own will upon you and disrupt your sense of inner harmony is not important—to *you*.

What presents itself to you has no inherent *value* or lack of *value* whatsoever. It is simply choice. You can choose to engage, energetically. Or you can choose to allow the energy to pass and leave you undisturbed. It is all simply choice. There is no *meaning* attached to any of it. It is all symbolism. And it is an opportunity to assess whether or not you feel a need to align with the energy of that opportunity and to taste the outcome, as experience, or not.

At this stage of your journey, the potential *price* in addressing certain energy is known to be too high. There is not even the slightest temptation for you. And as you consistently see yourself demonstrate that response, you begin to realize that you have transcended a cornerstone of material existence, and that you are experiencing reality at another level.

You recognize that you haven't *gone* anywhere. You have merely withdrawn your energies from the external comings and goings of the world that surrounds you. And you have taken up residence …within. This is the point of recognition at which you embrace the eternal child who is always asking the big question: "Are we *there* yet?" Now you no longer need to ask. Or do you?

chapter forty-two

The concept of harmony and the essence
of "difference" that sustains it.
How the "heaven on earth" of prophecy
will come to be.

Harmony is a concept that one begins to integrate as the fullness of that experience takes precedence over the infinite
shades of discord that have characterized most of this lifetime. At
first, the experience seems like a novelty, and is regarded with amusement. But then one becomes aware of the consistency of that
state of beingness and recognizes that the next stage in one's
metamorphosis is at hand.

One is struck, often dramatically, by the realization that all possibilities are now viable options. And the variable that determines
what is and what is not experienced is nothing more than choice.
For the limitations and constraints that once may have restricted
one's idea of what might be possible have been lifted vibrationally.
And one recognizes the arrival at a stage where one's priorities may
be scrutinized objectively, perhaps for the very first time.

Suddenly, the world is saying "yes." And instead of fending
off adversity, one begins to focus on identifying what it is that one
truly wants. For many, that focus shifts at this stage to one in which

personal gain takes a back seat to work that emphasizes the higher perspective of the worldview. One is inclined to dedicate the major thrust of one's life to efforts where the long-term benefit to humanity is the primary consideration. One understands that one's own personal welfare will be seen to as a by-product of that intent and need not command the primary focus of one's attention.

One need not be any less prosperous in making such a shift. For the key to sustaining the manifestation of abundance, under conditions where the idea of personal prosperity is irrelevant, is the subtle shift in where one chooses to focus one's intent. Beings who choose to dedicate their lives to humanity or to restoring the harmony of the environment are not required to choose poverty as a demonstration of that selflessness. Circumstances will manifest quite naturally that would ensure the physical comforts of those in question when one is aligned with one's own highest purpose.

The question then is not what one chooses to be doing, so much as the intent with which one chooses to be doing it. When one is focused upon material gain as an end in itself, as are the majority of beings in your world, the outcome is constricted by the foundation of *fear* upon which scarcity is based. When one is focused upon selfless service to the higher good of All Life, without fear for one's own well-being, the highest result is manifested for all.

Many who read these words will struggle with this concept, even after you have grasped the other aspects of your process. Many of you still have difficulty with the idea of abundance, despite the extent of your inner metamorphosis. Some of you actually presume that great self-sacrifice is required of you at this stage of your journey as a gesture of compensation for all you have accomplished in terms of personal growth. Nothing could be further from the truth.

There is absolutely no price to be paid for your spiritual journey. For, who is it that would be paying such a price? And to whom would it be paid? It is all Oneness. So be very clear that if you are choosing austerity and physical deprivation as a way of demonstrating your spiritual focus, it is you and you alone who is making such a choice. It is not being asked of you, nor is it expected. For a *demonstration* of any kind is a statement of separation from the *other* you are trying to impress with your action. And there is no *other*. Oneness is not impressed by deprivation. Oneness is not invested in your mundane choices. Choose as you will. And enjoy the results of those choices.

When your heart is clear that the focus of your life is toward the highest good of All Life, let it be through recognition of the Oneness that unites all aspects of that Life and includes you as a vital part of it. It is counterproductive to the thrust of all you would do, if you approach those efforts with an altruistic attitude of self-sacrifice. You are not here as a statement of separation from Life, but as a materialized statement of unification with it. You are not helping that *other person* in your well meaning activity. You are helping your Self. For that Self is the Oneness of which you are a part—and none *other*.

The sense of deep inner satisfaction that you may derive from efforts focused in humanitarian activity is not based on a *holier-than-thou* attitude toward one's fellow beings. It is based upon recognition of the sacredness of All Life and a vivid awareness of the part that each and every creature plays in its portrayal. There are infinite variations on the theme that manifests as your physical reality. And none of you is any different, in your core essence, than any other. You simply are here to hold a particular note in the resonance that is playing as a particular symphony of experience: this "here and now." How you choose to experience that aspect of the One Divine Presence is totally up to you.

If you choose to experience your recognition of your innate Divinity through an expression of austerity, then by all means do so. But be clear about your motives for that demonstration. If your purpose is to show *others* your level of connectedness with the One Divine Presence, you have defeated that purpose by demonstrating yourself to be separate from All that comprise it. If your purpose is to hide on a remote mountaintop and impress only God with your austerities, know that you have succeeded only in demonstrating your separation *from* that Source in so doing. For there is no need for you to try to *earn* what you already Are.

The more you try to prove, through self-effacement, the extent of your connectedness, the deeper the wedge that is driven between you and the harmony you yearn for. For harmony is achieved only within the context of *unison*. It cannot be achieved through acts of separation.

The levels of joy that you are capable of experiencing at this stage of your journey are your birthright. There is no limit to the levels of abundance with which you may choose to gift yourself— or not. It is simply choice. And there are no higher or lower aspects of it. All are simply options within the infinite range of possibility—an endless menu from which you have been invited to select what pleases you. And when you do so from a place that honors Self in that way, there is no limit to the joy that may be shared.

You may choose to experience your connectedness with Self in the company of another being. And in so doing, you harmonize certain aspects of your beingness with the vibrational essence of that other person. Yet the connectedness remains your own. And while you may travel on a parallel path with another and have certain experiences in common, your path remains your own.

You may radiate the levels of your own newfound connectedness, and others may reflect what they feel in your presence. Yet you are not required to carry those others up the mountain simply because you share a history of relationship. You have not cloned yourself in any respect, in your experience of physicality. And, it is not to be expected that the pace at which your growth proceeds will be duplicated by another being, regardless of how kindred the connection.

Each of you comes to this lifetime with a unique set of variables that will be worked out within the context of your relationships with the world at large, as well as with each other. You will serve as the catalyst for the growth of many, in the significant connections you have formed with other beings. Yet the pace at which the understandings are gleaned and integrated as knowingness varies with every exchange.

You may presume that you are in certain relationships to sustain levels of harmony. Yet, as you progress on your journey, that sublime state eludes you. It is easy to fault the other person with not living up to the level of your expectations and the pace of your own journey. But do not underestimate the role that that being is scripted to play for you. Harmony may well be a shared mutual objective. Yet to truly achieve it in tandem with another, it is necessary to allow the levels of density within the energy fields of each of you to rise to the surface and be released. Without a certain measure of abrasion, the smooth surface each hopes to sustain is not possible.

When two beings share the sacred journey at an intimate level, each has been factored in to the growth objective of the other. And relationships that at one time thrived on the ease at which the energy flowed between you are suddenly cast into turbulent waters of change. When you are aware of the nature of the process itself, you are able to step back from the intensity of certain clashes and recognize the vibrational foundation underlying it. It is far too easy to dismiss the process of another being, when the dynamic does not go according to your plan, and rob yourself of the potential in the clash of wills. For, before real harmony can be experienced within the context of a relationship, it is necessary to allow the fullness of the energy that resonates between you to be *expressed*.

It is no accident that some of you are sharing these times with a companion. You are the ones who have been given the tool of *relationship* through which to discover the intimate connection you share with your own inner being. For the intimate details of your innermost feelings are magnified for you vividly when contrasted with the conflicting priorities of a life partner. Without that catalyst you might drift along, peacefully enough, deluding yourself into believing that all was well with your world, when in fact, you had managed to camouflage the very essence of your gravest challenges. No one knows you like a partner. And no one is as skilled in stimulating your issues to rise to the surface of your awareness, where there is no denying what is really there.

The partner or close friend who appears to be lagging behind on his spiritual journey may well be enacting certain sacred agreements that force you to look at and see the density and patterns of denial that you've best kept hidden from yourself. It is these very issues that, as a soul approaching the interdimensional threshold, you most want to resolve. For you cannot complete the journey in a state of imbalance.

Those of you in long-standing relationships that have become discordant have been gifted with a partner who has enough at stake in the relationship not to walk out when the going gets rough. Each of you has a vested interest in recreating the sense of harmony that united you in the first place. For it is through this experience with each other that you have been permitted to taste the essence of *connectedness* itself. This is the bond that you share with your very own sacred essence. And this is the Divine connection that, ultimately, you will experience universally.

When you are able to transcend the ego focus with which you have each been equipped, you are able to truly embrace another being and to recognize Self in and through that connection. That does not presuppose that each of you is a duplicate of the other. That does not mean that one of you has acquiesced with regard to core issues. And it does not indicate that you have, necessarily, completed the work you have come together to do. The recognition of Self in the form of another is an attestation to the true essence of the very differences that prove most challenging. And it is evidence of the depth of *contrast* without which there can be no harmony.

For, in order for harmony truly to be experienced, there must be the essence of "difference" to comprise it. There is no harmony in a vacuum. And there is no harmony in a world where all are focused solely upon their own needs—both personally and as a collective. *Harmony is dependent upon a recognition of difference and a willingness to hold one's own truth intact in its presence.*

Until one is at the place where resonance with All Life is experienced, one is relegated to the joys of harmony. For once you are able to look at another being and see no difference at all, there is no need for harmony. For here, there Is only Oneness. There is no *other*. There is nothing through which to contrast oneself and taste the joys of harmony.

This is the place the story began. And this is the end toward which all consciousness now strives to return. You are destined to transcend the need for harmony and to experience the essence of Isness in unison with All Life. That does not mean that each of you will disappear and enter a state of nonexistence—absorbed forevermore by one all-consuming consciousness. Each of you will remain in a state of self-perception for all eternity. And as you enter the states of higher awareness, each of you will be graced with Self-Perception.

That is the essence of the Oneness of which we have spoken. For we Are that Oneness. We are the essence of each of you. And none of you will be lost in the momentum toward reunification that unites us All. The unity is in the recognition of the *other* as Self, not in the exclusion of any of you. None will be left behind. Not one fragment of the sacred essence of Oneness will cease to have self-awareness—and a sense of identity—at some level of existence. For that is the Divine Plan.

The opportunity for you who are moving through this experience of transcendence with your eyes wide open is to see that the concept of unification in Oneness is not to be interpreted in a physical sense. Rather, it is an experiential journey. Some will choose to experience that awareness through the context of form, and in so doing, will taste the concept of *difference* and experience the delights of harmony. Others will be content to remain within the embrace of the energy of Isness, perceiving themselves individually despite the absence of physical evidence, and at the same time, knowing themselves to be One with All Life.

What will have changed is the nature of what will be experienced—and by whom. Ultimately, the dictates of the Laws of Karma will have been relegated to a page in linear history. Those energies will have been brought to completion in the fullness of *time* within the context of the physical realms in which those dramas were enacted. They will no longer color the experience of those who choose to taste their Divinity in physical form.

Your physical realms will not cease to exist in the world to come. They simply will have experienced a spiritual transformation. They will offer the spiritual travelers amongst you a destination through which to rediscover your Sacred Essence, in physical form, under optimal conditions. There will no longer be the need to experience "that which you are not" in order to recognize, by contrast, "that which you Are." For all will be fully aware of the nature of Self and will recognize the Oneness in All Life.

That is the nature of the world that you may or may not choose to experience, at a higher dimensional level, in the times to come. You will not be *sentenced* to a physical lifetime as a means of *karmic compensation*. For, vibrationally, the slate will have been wiped clean.

Naturally, there will not be nearly the number of beings experiencing physical incarnation as there are in the present period. For, given the option of remaining within the essence of eternal Oneness, relatively few will opt for the adventure of the world of physical experience.

Those realms will have returned to the sanctity of a world uncompromised by conflict and unscarred by its inevitable aftermath. For the mass consciousness will have altered its collective mind-set significantly. And the perception of your world, as it *now* is, will manifest in the awareness of few. We are in the final moments of those times.

The others of you who have helped, with your collective presence, to sustain the vibration of the realities in which you have experienced yourself in this lifetime, will have moved on. You will have taken yourself, vibrationally, out of the range where perception of such conditions was possible. You will have ascended.

For reality *is* only as each of you experiences it. *The nature of your world is no more and no less than a reflection of the composite vision of the consciousness present.* In the times to come, the nature of the consciousness present will have transformed. And the world that reflects it, in which you may choose to experience Life, will resonate accordingly.

This world in the times to come will radiate the essence of harmony. It will hold the resonant frequency of the higher, non-physical realms and thus will Be the "heaven on earth" that has been prophesied, throughout your history, for the days to come. Not because some big, Almighty God, who is up there in the sky somewhere made it that way. But because You—each of you—exercised your Divine Will in harmony with Divine Intent. It is You who will have created this world anew, by recognizing yourself as Oneness—and resonating as One. Just as it was In The Beginning.

chapter forty-three

Viewing ancient prophecy about "The End Times"
from a heightened perspective.

There has been much wisdom and much speculation handed down through the ages with regard to the nature of the times now upon you. They have been referred to as "The End Times," by sages since time immemorial. In reading this text, you may have come to consider that that label has been interpreted in a literal and a linear sense by many in your reality. And as such, much fear and mass hysteria has been triggered unnecessarily.

It should be obvious to you that massive change is at hand. To resist that change and cling to an outmoded reality is surely not the answer for a world that is clearly growing in conscious awareness. For, just as radical change has transpired within your own life circumstances and within the depths of your inner being, so too is the reality reflected by the collective consciousness a product of that change.

To expect that catastrophic events will victimize your world and reduce it to rubble is to cast a literal interpretation upon words with which basic truth may have been given. That is not, in fact, what has been foreseen for these times, *as you will experience them.* For the collective mind-set presently representing your reality is not of the resonance to reflect that outcome.

There are other realms, where that is not the case. There are realities that are vastly denser variations on the theme that you regard as your world. In those realities, the environment that hosts and supports the life that experiences itself there is having a far more severe reaction to the universal upsurge in vibrational frequency. At those levels of experience, circumstances more in keeping with radical interpretations of "End Times" prophecy are manifesting as reality.

It was those diminished vibrational realms that were referenced by prophecies made so very long ago. It was anticipated that at those denser vibrational levels, more radical change was required in order to keep pace with the momentum of ascension that is being experienced at other levels of reality. You are not experiencing those conditions because your awareness is no longer focused at those levels.

It is for you, who have been made aware of the kinds of events predicted for these times, to know that the changes in question need not carry the density that many of you have given them. The maintenance of physical life is not the consummate goal here. Rather, it is *the vibrational elevation of All Life and the environment that sustains it* that is the objective in all that now transpires in and around you.

Consider carefully the possibility that the beings in question have come to completion with the life's work of this present incarnation, and the highest possible expression of their collective destiny is, in many cases, to relinquish their physical forms. In so doing, they are able to transcend the limitation of those physical identities. In many cases, such beings have paid much of their karmic debt. And with the one great contribution of their very life, have earned their liberation from continued incarnation at levels that have kept them bound in the experience of oppression.

The profound levels of release that are experienced as large populations of beings transition from such circumstances should not be underestimated.

There are no accidents in your physical world. All has been carefully orchestrated. And even though there are circumstances and levels of human condition which you may find horrifying, know that the individuals in question selected these very circumstances to illustrate, to *themselves*, the issues in which each was most profoundly invested at a soul level. Each volunteered to pay the price in terms of *suffering* in order to elevate themselves from the need to continue to experience incarnation at those levels.

Once the lesson is manifested and the understandings gleaned, there is simply not the need to continue an incarnation, simply because the physical form is still capable of sustaining life. Essentially, that lifetime is complete, whether it is one that terminates in infancy or in old age. Longevity is not the objective of a physical incarnation, but rather it is the fulfillment of one's life purpose.

The catastrophic events that are being experienced by large segments of the population in remote areas of the globe are indicative of a mass release of energy that has been liberated from the need to continue in oppressive conditions. Having experienced some of the "horrors" of those circumstances, these beings have transcended the need for much of the repetition of similar themes that might have been otherwise called for. They contracted for these conditions voluntarily, fully aware of the price to be paid and the liberation to be attained as a result.

Much that has been categorized, as "Earth Changes," were scenarios that were orchestrated to provide just such opportunities. For, in living out some of the most insidious of these experiences, quantum leaps in consciousness are possible. And this is a choice made by many who will be riding the crest of some of those waves.

There are other segments of your population that will be totally untouched by these kinds of circumstances. It is you, many of whom are tuned-in to the higher understandings also being made available en masse in these times, who will transcend the need to be caught in the grasp of any manifestation of environmental upheaval at all. Your earthquakes and tidal waves are transpiring within you, and the ravages of famine and disease are being experienced equally by you—symbolically.

You are not being asked to pay the supreme price of the relinquishing of your physical body in exchange for the lessons learned, as are some in other corners of your world. The price many of you have agreed to pay is far dearer than that. For you have dared to weather the virtual annihilation of an entire state of beingness that has kept you imprisoned in self-defeating patterns for lifetimes. The ravages of such an experience cannot be underestimated. And, depending upon just how invested some of you were in maintaining the stance in question, that is the extent to which the energies of change have come to bear upon you.

You entered into these agreements knowingly—fully aware of the trauma that would result when the time was at hand. But you were also fully aware of the possibility of transcendence that might be realized from having weathered those levels of upheaval. And you exercised your power of choice. And you prayed from the depths of your very soul, to be permitted to go through exactly what you're going through, for the chance that you might, at long last, be free of what has been your life pattern and taste what is truly there within you.

The prophecies for these times of transformation are not something to be feared. They are possibilities to be embraced by those of you who are fortunate enough to be touched by the sacred energies that deliver them. They are the monumental turning points you yearn for as a soul. They are the gift of deliverance.

The so-called "End Times" to which the attention of so many is now drawn is not an *ending* in the physical sense, so much as a transcendence of the limitations posed by linear perspective. The endings that may well transpire in the physical lives of many are not the objective of the events that may precipitate them. Rather, these endings are the doorway to another level of experience, whether or not in physical form.

What is being brought to completion in this "here and now" are the intense patterns of karmic compensation that were enforced vibrationally in a system that was ongoing and essentially inescapable. By altering the vibrational basis through which that aspect of reality has perpetuated itself, beings are once more being given the possibility to exercise their free will and to live their lives fully in the Now moment. By integrating the higher frequencies and elevating one's vibration, one is able to significantly expand the range of options for experiencing Life at levels of reality where the conditions are less challenging.

When viewed solely in the literal sense, it could be interpreted that "the world is coming to an end." That might be how it would appear to those who have chosen to be present in such realities when those times are at hand. But most of you will no longer have your focus of awareness invested at those levels. And you will not even know that cataclysmic events are, indeed, occurring *where you once were.* For you will no longer be "there" to experience them. You will have ascended out of that range of reality. And you will be experiencing a higher vibrational variation on the theme of those prophesied events.

From the perspective of the distant observer—some of the so-called *guides* that are filtering information through to many of you—the conditions being observed from afar appear to be transpiring according to *schedule.* For what has been prophesied is based solely on the logical, predictable outcome of combinations of variables, all of which are energy patterns. Those patterns can still be perceived from the vantage point of those who may be watching from a distance that is extraterrestrial and providing commentary on it.

However, these forms of consciousness are only able to perceive the level of reality to which *they* are vibrationally aligned. What they may not be able to sense is what each of you actually perceives as *your* reality in any given moment, which is based solely on your vibrational state of beingness. Thus, the level of reality upon which otherworldly observers may be reporting is not necessarily the one you are likely to experience.

Ancient prophecy is only as accurate as the moment in time in which the seer had the vision. From the perspective of certain moments in *the past* the probability of certain events manifesting as reality seemed likely. As the free will of the collective of consciousness present exercised its power to co-create its reality, that outcome may well have shifted in any of a number of ways. And the likelihood of certain prophecies actually occurring as envisioned is minimal, at best. For mass consciousness *has* shifted. And the reality that is a reflection of it has shifted accordingly.

Know that in these times of transformation, all things are possible. The script is being drafted anew, based on your willingness to embrace the layers of change that are erupting within each of you. Life in this tumultuous period of "history" is defined by the degree to which each is able to detach from the need to try to control the process. Clinging to the safety nets of the past places an energetic death grip on your ability to float through the turbulent patches and harness the powerful currents that have come to carry you through.

Those of you, who have become consumed with the "worst-case scenario" predictions that are presently flooding your reality, have created for yourself a fascinating test. For you have given yourself the option to choose to perceive the vision that once appeared in the mind's eye of another being. Or, alternatively, to experience a heightened expression of reality, custom-made for your eyes only, that has not yet been revealed.

The proverbial blind leap of faith presupposes that one is capable of ignoring what the logical mind is screaming about. For, that logic is often based on fears firmly entrenched by painful experiences of the past. In these times, that past—and all the ground rules that went with it—is, quite possibly, no longer relevant.

Whether or not you choose to give credence to fear based prophecies is certainly up to you. It is yet another of the fascinating variables you have chosen to factor into your script as part of *your* "End Times" saga. And watching yourself go through the mental gyrations of trying to *figure it out* can certainly be part of that experience.

But there often comes a moment, in the heat of your desperation, when you call a "time-out." And you withdraw from the cyclone of illusion that swirls around you. And you find, after all that drama, that the stillness within is still there waiting. It never left. You did. And you scattered a mind-boggling trail of chaos behind you. So that, when all else fails—as it inevitably does—you would find your way home.

chapter forty-four

Viewing your life through the eyes of Oneness.

The issues on which you have chosen to focus your attention will illustrate for you the level of your own involvement in the transformational process that has captured the attention of consciousness throughout all Creation. There is no specified timetable within which you have been programmed to complete certain phases of this exercise. All of this is being presented to you as choice. And, given that certain of these teachings may have struck a note deep within you, this opportunity for reflection is likely to initiate a monumental shift within you that will help you to halt your conditioned patterns of response—and be Still.

So long as you permit the programming of your mind to dominate every waking breath, and so long as you run your life as a mindless exercise of reflex responses calculated to prove that you are "right" about whatever your issues happen to be, you will not be capable of experiencing the exquisite connectedness that awaits you. So long as you hold your focus in the realm of mundane concerns, you will be unable to perceive the Divine essence that calls to you in silence.

There will come a moment, in the heat of some mentalized frenzy, when you will, at long last, stop dead in your tracks. You will have reached a saturation point with the unending series of illustrations that you have provided for yourself to underscore the point of the exercise upon which you have directed your focus. You will have reached the point where you are ready to walk out on all of it. For, clearly, the way it is—is not working. That is the moment you have been waiting for.

For until you have nothing left to lose and nothing left to gain by continuing in your ingrained patterns, you do not have the catalyst for initiating radical change. Until that moment, your circumstances will continue to depict for you example after example of the life themes on which you have been working all this time. And well after you have become aware of what is really happening, your life circumstances will continue to provide for you the testing conditions that can be the springboard for transcending those patterns.

You will continue to manifest life circumstances that will put your understandings to the test, long after you have mastered them in theory. For, until these issues are ingrained as knowingness to the extent that *they* become your reflex responses, you will continue to manifest opportunities to strengthen those new patterns of reaction. By being fully conscious of what you are doing in those moments when you feel those old familiar buttons being pushed, you can begin to dissipate the vibrational charge that is drawing those kinds of circumstances to you.

There comes a time, in the clarity of full, lucid awareness of this process, where your very life flashes before your eyes. And you are able to summarize, with the energy of joy and rapture, some of the agonies you have chosen to experience. In those moments of vivid awareness you will have set the stage for the episodes that represent the *waning* of those patterns of energy.

What follows is a virtual barrage of illustrations, all of them inconsequential, which will provoke you into shifting into a new mode of being. Your detachment from the need to be "right" bears the gift of transcendence. And you will discover within those depths, the Stillness within your own being that opens the door to your true essence.

You will continue to play out your role in your daily interactions with your fellow beings. Yet you will begin to see all of it very differently. They will appear to you as players on a stage, reciting the lines you have scripted, and drawing you into the Dance. Enjoy the Dance. You are not here to sit on the sidelines and watch life unfold without you. You are here to participate fully, and joyously—and consciously. And once you have begun to enact your life drama in that way, you will become aware that life is now unfolding in a very different way.

You will have begun to *experience* the higher octave of your own being that you will have embodied, vibrationally. And you will begin to recognize the others, discreetly playing their roles on the sidelines of your own dramas, who illustrate your newfound understandings. Where have they been all this time? Where have they been while you were struggling with your monsters and "going down for the third time," over and over again? Right where they have been all along, by your side, awaiting your imminent arrival.

The Dance will take on a new tempo as the harmony that emanates from within sets the pace for other kinds of experience. And life will have transformed into another kind of adventure: one you will be guided to enjoy with beings who are able to perceive reality as you do.

This physical incarnation offers the potential of infinite variations on the experience that is your life. You can veer off in a new and different direction any time you choose. You can deviate from what you believed was your life script, if it pleases you to do so. And you are obligated to no one, other than your own Sacred

Self. Naturally, there continues to be cause and consequence with regard to the choices you will continue to make in the course of a physical existence. But now, those choices will be made consciously. And they will result in the highest possible outcome for all concerned, when choices are made from that state of being.

For, when life is *working* for you, it cannot be to the detriment of another being. That's not how it works. Choices that give the illusion of putting your back against the wall are the very tests that hold the potential of monumental breakthroughs for all concerned. When you honor your own truth, unconditionally, it sets the stage for a chain reaction of transformation, all the way around.

The higher dimensional realities through which you now progress will provide a broad spectrum lens through which you will be able to focus your own unique perspective. What you perceive will be your own vantage point, with the coloration of a more universal outlook. You will instinctively view the world and your role within it from a place that sees All of it as you would see yourself. The qualities of compassion will have been stimulated to the surface of your awareness. And you will be able to *feel* deeply the sense of standing in the shoes of another. For you will perceive that *other* as your very own Self.

Now, the adversarial role that others have played throughout much of your life shifts quite naturally. And you discover that you have emerged into a state of being where life flows effortlessly and with relatively little conflict. For, vibrationally, you will have crossed the threshold from a reality where the mind-set of separation would have set up the building blocks of disagreement and the ensuing battles into which they once escalated. When one does not perceive oneself as *other* there is nothing with which one can clash. And life transforms into an experience that is there to be enjoyed.

This is the nature of the journey in which you are, by now, well invested. You would have encountered the proverbial point of no return any number of times on any number of counts. And you would have stumbled headlong into the crises that are calculated to push you over the edge and stimulate the shifts that herald real change.

You would, by now, have survived numerous episodes calculated to bring you to your knees, experientially. It cannot have been otherwise. For, if you are standing at the brink of that level of breakthrough, you would have weathered the virtual annihilation of your linear identity. You would be standing, still wet with the innocence of a birthing process, drawing your very first newborn breaths, and trusting completely that you are safe. And you would know, unquestioningly, that you have *arrived.*

The difference in this *beginning* is that you would know exactly from whence you have come, for you would have retained full lucid awareness of all of it. Throughout the process of this birthing into the next dimension of reality, you would be fully conscious. For, you would have *completed* the course of study. There would be no need to blank out the slate of your memory of similar experiences, in order to continue to put you to the test. This time you are not starting from scratch. You are beginning from where you left off—only a moment ago.

Your ascension into the range of realities where you know yourself to be One with all else you encounter, marks the turning point in your evolution as a pinpoint of consciousness with Self-perception. For, from this point forth, the thrust of your efforts will not be focused in erasing the vibrational residue of past action. Rather, you will embody the experiential reinforcement of your knowingness of the interconnectedness of All Life, in the ongoing Now moment.

You will be starting a fresh new page in the ongoing saga of your Self-awareness. And you will be creating a new track record of evidence to support your understanding of your Divine connection. That is the kind of experience you will be *co-creating* with those others, in physical form, with whom you choose to surround yourself. And the kind of experiential dramas you will enact will affirm for you, over and over and over again, the Oneness of which you are a part.

That is the nature of the journey of ascension that carries you. The birthing process can be relatively effortless. Or it can be agonizingly long and drawn out. You get to choose how it will play out for you—and the possibilities are limitless. That's the beauty of it. For, no matter how you manifest your emergence into the next level of awareness that awaits you, there will be no question that your journey is perfection. Through the eyes of Oneness, that is the only possibility. And those are the eyes through which you have witnessed all of it. Every priceless moment—captured for all time—within the never-ending moment of Now.

about Rasha

Author of Oneness and The Calling, Rasha awakened to her inner-calling as a conduit of Divine guidance in 1987. As a messenger of Divine wisdom, Rasha has dedicated herself to addressing the profound spiritual awakening that is the hallmark of these times. Her teachings are universal in nature and do not represent the beliefs of any religion, spiritual movement or guru. An incurable world traveler with an affinity for India and Northern New Mexico, Rasha actively continues to document the teachings of Oneness for future volumes from the home she found within.